A COURSE ON
WORDS

A COURSE ON
WORDS

Waldo E. Sweet

Glenn M. Knudsvig

Ann Arbor
The University of Michigan Press

Acknowledgments

Entries from *The American Heritage Dictionary of the English Language, New College Edition*, are reprinted by permission of Houghton Mifflin Company, copyright © 1981 by Houghton Mifflin Company.

The entry from *The Shorter Oxford English Dictionary* is reprinted by permission of Oxford University Press, copyright © 1973.

The entries from *Webster's Ninth New Collegiate Dictionary*, copyright © 1989 by Merriam-Webster, Inc., publisher of the Merriam-Webster ® dictionaries, are reprinted by permission.

Entries from *Webster's New World Dictionary*, Second College Edition, are reprinted by permission of Simon & Schuster, Inc., copyright © 1984.

Originally published © 1982 by Harcourt Brace Jovanovich, Inc.
Copyright © 1989 by the University of Michigan Press
All rights reserved
ISBN 0-472-08101-2
Library of Congress Catalog Card Number 81-85553

2017   2016   12   11

ISBN 978-0-472-08101-1

To the Instructor

"I feel like I am actually learning to think about words, not just memorize words."

"This book makes you feel as if there is someone studying along with you, and helping you."

"This book constantly reinforces the main facts and ideas so the reader really gets them."

"The text is very supporting in that you are rewarded immediately for correct responses and corrected immediately for incorrect responses. If all learning was as much fun and as interesting as this, we would all be scholars."

"This book allows me to learn by practicing and thinking, not like the other books I tried to learn from."

"I never realized that so little could give me so much; that is, learning a few stems gives me so many words."

"The self-testing type of approach helps me a lot — the material stays with a person better than by just reading or note taking."

"I only wish I could have had this course and this book a lot earlier in school. Vocabulary learning would have been something other than just boring, and tough, memorizing."

These comments from students are typical reactions to this book. . . . They highlight some of the features and benefits that both students and instructors have come to expect from the book.

A great many students enter an etymology course with only one goal — to learn new words with the hope that they will be more successful in classwork, in standardized exams, or in a variety of work-related situations. In *A Course on Words* students will indeed learn new words, but, more important, they will gain an understanding of how words are built and how they can use this information to analyze new words that they will encounter outside the classroom. They will spend most of the time learning elements of words that will enable them to determine the meanings of many new words in the future. As one student put it, this book seems to "sensitize us to words and get us to think about words."

The extensive and varied practice items and exercises throughout the book seem to be the primary inspiration for students to make such comments as "This book really:

— helps you
— makes studying easy
— reinforces facts and ideas
— rewards immediately
— corrrects immediately
— allows for self-testing
— allows you to understand before you memorize.

The most appealing feature of the book to most students is that it avoids giving one the feeling that the course is nothing but the memorization of lists, whether of words, or bases, or prefixes, or whatever. Memorization of material in this book is natural and an easy step since the material to be memorized has already become familiar through use in the practices.

The words that occur in this course represent various areas of study, such as history, science, and literature. The words and word elements were chosen according to one of these criteria:

1. Productivity. For example, the base [phob], meaning "fear," is used in scores of words, as is the base [fer], meaning "carry."

2. Value in illustrating linguistic principles, in keeping with our avoidance of mindless rote memorizations.

3. Usefulness in conveying to the student that new and unfamiliar words can be understood on the basis of morphemes that have already been mastered.

The words range from high-frequency terms that are likely to be familiar to most students, such as "diameter" and "refer," to low-frequency terms, such as "antipathy" and "periodontist," that may be unfamiliar to many students.

Not too surprisingly, in a questionnaire given to students who were enrolled in a course using this book, most of the students indicated that they use their dictionaries only infrequently, usually to check on the spelling of a word. *A Course on Words* provides exercises based on actual dictionary entries to teach students how to extract all possible information from a dictionary. Most students have expressed amazement at how interesting and useful the dictionary can be, relief at how nonthreatening it is, and regret that they hadn't discovered all this much earlier in their schooling.

The book is unusual in that it offers both programmed and nonprogrammed material. Each type of material is designed to provide students with the maximum amount of involvement and practice. The students do not simply read definitions of words, as is the case with some courses. Rather, they engage in many different activities; not only defining words but analyzing and building them, and learning to use context to derive meaning. The programmed approach enables students to do the work on their own and receive immediate checks of their answers. Classroom time, therefore, is free for review, reinforcement of programmed activities, work on the nonprogrammed material, and attention to the needs of individual students. The book also includes at the end a set of Supplementary Exercises for each unit. The nonprogrammed materials include "Review Exercises," "Words of Interesting Origin," "Easily Confused Words," and "Latin Phrases." These provide practice in concepts learned in the unit and an opportunity to explore a wide variety of topics, such as eponymous words and the literal meanings of Latin expressions used in English.

To the Student

The aim of this course is for you to increase your vocabulary, not only by learning new words but by learning certain *elements* of words which will enable you to determine the meaning of many words you encounter in the future. This book does not teach in the ordinary manner of a textbook; rather, it is programmed instruction. The tasks are broken down into small steps, and after each step you find out immediately whether your answer is correct. To succeed in learning all the material, it is important that you make a reasonable attempt to answer every question before looking at the answer printed below.

Here is the way to proceed. Use a piece of blank paper, or a card, wide enough to go all the way across the page. The beginning of each frame is signaled by a number in boldface on the left. Lower the paper down the page until you reach a row of boxes like this:

▶ □ ◀

Hold your paper level with this line so that you cover the answer printed beneath. Read the discussion if there is one; then answer the question by writing on the line or lines provided. Next, check your response by uncovering the answer. If your answer is incorrect, go back as far as necessary until you understand why the answer given is the correct one. Then move your paper down and go on to the next numbered frame.

Ask your instructor for clarification if you have any questions. And enjoy the course!

Contents

UNIT ONE

Extent of Borrowing in English from Greek and Latin — 1

Introduction: Analysis of a Newspaper Advertisement	2
Content Words and Function Words	3
Ancestors of Modern English	5
Modern English Vocabulary Borrowed from Latin and Greek	6
More English Derivatives from Latin and Greek Words	9
Morphemes: Prefixes and Bases of Latin Origin	10
Empty, Full, and Intensifying Morphemes	18
New Prefixes	22
Three Main Types of Morphemes: Prefix, Base, and Suffix	25
Your Dictionary as a Tool	27
Word List	34
Exercises	35

UNIT TWO

Classes of Words in English — 39

English Nouns	40
A Second Class of Word: English Adjectives	45
Nouns Used as Modifiers of Other Nouns	52
A Third Class of Word: English Verbs	55
The Fourth Class of Words: Adverbs	59
Word List	62
Exercises	62

UNIT THREE
Analysis of a Literary Text

67

Introduction	68
A Common Noun Suffix	69
A Common Adjective Suffix	71
Substitution of Synonyms in the First Sample Text	75
Substitution of Synonyms in the Second Sample Text	76
Dictionaries as Tools	81
Word List	91
Exercises	92

UNIT FOUR
Derivatives from Greek

97

A Review of Latin Examples of Three-Part Words	98
Prefix, Base, and Suffix: Eleven Examples Derived from Greek	98
Words with Two Bases: Examples Derived from Greek	104
Unusual Words Derived from Greek	110
Optional Exercises	118
Word List	120
Exercises	120

UNIT FIVE
Productive Greek Morphemes

125

The Greek Prefixes {a}, {anti}, {epi}, and {syn}	126
The Greek Prefixes {ana}, {cata}, {dia}, and {peri}	128
The Greek Prefixes {ec}, {en}, {hyper}, and {hypo}	131
Review of Greek Prefixes	135
The Greek Prefixes {meta}, {palin}, {para}, and {pro}	140
The Greek Prefixes {amphi}, {apo}, and {exo}	144
Review of Greek Suffixes	147
Word List	149
Exercises	150

UNIT SIX
The Most Useful Latin Prefixes

157

Review	158
Four Latin Prefixes and Five Latin Bases	159
Allomorphs of Latin Prefixes	161
Combinations of the Base {gress} with Both Old and New Prefixes	167
Combinations of the Base {ced / cede / ceed / cess} with Both Old and New Prefixes	168
Review of {empty}, {full}, and {intens} Morphemes	170
Review of Eight Prefixes	174
Combinations of the Base {fer} with Old and New Prefixes	176
Combinations of the Base {pose / pone / posit} with Old and New Prefixes	179
Four More Latin Prefixes	183
Two Latin Prefixes Meaning "Not"	184
Four New Latin Prefixes	187
Word List	190
Exercises	191

UNIT SEVEN
Useful Suffixes, Greek and Latin

195

Review	196
The Greek Suffix {oid}	197
Greek Suffixes Common in Medicine	200
Review Frames for Greek Suffixes	206
Seven Noun Suffixes from Latin	210
Review of Material in Frames 103–135	215
Five Adjective Suffixes from Latin	218
Review Frames for the Last Sequence	222
Word List	226
Exercises	227

UNIT EIGHT
More Compound Words

233

Review	234
Ten Greek Combining Forms	234
Review of {logy} and {logist} Words	236
More Combining Forms	238
Review of Preceding Frames	242
Combining Forms, Both Old and New, Derived from Latin	246
Six Latin Bases	250
Six More Latin Bases	252
Literal and Figurative Meanings	255
Word List	259
Exercises	260

UNIT NINE
What Number, Please?

263

Latin Cardinal Numbers	264
Latin Ordinal Numbers	272
Greek Cardinal Numbers	276
Greek Ordinal Numbers	280
Other Words Showing Number	281
Irregular Plurals	286
Latin Words like One *Alumnus* / Two *Alumni* and One *Alumna* / Two *Alumnae*	288
Latin Words like One *Stratum* and Two *Strata*	291
Greek Words like One *Analysis* / Two *Analyses*	293
Review of Greek and Latin Plurals	293
Word List	296
Exercises	297

UNIT TEN
Cognates and Borrowings

303

Introduction	304
The Indo-European Language System	305
Review of Cognates and Borrowings	312
Norman French Words in English	315
Modern French Words in English	317
Italian Words in English	327
Spanish Words in English	331
Words from Other Languages	334
Word List	338
Exercises	338
Supplementary Exercises	343
List of Words Taught in This Course	357
Glossary	363

UNIT ONE

Extent of Borrowing in English from Greek and Latin

In this unit you will begin to see the rich background from which the vocabulary of English comes. Specifically, you will get an idea of how many common words are borrowed from the ancient languages Greek and Latin. To illustrate this we will show you borrowed words as they appear in a current newspaper ad and in the Declaration of Independence. You will also see that most of these borrowed words have been changed somewhat when they were borrowed into English. Second, you will learn how individual building blocks are put together to make words. Finally, you will learn how to get more information from a dictionary than you may be getting at present.

Those of you who know the structure of English or of another language, especially Latin, may find parts of this unit (and Unit Two) too easy. If so, work through the unit quickly, but be sure that you do not let your familiarity with the words being used cause you to miss the general concepts being taught. We have purposely used many easy words in these first two units in order to teach concepts instead of emphasizing vocabulary.

You are responsible for knowing the meanings of *all* words introduced in this unit. You are also responsible for *all* the terms used in talking about language, such as "derivatives," "content words," and "morphemes."

Note that in the book, in order to emphasize *how* words are built, we often have given only one of several common meanings of a word part.

CONTENTS

1–3	Introduction: Analysis of a Newspaper Advertisement
4–13	Content Words and Function Words
14–19	Ancestors of Modern English
20–38	Modern English Vocabulary Borrowed from Latin and Greek
39–49	More English Derivatives from Latin and Greek Words
50–112	Morphemes: Prefixes and Bases of Latin Origin
113–141	Empty, Full, and Intensifying Morphemes
142–160	New Prefixes
161–176	Three Main Types of Morphemes: Prefix, Base, and Suffix
177–206	Your Dictionary as a Tool

SAMPLE TEXTS IN THIS UNIT   Bank Advertisement in a Newspaper
Excerpt from the Declaration of Independence

Introduction: Analysis of a Newspaper Advertisement
(Frames 1–3)

1   Read the following newspaper advertisement:

Your Daily Working 5¼% Account

Here's What It Can Do for You . . .

With all the recent emphasis on high interest rates for investment certificates, you may be overlooking a very important family financial tool . . . the five and one quarter percent per annum passbook savings account.

This is your "daily working" savings account. It earns daily interest—from day of deposit to day of withdrawal. The money is always available, so you can use this account to accumulate dollars, take them out when you need to pay a medical bill, a repair bill, taxes, a trip. It's about as convenient as a wallet, but your money is earning a good return every day it is on deposit and it is safely insured with an agency of the federal government.

A bonus feature is that by maintaining a balance of $1000 or more in savings you are entitled to all of the travelers checks and money orders you can use. No charge.

So invest all the money you can in our top interest paying certificate accounts for long term requirements, but for day to day needs and emergencies keep a healthy balance in a five and one quarter percent daily working account where it will be immediately available and earn a good return.

SOURCE: Reprinted by permission of Great Lakes Federal Savings, *Ann Arbor News,* August 29, 1978.

In your opinion is this advertisement written (a) in language that would be understood by the average reader? Or (b) in language that would be intelligible only to a person with

a college education? _____

(A card should be covering everything below the row of boxes. Pull down your card *only* when you have come to a decision and have written your answer.)

► □ ◄

A: Of course, we asked for your opinion, so either choice would have to be considered correct. But certainly the people who placed the advertisement were trying to reach a large number of people. Therefore, (a) seems like the better answer.

2   Here is the same advertisement with all the words which are **borrowed (= derived)** from Latin and Greek printed in boldface type.

With all the **recent emphasis** on high **interest rates** for **investment certificates,** you may be overlooking a very **important family financial** tool . . . the five and one **quarter percent per annum** passbook **savings account.**

(continued)

This is your "daily working" **savings account.** It earns daily **interest**—from day of **deposit** to day of withdrawal. The **money** is always **available,** so you can **use** this **account** to **accumulate** dollars, take them out when you need to **pay** a **medical bill,** a **repair bill, taxes,** a trip. It's about as **convenient** as a wallet, but your **money** is earning a good **return** every day it is on **deposit** and it is **safely insured** with an **agency** of the **federal government.**

A **bonus feature** is that by **maintaining** a **balance** of $1000 or more in **savings** you are **entitled** to all of the **travelers** checks and **money orders** you can **use.** No **charge.**

So **invest** all the **money** you can in our top **interest paying certificate accounts** for long **term requirements,** but for day to day needs and **emergencies** keep a healthy **balance** in a five and one **quarter percent** daily working **account** where it will be **immediately available** and earn a good **return.**

What does this tell you about the frequency of Latin and Greek **borrowings** in English? (In your own words) _____

_____

▶ □ ◀

A: It certainly suggests that Latin and Greek borrowings in English are very common. (In fact, the majority of words in English are borrowed from Greek and Latin; that is why we begin this course with these two languages.)

3 Here is the first sentence of the Sample Text again with all the Latin and Greek derivatives removed. (We will refer to the advertisement from now on as the Sample Text.)

With all the ------ -------- on high -------- ----- for ---------- ------------, you may be overlooking a very --------- ------ --------- tool . . . the five and one ------- ------- --- ----- passbook ------- -------.

How much information do you get with the Greek and Latin derivatives removed?

_____

▶ □ ◀

A: Not very much. (Did you write an answer *before* you looked here? You'll learn much more from this program if you try to think of your own answer before checking below.)

Content Words and Function Words
(Frames 4–13)

■ Words may be divided into two classes called **content words** and **function words.** The content words in our Sample Text are such words as *recent, emphasis, high, interest,* and *rates.* Content words in English are usually derived from Greek or Latin. Function words, in general, are short words which serve as cement to hold the content words together. Examples of function words in the first sentence of the Sample Text are *with, the,* and *on.* It is difficult to provide a meaning for many of these words.

4 The meaning of content words is comparatively easy to provide. For example, if asked what the meaning of *emphasis* was, in the sentence "There is an *emphasis* on winning," what would you say? (in your own words) _____

▶ □ ◀

A: "Special attention," "stress," etc.

5–6 You can easily distinguish function words from content words after a few examples. Which two of these words from the first sentence of our Sample Text do you think are function words? (Circle your answers.) *For, investment, a, family.*

▶ □ ◀

A: For; a.

■ We will now ask you to distinguish between content words and function words, using examples from the Sample Text.

7 Is *certificate* a content word or a function word? _____

▶ □ ◀

A: Content word.

8 Is *money* a content word or a function word? _____

▶ □ ◀

A: Content word.

9 Is *by* a content word or a function word? _____

▶ □ ◀

A: Function word.

10 Is *overlooking* a content word or a function word? _____

▶ □ ◀

A: Content word.

11 Is *and* a content word or a function word? _____

▶ □ ◀

A: Function word.

12   Is *interest* a content word or a function word?   _____

▶ □ ◀

    A: Content word.

13   Is *with* a content word or a function word?   _____

▶ □ ◀

    A: Self-test item. No answer given. (If you are not sure of your answer, it means that you did not learn the material. Reread frames 4–12.)

Ancestors of Modern English
(Frames 14–19)

■ As we have seen, Modern English has borrowed many content words from Greek and Latin. However, Modern English is descended from a language spoken by the Angles and the Saxons, who were people from northern Europe who invaded England in the fifth and sixth centuries A.D. The earliest form for which we have written records is called **Anglo-Saxon** (or **Old English**), the form of the language from about A.D. 400 to A.D. 1100. In the form used from A.D. 1100 to A.D. 1500, this language is known as **Middle English.** Modern English has Anglo-Saxon **structure.**

We use the word "structure" to describe the way a language is put together. An English sentence is put together on the model of an Anglo-Saxon sentence. The structure depends partly on **function words** and partly on **word order.** You have already been introduced to function words; here are examples of word order as a signal of structure.

14   Observe the word order in "The dog bites the boy." Who does the biting?   _____

▶ □ ◀

    A: The dog.

15   Again, from the word order, who does the biting in "The boy bites the dog"?   _____

▶ □ ◀

    A: The boy.

16   So, what is the *structural signal* that distinguishes the meaning of "The boy bites the dog" from the meaning of "The dog bites the boy"?   _____

▶ □ ◀

    A: Word order.

17   What is the structural signal that distinguishes the meaning of "race horse" from "horse race"?   _____

▶ □ ◀

    A: Word order.

18 Do we get this structural signal, word order, from the Greek and Latin languages or from the Anglo-Saxon language? _____

▶ □□ ◀

    A: The Anglo-Saxon language.

19 What two important parts of the structure of English come from Anglo-Saxon?
_____ and _____

▶ □□ ◀

    A: Self-test item. No answer given.

Modern English Vocabulary Borrowed from Latin and Greek
(Frames 20–38)

■ Here is the first paragraph of our Sample Text again:

> With all the **recent emphasis** on high **interest rates** for **investment certificates,** you may be overlooking a very **important family financial** tool . . . the five and one **quarter percent per annum** passbook **savings account.**

20 What language do the function words such as *with*, *on*, and *for* come from?
_____

▶ □□ ◀

    A: Anglo-Saxon (or Old English).

21 From what two languages do the words come that are shown in boldface letters?
_____

▶ □□ ◀

    A: Latin and Greek.

22–24 However, not *all* content words are derived from Latin and Greek. In the Sample Text preceding frame 20 there are six content words that are Anglo-Saxon in origin and are therefore not given in boldface. Identify three of them.

_____ , _____ , _____

▶ □□ ◀

    A: (Any three) High, overlooking, tool, five, one, passbook.

NICE-TO-KNOW ■ Some words are borrowed directly into Modern English from Latin or Greek; others come in indirectly. We have included *financial* as a Latin derivative, but it has come into English indirectly from Latin. If you wish to know the origin of "financial," you can look it up in your dictionary: it comes to us through French. You will learn more about borrowing from French later.

Unless your instructor wishes, you do not need to remember the material presented in the "Nice-to-Know" sections. It is for your entertainment and education.

■ We will now give the original Latin or Greek words from which some words in the Sample Text are borrowed. You are to give the English derivatives that appear in the bank advertisement. Sometimes the words will be identical in spelling; at other times they will be a little different.

You are not responsible for memorizing the Latin and Greek words in the series of frames that follows. The exercises are designed to give you a clearer picture of the relationship of the vocabulary of Modern English to the vocabulary of the Greeks and Romans. Refer to the Sample Text (preceding frame 20) as needed.

25 What Modern English word would you guess comes from Latin *recens*? _____

▶ □□ ◀

   A: Recent.

26 What Modern English word would you guess comes from the Greek word *emphasis*?

   _____

▶ □□ ◀

   A: Emphasis.

27 What Modern English word comes from the Latin word *interest*? _____

▶ □□ ◀

   A: Interest.

28 What did Latin *rata* become in Modern English? _____

▶ □□ ◀

   A: Rate. (In the Sample Text, the word "rate" has the form "rates." This contrast will be explained later.)

29 What did Latin *investimentum* become in English? (From now on, the term "English" will be used to refer to "Modern English.") _____

▶ □□ ◀

   A: Investment.

30   What derivative does Latin *certificatum* have in English? _____

▶ □ ◀

   A: Certificate.

31   What derivative does Latin *importans* have in English? _____

▶ □ ◀

   A: Important.

32   What derivative does Latin *familia* have in English? _____

▶ □ ◀

   A: Family.

33   What derivative does Latin *quartus* have in English? _____

▶ □ ◀

   A: Quarter.

34   What derivative does Latin *per centum* have in English? _____

▶ □ ◀

   A: Percent.

35   The two-word Latin phrase *per annum* comes to us from Latin with no change. *Per annum* tells how often the interest is added to the principal. Thus, the bank which is advertising says that it pays $5\frac{1}{4}$ percent _____ (hourly / daily / monthly / annually).

▶ □ ◀

   A: Annually. (Latin *per annum* means in English "per year.")

36   What language would you assume the Modern English word *annually* comes from?

   _____

▶ □ ◀

   A: Latin (from the resemblance to *annum* in the Latin phrase *per annum* = per year).

37–38   In the Sample Text preceding Frame 20, you saw some words borrowed from Latin and Greek with no change. There were three such words (or phrases). Give two of the three.

   _____ and _____

▶ □ ◀

   A: (Any two) Emphasis, interest, per annum.

NICE-TO-KNOW ■ While our Sample Text contains some words that have been taken from Latin or Greek with no change at all, there are some words at the opposite end which have changed very much as they came into English. The word *saving*, for example, comes to us through Middle English and Old French from Latin *salvare*. Not very close, is it? *Account* comes to us also through Middle English and Old French from Latin *computare*. And *financial* also comes by the same Middle English and Old French route from Latin *finis*, meaning "finish," the connection being that in financial matters one brings an account to an end. Some of these connections may seem unlikely, but evidence for the derivations is found in old manuscripts that reflect gradual changes in the usages of these words.

More English Derivatives from Latin and Greek Words
(Frames 39–49)

■ We will now examine another Sample Text, the opening paragraph of the Declaration of Independence. Once again, words of Greek or Latin origin are printed in boldface type. First, read the text.

> When in the **course** of **human events**, it becomes **necessary** for one **people** to **dissolve** the **political** bonds which have **connected** them with another, and to **assume** among the powers of the earth **separate** and **equal station** to which the laws of **nature** and of **nature's** God **entitle** them, a **decent respect** to the **opinions** of mankind **requires** that they should **declare** the **causes** which **impel** them to the **separation**.

The following frames provide another opportunity for you to see the relationship between English words and Greek and Latin words. For each word provided give the English derivative which appears in the Sample Text.

39   Latin *respectus* > (= has as a derivative) English _____

▶ □ ◀

    A: Respect. (Another word derived from Latin *respectus* is "respectable," but it is not the right answer because it is not in the Sample Text.)

40   Latin *statio* > (= has as a derivative) English _____

▶ □ ◀

    A: Station. (From now on, we will use the symbol > to mean "has as a derivative.")

41   Latin *separatio* > English _____

▶ □ ◀

    A: Separation.

42   Latin *cursus* > English _____

▶ □ ◀

    A: Course.

43   Latin *natura* > English _____

▶ ▫ ◀

     A: Nature.

44   Greek *politikos* > English _____

▶ ▫ ◀

     A: Political.

45   Latin *opinio* > English _____

▶ ▫ ◀

     A: Opinion.

46   Latin *eventus* > English _____

▶ ▫ ◀

     A: Event.

47   Latin *populus* > English _____

▶ ▫ ◀

     A: People.

48   Latin *causa* > English _____

▶ ▫ ◀

     A: Cause.

49   Latin *humanus* > English _____

▶ ▫ ◀

     A: Human. In the test for Unit 1, and in later tests, you will *not* be asked to remember
     Latin or Greek words.

Morphemes: Prefixes and Bases of Latin Origin
(Frames 50–112)

■ As you will soon see, words are often made up of two, three or even more **morphemes** (=
minimum units of meaning). In the next sequence of frames you will learn to **analyze** (= break
down) words made up of two morphemes. The words come from the opening paragraph of the

Declaration of Independence: *event, dissolve, assume, require,* and *impel.* Here are the same words rewritten to show the division into their two morphemes: *e-vént, dis-sólve, as-súme, re-quíre,* and *im-pél.* We have also indicated which syllable is accented.

50–54 A morpheme that occurs *at the front* of a word is called a **prefix.** It is customary to put morphemes in braces, like {**dis**}, in order to identify them. Write the five different prefixes in the words *event, dissolve, assume, require,* and *impel:* {_____}, {_____}, {_____}, {_____}, {_____}.

▶ □ ◀

    A: {e}, {dis}, {as}, {re}, {im}.

55 The morpheme to which a prefix is added is called the **base.** In the word *event,* {**vent**} is an example of such a base. What is the base of the word *dissolve?* {_____}

▶ □ ◀

    A: {solve}

56 What is the base of the word *impel?* {_____}

▶ □ ◀

    A: {pel}

57–58 What is the prefix in the word *event?* {_____} What is the prefix in *impel?* {_____}

▶ □ ◀

    A: {c}, {im}.

59–60 In the word *require,* what is the morpheme {**re**} called? _____.
What is the morpheme {**quire**} called? _____.

▶ □ ◀

    A: Prefix. Base.

61 As we have said, morphemes like {**re**} are minimum units of meaning. As an example, *impel* means to "push (someone or something) into something else." The morpheme {**pel**} means "push"; what does the morpheme {**im**} mean? _____

▶ □ ◀

    A: Into.

62–66 Write the five prefixes which occur in these new words: *return, eject, impose, assign,* and *dispose:* {_____}, {_____}, {_____}, {_____}, and {_____}.

▶ □□□ ◀

    A: {re}, {e}, {im}, {as}, and {dis}.

67 What do the braces around {**dis**} and {**solve**} signal? _____

_____

▶ □□□ ◀

    A: That these forms are morphemes.

68–70 There are now three technical terms you should know:

    1. What is a minimum unit of meaning called? _____

    2. What is a morpheme like {**dis**}, which comes at the *beginning* of a word, called?

       _____

    3. What is the {**pel**} part of *impel* called? _____

▶ □□□ ◀

    A: Self-test item; the answers can be found in frames beginning with 50.

71 It is often possible to determine the meanings of the five prefixes we have been examining from the contexts in which they occur. The prefix {**e**} is seen in *e-mérge,* as in "The frog *emerged* from the water and climbed onto a lily pad," and in *e-vict,* as in "After the party the landlord forcibly *evicted* John from his apartment." From the context, what is the meaning of {**e**} in these words? _____ (in / out / to / with)

▶ □□□ ◀

    A: Out (or from). Use your dictionary if you have any questions.

72 The prefix {**dis**} occurs in *dis-míss,* as in "The king *dismissed* the court jester with anger," and in *dis-pél,* as in "My uncle immediately started the group members singing, to *dispel* their fears aroused by the storm." From the context, what is the meaning of {**dis**} in these words? _____ (away / in / on / with)

▶ □□□ ◀

    A: Away.

73 The prefix {**as**} occurs in *as-sént,* as in "The teacher quickly gave his *assent* to our request," and in *as-sígn,* as in "The principal *assigned* an extra crossing guard to that corner." What is the meaning of {**as**} in the two words? _____

(from / to / under / with)

▶ □□□ ◀

    A: To (or toward).

NICE-TO-KNOW ■ The morpheme {as} is a common variant of {ad}, which occurs in the words *adjacent, admit,* and *adhesive.* Later we will explain the reason for this difference.

74   The prefix {re} occurs in *re-túrn,* as in "Mary *returned* our punch bowl just in time," and in *re-ject,* as in "The officer *rejected* my explanation without hesitation." What is the-

    meaning of {re} in these words? _____ (back /out / under / with)

▶ □□ ◀

    A: Back.

75   The prefix {im} is a variant of {in}. The {im} form occurs in the word *im-migrate,* as in "My grandfather *immigrated* to this country in 1910"; the {in} form occurs in the word *in-ject,* as in "The doctor *injected* a heavy dose of sedative into my sister's arm." What seems

    to be the meaning of {im} and {in} ? _____ (by / into / near / on)

▶ □□ ◀

    A: Into.

76   Here are the prefixes and bases of some of the words that appeared in the first paragraph of the Declaration of Independence. Notice that almost all of them have *variant forms* (that is, different forms with the same meaning). In the following sequence of frames you may refer to this list as you need to.

PREFIXES:
{**ad**}, {**as**} = to, toward
{**dis**} = away, apart
{**e**}, {**ex**} = out, from
{**in**}, {**im**} = in, into
{**re**} = back, again

BASES:
{**pel**}, {**pulse**} = push, drive
{**quire**} = ask, seek
{**solve**}, {**solut**} = loosen
{**spic**}, {**spect**} = look at, see
{**sume**} = use up, take
{**vene**}, {**vent**} = come

First, let's look at the meaning of some of the words that appear in the Sample Text:

> When in the **course** of **human events,** it becomes **necessary** for one **people** to **dissolve** the **political** bonds which have **connected** them with another, and to **assume** among the powers of the earth **separate** and **equal station** to which the laws of **nature** and of **nature's** God **entitle** them, a **decent respect** to the **opinions** of mankind **requires** that they should **declare** the **causes** which **impel** them to the **separation.**

What does *dis-sólve* mean in the phrase "it becomes necessary for one people to *dissolve* the political bonds"? (In your own words; use the list of morphemes above if necessary.)

_____

▶ □□ ◀

    A: Loosen themselves away from them.

77   What word in the Sample Text that means "take to oneself" is built on the base {**sume**}?

_____

▶ □□ ◀

A: Assume.

78   The Sample Text says that the authors will give the reasons that drove them to separation. What word means "drive to"?   _____

▶ □□ ◀

A: Impel.

79–83   Write the meaning of these prefixes.

{**ad**}, {**as**} = _____   {**dis**} = _____   {**e**}, {**ex**} = _____

{**in**}, {**im**} = _____   {**re**} = _____

▶ □□ ◀

A: Self-test item.

84   Now for an important fact about morphemes before we continue our study of prefixes and bases. A morpheme often has variant forms (i.e., different forms or spellings), depending on what base it is attached to. For example, the prefix you saw in _im-pél_ also occurs in _in-vént_ and _in-quíre_. What is the form of the prefix {**im**} in these two words?   _____

▶ □□ ◀

A: {in}

85   These variant forms, like {**in**} and {**im**}, which both mean "in" or "into," are called **allomorphs.** We say that {**in**} and {**im**} are allomorphs of each other. Likewise, the base {**pulse**} of the word _im-púlse_ is an allomorph of {**pel**} in _im-pél_. Thus, both {**pulse**} and {**pel**} have the same meaning. What is this meaning?   _____

▶ □□ ◀

A: Push or drive.

86   What do we call the variant forms of morphemes that have the same meaning, such as {**im**} and {**in**} in _impel_ and _inquire_?   _____

▶ □□ ◀

A: Allomorphs.

87 According to the list of prefixes and bases in frame 76, what is an allomorph of {**ex**}? _____

▶ □ ◀

A: {e}

88 What is an allomorph of {**ad**}? _____ (Use frame 76 if you need to.)

▶ □ ◀

A: {as}

89 What is an allomorph of the base {**vene**}? _____

▶ □ ◀

A: {vent}

90 What is an allomorph of the base {**solve**}? _____

▶ □ ◀

A: {solut}

91 What is an allomorph of the base {**spic**}? _____

▶ □ ◀

A: {spect}

92 What is the allomorph of {**in**} that appears when {**in**} is added to {**pel**}? _____

▶ □ ◀

A: {im}

93 We will now use these morphemes, both bases and prefixes, to form new combinations.

PREFIXES:
{**ad**}, {**as**} = to, toward
{**dis**} = away, apart
{**e**}, {**ex**} = out, from
{**in**}, {**im**} = in, into
{**re**} = back, again

BASES:
{**pel**}, {**pulse**} = push, drive
{**quire**} = ask, seek
{**solve**}, {**solut**} = loosen
{**spic**}, {**spect**} = look at, see
{**sume**} = use up, take
{**vene**}, {**vent**} = come

When someone *in-vénts* something, that person _____s into or upon that idea.

▶ □ ◀

A: Comes.

94 When people *in-quíre* about something, they make an investigation that looks _____ the matter.

▶ □ ◀

    A: Into.

95 What term is used to refer to both {in} and {quire}? They are both _____s.

▶ □ ◀

    A: Morphemes.

96 When we *re-pél* something, in what direction do we drive it? _____

▶ □ ◀

    A: Back.

97 When we *ex-pél* someone, where do we drive him? _____

▶ □ ◀

    A: Out.

98 When we say that the sun has *dis-pélled* the shadows of night, in what direction did the sun drive them? _____

▶ □ ◀

    A: Away.

99 What word is made up of the prefix {ad} and the base {vent} and means "arrival"? _____

▶ □ ◀

    A: Advent.

100 When we *re-súme* a task, we take it up _____.

▶ □ ◀

    A: Again.

101 How many morphemes are in the word *resume?* _____

▶ □ ◀

    A: Two.

102 The meanings of these and other prefixes is sometimes easy to see and sometimes difficult to see in English derivatives. In the Sample Text you saw the phrase "a decent *respect* to the opinions of mankind." The meaning of {**re**} in *respect* is not easy to see, for in English we think of *looking up* to someone we admire, but not *looking back*. It is therefore difficult to see the meaning of the {**re**} in *respect*. But the meaning of the base {**spect**} is clear. What does it mean? _____

▶ ◻ ◀

   A: Look at or see.

103 When someone *in-spécts* a shipment of goods, that person _____s into them.

▶ ◻ ◀

   A: Looks.

104 Now we will use a new prefix, {**con**}, which also appears in the form {**com**}. This prefix often means "together." When a group of people *con-véne* in a city for a meeting they come _____ for the meeting.

▶ ◻ ◀

   A: Together.

105 What do we sometimes call a large meeting or assembly of people who have *convened* (come together) for the purpose of carrying on some sort of business? A _____.

▶ ◻ ◀

   A: Convention.

106–107 In the last two frames you have seen two allomorphs that mean "come." What are they? {_____} and {_____}.

▶ ◻ ◀

   A: {vene}, {vent}.

108 Now we will use the prefix {**re**} again. The prefix {**re**} occurs with the bases {**solve**}, {**sume**}, {**spect**}, {**quire**}, and {**pel**}. What does an army do when it *repels* an attack of the enemy? It _____ them _____.

▶ ◻ ◀

   A: It pushes them back.

109 When a person *resumes* the study of the piano, that person _____
(begins it / improves / stops it / takes it up again).

▶ □ ◀

   A: Takes it up again.

110 In *repel* the prefix {**re**} means "back." But what does {**re**} mean in *resume?* _____

▶ □ ◀

   A: Again.

111 You have now learned two important facts about these minimum units of meaning which
are called morphemes. In your own words, what was the first fact about the *forms* of
morphemes, illustrated by the morpheme {**as**} or {**ad**} in the words *assign* and *advent?*

_____

▶ □ ◀

   A: That morphemes have allomorphs.

112 Considering the meanings of the prefix {**re**} in the words *repel* and *resume,* what is the
second important fact about the meaning of morphemes? (In your own words.)

_____

▶ □ ◀

   A: They sometimes have different meanings.

Empty, Full, and Intensifying Morphemes
(Frames 113–141)

113 While {**re**} means "back" in *repel* and "again" in *resume,* it is difficult to assign a meaning
to {**re**} in *respect* and *require.* We therefore say that the {**re**} in *respect* and *require* is an

empty morpheme. In your own words, what does this term seem to mean? _____

_____

▶ □ ◀

   A: That this morpheme has no clear meaning.

114 The {**re**} in *repel* is called a **full morpheme** because a meaning can be assigned to it. Is the

morpheme {**re**} in *resume* full or empty? _____

▶ □ ◀

   A: Full.

115 The distinction between empty morphemes and full morphemes is a useful learning device, but the distinction is not always clear. Is the {con} in *convention* full or empty?

_____

▶ □ ◀

A: Full. (People come *together*, rather than come back, for example.)

> **NICE-TO-KNOW** ■ It would be tidy if all morphemes had just one meaning. If we face the facts we find that not only do most morphemes have several meanings, but even the distinction between full and empty is not always clear. Therefore, do not be surprised if occasionally what we call empty seems to you to be full, or vice versa.

116 It is sometimes advantageous to use a shorthand form for concepts. In the sentence "The prefix {con} in *convention* is a {**full**}," how would you interpret {**full**}?

_____

▶ □ ◀

A: Full morpheme.

117 Therefore, how would you interpret {**empty**} in the sentence, "The {**re**} in *respect* in an {**empty**}"? _____

▶ □ ◀

A: Empty morpheme.

118 Morphemes need not be just full or empty. For example, often the prefix {**con**} or {**com**} does not mean "together" but has the effect of *strengthening the meaning* of the base. When we say, "John's boss *compelled* him to work under unsanitary conditions," from the context does the action of the boss seem weak, moderate, or forceful? _____

▶ □ ◀

A: Forceful.

119 We say that a morpheme like {**con**} in *compel* **intensifies** the base. Does this mean that it makes the base stronger or weaker? _____

▶ □ ◀

A: Stronger.

120 Just as we have the symbols {**full**} and {**empty**}, we will add a third symbol, {**intens**}. How would you interpret {**intens**}? _____

▶ □ ◀

A: Intensifying morpheme.

121   What kind of prefix is {**con**} in *compel*—empty, full, or intensifying? _____

▶ □□ ◀

    A: Intensifying.

122   What allomorph of {**con**} did you see in the last frame? _____

▶ □□ ◀

    A: {com}

123   When we say that the fire *consumed* the building, was the damage light, moderate, or heavy? _____

▶ □□ ◀

    A: Heavy.

124   The base {**spect**}, which means "see," has an allomorph {**spic**}. The word *conspicuous*, as in "After four drinks Harry made himself *conspicuous* by boisterous talking and by telling terrible jokes," means about the same as "visible." But which is stronger, *conspicuous* or *visible*? _____

▶ □□ ◀

    A: Conspicuous.

125   *Conspicuous* means not just visible but highly visible. What morpheme conveys the general idea of "highly" or "very"? _____

▶ □□ ◀

    A: {con}

126–127   What is the prefix in the word *conspicuous*? {_____} Does this prefix seem to be {**empty**}, {**full**}, or {**intens**} in this word? _____

▶ □□ ◀

    A: {con}, {intens}.

128   Following are examples of {**empty**}, {**full**}, and {**intens**} morphemes. Look at the two sentences "Suddenly the speaker observed a *motion* among her listeners," and "Suddenly the speaker observed a *commotion* among her listeners." Which word is stronger, *motion* or *commotion*? _____

▶ □□ ◀

    A: Commotion. (Somebody might get hurt in a commotion.)

129   Therefore, what kind of morpheme is {**com**} in *commotion?* _____

▶ □□ ◀

    A: {intens}

130   Morphemes like {**re**} in *repel* and a new prefix, {**pro**} in *propel*, are full morphemes. In which direction do we *propel* something? _____

▶ □□ ◀

    A: Forward.

131   In which direction do we *repel* something? _____

▶ □□ ◀

    A: Back (or backwards).

132   The {**con**} in *conspicuous* means that something is not just visible but is _____.

▶ □□ ◀

    A: Highly visible.

133   What symbol is used for a morpheme with this meaning of strengthening?

    {_____}

▶ □□ ◀

    A: {intens}

134   In the second paragraph of the bank advertisement we read "You can use this account to *accumulate* dollars." The English word *cumulus* refers to a certain type of cloud. These clouds are not thin, streaky clouds but thick, massive clouds that look like heaps of hay. In the sentence "The winter storms *cumulated* shells upon the beach in great numbers,"

    what does *cumulate* mean? _____

▶ □□ ◀

    A: Heap (or heap up).

135   What does the Sample Text say you can do to dollars? _____

▶ □□ ◀

    A: Accumulate them.

136 The morpheme {**ac**} is an allomorph of {**ad**} and often means "to" or "toward." The base {**cess**} means "go" or "come"; *access* is a going or coming _____ something.

▶ □ ◀

A: Toward.

137 But it is hard to see how {**ac**} in *accumulate* means "heap up towards." Consequently we identify {**ac**} here as an {_____}.

▶ □ ◀

A: {**intens**}. (A good argument can also be made for {**empty**}: as we have explained, the distinctions are not always clear in most areas of analysis of meaning.)

138 Which kind of morpheme is {**re**}, as in "earn a good return," {**full**} or {**intens**}? _____

▶ □ ◀

A: {full}

139 When we *return* something, in which direction do we turn it? _____

▶ □ ◀

A: Back.

140 When we *overturn* something, in which direction do we turn it? _____

▶ □ ◀

A: Over.

141 And what direction is an *upturn* taking? _____

▶ □ ◀

A: Up.

NICE-TO-KNOW ■ The morpheme {**over**} is an Anglo-Saxon prefix; {**turn**} is a derivative from Latin. The morpheme {**up**} is also an Anglo-Saxon prefix.

New Prefixes
(Frames 142–160)

142–147 In this section, some new prefixes will be presented. But first review the meanings of the bases you have already used. One meaning for each is enough.

{pel}, {pulse} = _____   {spic}, {spect} = _____

{quire} = _____   {sume} = _____

{solve}, {solut} = _____   {vene}, {vent} = _____

▶ □ ◀

A: Push, drive; ask, seek; loosen; see, look at; use up, take; come.

148 Now for four new prefixes. The first is {pre}, as in "He got to the gym earlier because he enjoyed the *pré-game* shows." What does {pre} mean? Pay attention to the context in which the word was used. _____

▶ □ ◀

A: Before.

149 "Jane had *pre-suppósed* that she would be welcome at the party, but she soon learned that she was not." That is, she supposed _____ (after / before) the party that she would be welcome.

▶ □ ◀

A: Before.

150 If someone *pre-vénts* an accident, it means that he does something _____ (after / before) an accident happens.

▶ □ ◀

A: Before.

151 Next is {retro}, as in "John was happy to read that his pay raise was *retro-áctive* to the first of the year." This means that his employer will go _____ (back / forward) to January 1 to figure his rate of pay.

▶ □ ◀

A: Back.

152 When we look at something in *rétro-spect*, in what direction do we look? _____

▶ □ ◀

A: Back.

153 Next comes {intro}, as in "The *intro-dúction* of goats was a disaster to the ecology of Hawaii." In what direction did the early travelers to Hawaii move the goats, into Hawaii or away from it? _____

▶ □ ◀

A: Into.

154 "Janice has an *intro-spéctive* nature." Does Janice focus her thoughts inward or outward?

_____

▶ □ ◀

A: Inward.

155 The fourth new prefix is {**contra**}, as in "Dinner at the Wilsons' that night was noisy because Mike *contra-dicted* everything his sister said." Did Mike speak for or against her?

_____

▶ □ ◀

A: Against.

156 Finally, {**pro**}, as in "Andy *pro-pélled* the rock against the bear with all his might." In what direction did he throw the rock? _____

▶ □ ◀

A: Forward.

157 On the other hand, the prefix {**pro**} frequently has the meaning of "in favor of." What are the feelings of someone who is *pro-revolútionary?* _____

▶ □ ◀

A: He or she is in favor of revolution.

158 You have heard the expression *pro and con*, meaning "for and against," as in "After we had heard all the *pros and cons* about the program we put the matter to a vote." The *pro* is the prefix {**pro**}, meaning "in favor of." The *con*, however, is not the prefix {**con**} meaning "together"; it is rather a shortened form of {**contra**}, which means _____.

▶ □ ◀

A: Against.

159 People voting for a motion are said to be _____ (pro / con).

▶ □ ◀

A: Pro.

160 The opposition is said to be _____.

▶ □ ◀

A: Con.

Three Main Types of Morphemes: Prefix, Base, and Suffix
(Frames 161–176)

161 The base {**creat**} means "make" or "build." What then is a *creát-or?*

_____

▶ □ ◀

    A: A person who creates (or makes or builds).

162 What is a *creát-ion?* _____

▶ □ □ □ □ □ □ □ □ □ □ □ U □ ⊓ □ □ □ □ □ □ □ □ □ ◀

    A: A thing that is created (or made or built).

163 Someone who *re-creátes* a Greek temple in an American city does not design from scratch but builds this temple _____.

▶ □ U U U □ □ □ □ □ □ □ □ □ □ ◀

    A: Again.

164 What is the prefix in *re-creáte* that means "again"?   {_____}

▶ □ ◀

    A: {re}

165 A **suffix** is a morpheme that comes at the end of a word. In *re-creátion*, the prefix is {**re**}, the base is {**creat**}, and {**ion**} is the suffix, meaning "act of." What is the suffix of *creator?* {_____}.

▶ □ ◀

    A: {or}

166 What is the meaning of the suffix {**or**}, as in *creator, inventor,* or *conductor?*

_____

▶ □ ◀

    A: A person (or thing) who acts or does something.

167 Let us examine *re-pláce-ment,* another word of Latin origin, as in "It was not easy to find a *replacement* for the star of the play." The word means "a person (or thing) which takes the place of another person (or thing)." What is the suffix in *replacement?*   {_____}

▶ □ ◀

    A: {ment}

We will now return to our Sample Text, the bank advertisement, to find words that can be used to analyze bases, prefixes, and suffixes.

With all the **recent emphasis** on high **interest rates** for **investment certificates,** you may be overlooking a very **important family financial** tool . . . the five and one **quarter percent per annum** passbook **savings account.**

This is your "daily working" **savings account.** It earns daily **interest**—from day of **deposit** to day of withdrawal. The **money** is always **available,** so you can **use** this **account** to **accumulate** dollars, take them out when you need to **pay** a **medical bill,** a **repair bill, taxes,** a trip. It's about as **convenient** as a wallet, but your **money** is earning a good **return** every day it is on **deposit** and it is **safely insured** with an **agency** of the **federal government.**

A **bonus feature** is that by **maintaining** a **balance** of $1000 or more in **savings** you are **entitled** to all of the **travelers** checks and **money orders** you can **use.** No **charge.**

So **invest** all the **money** you can in our top **interest paying certificate accounts** for long **term requirements,** but for day to day needs and **emergencies** keep a healthy **balance** in a five and one **quarter percent** daily working **account** where it will be **immediately available** and earn a good **return.**

168–170 There are three words in this Sample Text that have the suffix {**ment**}. What are they?

_____, _____, _____.

▶ □ ◀

A: Investment, government, and requirements.

171 An *investment* is something (like money) that has been _____ in something else, like stocks or a bank account.

▶ □ ◀

A: Invested.

172 Which meaning does the suffix {**ment**} have in *requirement*, as in "The main *requirement* for the course is the ability to swim"? Is a *requirement* (a) a thing that is required, or (b) an agency that does the requiring? _____

▶ □ ◀

A: (a) A thing that is required.

173 Now to another common suffix. The Sample Text included the phrase "to pay a medical bill." The word *medical* means "connected with the science of _____."

▶ □ ◀

A: Medicine.

174 The base in *médic-al* is {**medic**}. What is the suffix and what does it mean? {_____}

_____

▶ □ ◀

    A: {al}. It means "connected with, pertaining to."

175 The Sample Text speaks of "the federal government." The base {**feder**} means "a union of states." In the War Between the States, the Southern states were known as the

_____

▶ □ ◀

    A: Confederacy (or Confederate states).

176 Today, *federal* means on a national level rather than a state level or municipal level. What does the suffix {**al**} mean in *federal?* _____

▶ □ ◀

    A: Connected with (or pertaining to).

Your Dictionary as a Tool
(Frames 177–206)

177 Some people expect that if they learn these prefixes, suffixes, and bases, they will hardly ever have to use a dictionary. In the light of your experience with this program so far, evaluate this statement. _____

_____

▶ □ ◀

    A: It is most misleading; language is not that simple. For example, morphemes often have more than one meaning.

178 Since language is so complex, we expect that as a result of the program you will use a dictionary _____ (more than / the same as / less than) before.

▶ □ ◀

    A: More than (*much* more!).

179 The first thing to realize about a dictionary is that it gives you an enormous amount of material, perhaps more than you can use at the present time. In this series of frames we will have you concentrate mainly on the meanings of the words you will be asked to look up. We will begin with the first paragraph of the bank advertisement, which is reprinted again here.

> With all the recent emphasis on high interest rates for investment certificates, you may be overlooking a very important family financial tool . . . the five and one quarter percent per annum passbook savings account.

We will give the entry for *emphasis* from four different dictionaries. First, here is the entry for the word as it appears in the *American Heritage Dictionary* (New College Edition):

em·pha·sis (ĕm′fə-sĭs) *n., pl.* **-ses** (-sēz′). **1.** Special importance or significance placed upon or imparted to something. **2.** Stress applied to a syllable, word, or passage by the use of a gesture, italics, or other indication. **3.** Force or intensity of expression, feeling, or action. **4.** Sharpness or vividness of outline; prominence. [Latin, from Greek, reflection, meaning, significance, from *emphainein*, to exhibit, indicate : *en-*, in + *phainein*, to show (see **bhā-¹** in Appendix*).]

One objective is for you to be able to understand the information following the numerals, which gives the different meanings of *emphasis*. First, then, how many different meanings does this dictionary say *emphasis* has? _____

▶ □ ◀

    A: Four.

180   Which of these four definitions describes the meaning that *emphasis* has in the first paragraph of the advertisement? _____ (1 / 2 / 3 / 4)

▶ □ ◀

    A: Meaning 1 ("special importance," etc.).

NICE-TO-KNOW ■ Here is a brief explanation of the rest of the information. The characters in parentheses (including the upside-down e) indicate the pronunciation of *emphasis*.
    The abbreviation **n.** means that *emphasis* belongs to the word class **noun** (as opposed to being a verb, adjective, or other part of speech). Some of you will not know what terms such as "noun" mean, but you will learn them in the next unit.
    The abbreviation **pl.** *-ses (-sēz′)* means that the irregular plural (= more than one) form of *emphasis* is *emphases,* and *(-sēz′)* shows its pronunciation.
    Remember, you are not expected to learn all this at the present time.

181   Look at the information at the end of the dictionary entry, printed inside square brackets, which gives the **etymology** (= origin) of the word. From what language did *emphasis* come directly into English? _____

▶ □ ◀

    A: Latin.

182   And from what language did the speakers of Latin borrow the word *emphasis?*

_____

▶ □ ◀

    A: Greek.

NICE-TO-KNOW ■ The information in parentheses ("see **bhà-**¹ in Appendix*") refers you to the section at the end of the *American Heritage Dictionary* labeled "Indo-European Roots." Most languages spoken in Europe and some used in India come from a common language called "Indo-European." You will learn more about this in Unit Ten.

183–186 Here is the entry from the *American Heritage Dictionary* again. Answer all four of the questions below before checking your answers.

> **em·pha·sis** (ĕm′fə-sĭs) *n., pl.* **-ses** (-sēz′). **1.** Special importance or significance placed upon or imparted to something. **2.** Stress applied to a syllable, word, or passage by the use of a gesture, italics, or other indication. **3.** Force or intensity of expression, feeling, or action. **4.** Sharpness or vividness of outline; prominence. [Latin, from Greek, reflection, meaning, significance, from *emphainein*, to exhibit, indicate : *en-*, in + *phainein*, to show (see **bhà-**¹ in Appendix*).]

How many different meanings does the *American Heritage Dictionary* say *emphasis* has?

_____

Which meaning does *emphasis* have in the phrase "with all the recent emphasis on high interest rates"? _____

What language does *emphasis* eventually go back to? _____

From what language did we get *emphasis* directly? _____

▶ □ ◀

A: Four. The first. Greek. Latin.

187 Here is the entry for the same word as it appears in *Webster's New World Dictionary* (Second College Edition):

> **em·pha·sis** (ĕm′fə sĭs) *n., pl.* **-ses′** (-sēz′) [L. < Gr. *emphasis*, an appearing in, outward appearance < *emphainein*, to indicate < *en-*, in + *phainein*, to show < IE. base *bha-*, to shine, whence OE. *bonian*, to ornament] **1.** force of expression, thought, feeling, action, etc. **2.** special stress given to a syllable, word, phrase, etc. in speaking **3.** special attention given to something so as to make it stand out; importance; stress; weight [to put less *emphasis* on athletics]

First, we will take up the different meanings. How many different meanings does this dictionary give for *emphasis*? _____

▶ □ ◀

A: Three.

188 And how many meanings did the *American Heritage Dictionary* give? _____

▶ □ ◀

A: Four.

189 Which of the three meanings in the entry given in *Webster's New World Dictionary* (frame 187) does *emphasis* have in our Sample Text? _____

▶ □□ ◀

 A: The third.

190 Through the abbreviations [L. < Gr.], this entry tells us that the word *emphasis* comes to us originally from the _____ language through the _____ language.

▶ □□ ◀

 A: Greek, Latin.

191 Here is the entry for *emphasis* as it appears in *Webster's New Collegiate Dictionary*:

> em·pha·sis \'em(p)-fə-səs\ *n, pl* -pha·ses \-,sēz\ [L, fr. Gk, exposition, emphasis, fr. *emphainein* to indicate, fr. *en-* + *phainein* to show — more at FANCY] (1573) **1 a** : force or intensity of expression that gives special impressiveness or importance to something ⟨writing with ～ on the need for reform⟩ **b** : a particular prominence given in reading or speaking to one or more words or syllables **2** : special consideration of or stress or insistence on something ⟨their ～ on discipline⟩

As before, we will begin with the meanings. How many *main* divisions of meaning do the editors of this dictionary present? _____

▶ □□ ◀

 A: Two.

192 Into how many meanings do the editors divide the first main meaning? _____

▶ □□ ◀

 A: Two (labeled *1a* and *b*).

193 So how many meanings in all do the editors give for *emphasis*? _____

▶ □□ ◀

 A: Three (1*a*, 1*b*, and 2).

194 Which meaning does *emphasis* have in our Sample Text? _____ (1*a*/1*b*/2)

▶ □□ ◀

 A: 2 ("special consideration," etc.).

195 Finally, here is the entry from *The Shorter Oxford English Dictionary*, an abridgment (= shortened version) of *The Oxford English Dictionary*. This entry from the abridgment is more than twice as long as the three "desk dictionary" entries we have been examining.

Emphasis (e·mfăsis). Pl. **emphases.**
1573. [– L. *emphasis* – Gr. ἔμφασις, orig.
(mere) appearance, f. *ἐμφα-* in ἐμφαίνειν
exhibit, f. *en* EM-¹ + φαίνειν show (see
PHASIS).] †1. (The Gr. and L. sense.) A
figure of speech in which more is implied than
is actually said; a meaning conveyed by
implication –1764. **2.** Vigour of expression.
Now as *transf.* from 4. 1573. **3.** Force of feeling, action, etc. 1602. **4.** Stress of voice laid
on a word or phrase to indicate its implied
meaning, or simply to mark its importance
1613. **5.** *transf.* Stress laid upon, or importance assigned to, a fact or idea 1687. **6.**
Prominence 1872. †**7.** A mere appearance.
WHARTON.
    2. Tertullian doth add the greater E. to his
Arguments BP. STILLINGFL. **3.** *Haml.* v. i. 278. **4.**
The e. is wrongly placed JOWETT. **5.** My laying e.
on the previous effect of the vaccine inoculation
1805. **6.** The bones which mark the features. .
lose their e. BLACKIE. var. †**E·mphasy.**

The first difference between the entry in the *SOED (Shorter Oxford English Dictionary)*
and the other three is the numerals "1573" immediately following the word *emphasis.*

What do you suppose they stand for? _____

_____

▶ □□□ ◀

A: They show the date of the first recorded use of the word.

196 How many meanings does the *SOED* list for *emphasis*? _____

▶ □□□ ◀

A: Seven.

197 Which meaning does *emphasis* have in the phrase from the Sample Text "with all the
recent *emphasis* on high interest rates"? _____

▶ □□□ ◀

A: The fifth ("stress laid upon," etc.).

198 According to the *SOED*, in what year was the word first used in the sense used in our
Sample Text? _____

▶ □□□ ◀

A: 1687.

199 Before meanings 1 and 7 there is a dagger. This dagger is a conventional sign meaning
obsolete. We often use *obsolete* in a sense like this: "The battleship, once the major
weapon in a country's navy, has now become *obsolete* because of such weapons as submarines and airplanes." What does *obsolete* mean when applied to words?

_____

▶ □□□ ◀

A: That they are no longer used.

NICE-TO-KNOW ■ The abbreviation **transf.** stands for "transferred meaning." When used with the fifth definition in the *SOED* it indicates that the meaning of *emphasis* has been transferred from such things as loudness of voice to the wider field of ideas.

200 There are other large dictionaries which you may sometimes wish to use, but in this program we will concentrate on showing you how to use the desk-sized editions. Here are the entries from *American Heritage*, *Webster's New World*, and *Webster's New Collegiate* for the word *investment*.

American Heritage Dictionary

in·vest·ment (ĭn-věst′mənt) *n.* **1.** The act of investing or the state of being invested. **2.** An amount invested. **3.** Property or another possession acquired for future income or benefit. **4.** Investiture. **5.** *Archaic.* A garment; vestment. **6.** An outer covering or layer. **7.** *Military.* A siege.

Webster's New World Dictionary

in·vest·ment (in vest′mənt) *n.* **1.** an investing or being invested **2.** an outer covering **3.** *same as* INVESTITURE (sense 1) **4.** *a)* the investing of money *b)* the amount invested *c)* anything in which money is or may be invested

Webster's New Collegiate Dictionary

¹**in·vest·ment** \in-′ves(t)-mənt\ *n* [¹*invest*] (1597) **1 a** *archaic* : VESTMENT **b** : an outer layer : ENVELOPE **2** : INVESTITURE 1 **3** : BLOCKADE. SIEGE
²**investment** *n* [²*invest*] (1615) : the outlay of money usu. for income or profit : capital outlay; *also* : the sum invested or the property purchased

How many meanings for *investment* does *American Heritage* have? _____

▶ □ ◀

 A: Seven.

201 Which of these seven meanings applies to the use of *investment* in the phrase "investment certificates" in the Sample Text (frame 179)?) _____

▶ □ ◀
 A: The third.

202 How many meanings for *investment* does *Webster's New World* have? _____

▶ □ ◀

 A: Four (one with three subdivisions, giving a total of six meanings).

203 How many meanings does *Webster's New Collegiate* give for *investment*? (Careful! This is tricky.) _____

_____

▶ □□ ◀

   A: First, there are two separate entries, meaning that the editors thought the meanings were so different that they are separate words. There are four meanings (1*a*, 1*b*, 2, and 3) for the first word; the second word has two meanings.

204 Here are the entries for the suffix {**ment**} as given by *Webster's New World* and *Webster's New Collegiate*. (*American Heritage* does not list the morpheme {**ment**} separately.)

Webster's New World

> **-ment** (mənt, mint) [ME. < OFr. < L. *-mentum*] *a n.-forming suffix meaning:* **1.** a result or product [*improve*-*ment, pavement*] **2.** a means, agency, or instrument [*adornment, escapement*] **3.** the act, fact, process, or art [*measurement, movement*] **4.** the state, condition, fact, or degree [*disappointment*] Final *y* after a consonant becomes *i* before *-ment* [*embodiment*]

How many meanings for {**ment**} does *Webster's New World* list? _____.

▶ □□ ◀

   A: Four.

205   *Webster's New Collegiate*

> **-ment** \mənt; *homographic verbs are* ‚ment *also* mənt, *the latter less often before a syllable-increasing suffix*\ *n suffix* [ME, fr. OF, fr. L *-mentum;* akin to L *-men,* suffix denoting concrete result, Gk *-mat-, -ma*] **1 a** : concrete result, object, or agent of a (specified) action ⟨embank*ment*⟩ ⟨entangle*ment*⟩ **b** : concrete means or instrument of a (specified) action ⟨entertain*ment*⟩ **2 a** : action : process ⟨encircle*ment*⟩ ⟨de-velop*ment*⟩ **b** : place of a (specified) action ⟨encamp*ment*⟩ **3** : state or condition resulting from (a specified action)

How many meanings does *Webster's Collegiate* list? _____

_____

▶ □□ ◀

   A: Three main meanings, but with two subdivisions for the first meaning and the second.

206 How do you account for the fact that the definitions of these words varies from dictionary to dictionary? (In your own words). _____

_____

▶ □□ ◀

   A: Dictionaries are composed by editors who, naturally enough, analyze words differently.

WORD LIST

This unit introduced a number of important concepts. The names of these concepts were printed in boldface type in the program. Here is a list of them; each item is followed by the frame number in which it was introduced. Make sure you understand *all* the concepts and can give examples of each. Use a dictionary if you need to.

allomorphs 85	derivative 2	intensifying morpheme 119	Old English 14
analyze 50	empty morpheme 113		prefix 50
Anglo-Saxon 14	etymology 181	Middle English 14	structure 14
base 55	full morpheme 114	morpheme 50	suffix 165
borrowings 2	function word 4, 14	obsolete 199	word order 14
content word 4			

Use the list below in the following way. Scan it rapidly and check any word that does not seem familiar. Using the frame number to the right of the word, look up the frame where the word first appeared.

access 136	cumulate 134	inquire 84	pro 158
account 37	cumulus 134	inspect 103	propel 130
accumulate 134	dismiss 72	interest 4	pro-revolutionary 157
advent 99	dispel 72	introduction 153	quarter 33
annually 36	dissolve 50	introspective 154	rate 4
assent 73	emerge 71	invent 84	recent 4
assume 50	emphasis 4, 179	inventor 166	re-create 163
cause 48	event 46	investment 5–6, 171	reject 74
certificate 7	evict 71	medical 173	repel 96
commotion 128	expel 97	motion 128	replacement 167
compel 118	family 5–6	nature 43	require 50
con 158	federal 175	opinion 45	requirement 170
conductor 166	financial 22	overlooking 10	respect 39
conspicuous 124	government 169	overturn 140	resume 100
consume 123	high 4	people 47	retroactive 151
contradict 155	human 49	per annum 35	retrospect 152
convene 104	immigrate 75	percent 34	return 74
convention 105	impel 50	political 44	separation 41
course 42	important 31	pregame 148	station 40
creation 162	impulse 85	presuppose 149	upturn 14
creator 161	inject 75	prevent 150	

Following is a series of non-programmed exercises. You and your instructor will decide which exercises would be useful to you. This unit, like all the others, has the following four types of exercises:

1. Review Exercises on some selected point of the unit (dictionary useful but not required)
2. Words of Interesting Origin (dictionary required)
3. Easily Confused Words (dictionary not required)
4. Latin Phrases (dictionary required)

REVIEW EXERCISES

Purpose: To practice determining the meanings of words on the basis of their prefixes.

Directions: Basing your decision only on the meaning of the prefix, copy from the choices provided the word that you think matches the definition. Write the prefix of the word and its meaning. Notice that there is not the usual context to assist you.

1. a moving backward _____

   The prefix is _____, which means _____

   (a) introgression
   (b) digression
   (c) regression

2. to put in, to let in _____

   The prefix _____ = _____

   (a) to emit
   (b) to intromit
   (c) to remit

3. to agree to (something) _____

   The prefix _____ = _____

   (a) to resent
   (b) to dissent
   (c) to assent

4. to indicate beforehand _____

   The prefix _____ = _____

   (a) to consign
   (b) to presignify
   (c) to resign

5. opposition, violation _____

   The prefix _____ = _____

   (a) contravention
   (b) convention
   (c) prevention

6. to stretch forth _____

   The prefix _____ = _____

   (a) to retract
   (b) to protract
   (c) to distract

7. something copied _____

   The prefix _____ = _____

   (a) conscription
   (b) prescript
   (c) rescript

8. to move forward _____

   The prefix _____ = _____

   (a) to emote
   (b) to promote
   (c) to demote

Directions: Circle the correct meaning of each of the italicized words. Base your decision on the information that the prefix gives you. Copy the prefix and give its meaning.

1. Mr. Long will *contravene* the proposal.

   Prefix _____ = _____

   (a) go with
   (b) go against
   (c) go before
   (d) go beyond

2. Ms. Davis gave a *proleptic* account of the event.

   Prefix _____ = _____

   (a) looking ahead
   (b) summary
   (c) contradictory
   (d) degrading

3. Gary's friends hoped to *dissuade* him.

   Prefix _____ = _____

   (a) encourage him
   (b) turn him against
   (c) turn him aside
   (d) assist him

4. The doctor will *excise* the kidney.

   Prefix _____ = _____

   (a) repair
   (b) remove
   (c) transplant
   (d) examine

5. Art's explanation was *convoluted*.

   Prefix _____ = _____

   (a) drawn out
   (b) filled in
   (c) separated
   (d) twisted together

6. The youth *accosted* Mr. Miller.

   Prefix _____ = _____

   (a) approached
   (b) returned to
   (c) followed
   (d) preceded

7. We considered Janice's position a *retroversion*.

   Prefix _____ = _____

   (a) a turning inward
   (b) a turning back
   (c) a turning toward
   (d) a turning around

8. We *imbibed* the radical views of the new instructor.

   Prefix _____ = _____

   (a) ridiculed
   (b) drank in
   (c) publicized
   (d) rejected

WORDS OF INTERESTING ORIGIN

Directions: Use this list to help complete the exercises. Consult a dictionary where necessary.

L. {nas} = nose
L. {turt} = twist
Gr. {skia} = shadow
Gr. {oura} = tail
L. {scrupus} = sharp stone

L. {ulus} = small
L. {villanus} = servant working on a farm
Hawaiian {uku} = flea
Hawaiian {lele} = jump

1. "The minute I saw the *nasturtium* in your garden, I could feel myself getting ready to sneeze." If you consider the Latin morphemes, what is the etymological meaning of the flower called *nasturtium*? _____

_____

2. From what two Greek morphemes does *squirrel* come? _____

3. "Thomas has no *scruples* about climbing in his neighbor's kitchen window."

   What does *scruple* mean today? _____

   What was the etymology of *scruple*? _____

   _____

4. "Aha," said the *villain*, "at last you shall be mine." What did *villain* mean in Roman times?

   _____

5. "Ike was a great favorite when he strummed his *ukulele* and sang." Explain the etymology of

   ukulele. _____

   _____

EASILY CONFUSED WORDS

There are many words that are commonly confused. At the end of each unit there will be an exercise intended to help you keep them straight. Use a dictionary as needed.

1. **Sanguine / sanguinary.**   Both of these words came from Latin {**sanguin**}, meaning "blood." *Sanguine* was originally a medical term, meaning that the sanguine person has the right amount of blood in his body and is therefore healthy and cheerful. Today its common meaning is "optimistic," as in "John's nature was so *sanguine* that we all felt cheered up when we saw him." *Sanguinary* means "covered with blood," as in "The battle was so *sanguinary* that hardly a combatant on either side was without a wound." The word also means "cruel" or "bloodthirsty," as in "John's nature was so *sanguinary* that we felt we could not trust him with any of the prisoners."

2. **Desiccated / dissected.**   These words come from different Latin origins. *Desiccate* means "dry out," from Latin *siccus* (= dry), as in "The corpse had been so *desiccated* over several centuries in the dry desert that the flesh was as hard as iron." *Dissect* comes from Latin *dis* (= apart) and Latin *sect* (= cut), as in "The surgeon carefully *dissected* the body, laying each organ in a special order."

3. **Disinterested / uninterested.**   Both words are the opposite of *interested*. *Disinterested* means "not influenced by selfish motives," as in "We could not have had a better judge than Judge Blandford; he was friendly, knowledgeable, and above all completely *disinterested*." *Uninterested*, on the other hand, means "not interested," "indifferent," "not paying attention," as in "We could not have had a worse judge than the one we had; he was completely *uninterested* in the case and the participants, and even read a magazine during some of the testimony."

Use the six words in the sentences where each makes sense.

1. We could never understand Larry's enthusiasm for showing us the bodies of animals he had

   _____ .

2. The scrap between the two boys appeared to be more _____ than it actually proved to be when we wiped away the gore.

3. After our eight hours on the trail, the _____ food we had brought tasted like something from the finest restaurant.

4. "If you were so _____ in football, why did you have me buy these expensive seats?" Dick asked bitterly.

5. "Can you assure me that you will be completely _____ in this case?" Nell asked suspiciously.

6. Walt was so _____ about the possibilities of fair weather that we didn't even take waterproof clothes.

LATIN PHRASES

NOTE: Latin words and phrases are common in English, particularly in the writings and speech of certain groups of highly educated people. There is, however, considerable variation in pronunciation.

First try to get the meaning of each Latin phrase from the context of the sentences below, choosing a definition from the list that follows. Write the number of the Latin phrase beside the definition that fits.

1. *Sine die*, as in "The judge had adjourned the court *sine die*, so we had no idea when our case would be resumed."

2. *Per diem*, as in "The travel expenses were on a *per diem* basis, so we did not need to keep our receipts."

3. *Post meridiem*, as in "The plane takes off at 2:05 *p.m.*"

4. *Tabula rasa*, as in "After six years as a prisoner Cliff felt that his mind was a *tabula rasa*."

5. *Ad nauseam*, as in "Grubbs talked about his accomplishments *ad nauseam*."

_____ a clean slate		_____ after noon	
_____ special mail		_____ throughout the day	
_____ daily allowance		_____ without a definite date	
_____ let me perish		_____ disgusting advertisements	
_____ an eroded tabletop mountain		_____ to the point of making one ill	

Use a dictionary to find the word-by-word translation and modern meaning for each phrase.

	Word-by-Word Translation	Modern Meaning
sine die	_____	_____
per diem	_____	_____
post meridiem	_____	_____
tabula rasa	_____	_____
ad nauseam	_____	_____

UNIT TWO
Classes of Words in English

If you were to take a course in identifying birds you would expect to learn a number of technical terms. Likewise when people learn to sail they must learn names for parts of the boats and orders that must be carried out exactly. So too there is the need for some terms like *morpheme* and *prefix* if we are to study words.

This unit will introduce to you, or perhaps review for you, some terms which dictionaries use in explaining words as well as other terms useful in working with words. Without a knowledge of these terms, it is impossible for you to use a dictionary effectively.

CONTENTS

1–41	English Nouns
42–103	A Second Class of Word: English Adjectives
104–126	Nouns Used as Modifiers of Other Nouns
127–154	A Third Class of Word: English Verbs
155–176	The Fourth Class of Word: English Adverbs

SAMPLE TEXTS IN THIS UNIT

Excerpts from the Declaration of Independence
Excerpts from the Constitution of the United States

English Nouns
(Frames 1–41)

1 English content words may be divided into four classes: **nouns, verbs, adjectives,** and **adverbs.** First you will learn the content words that are called **nouns.** Here again is the first paragraph of the Declaration of Independence. The italicized words are nouns in this passage.

> When in the *course* of human *events,* it becomes necessary for one *people* to dissolve the political *bonds* which have connected them with another, and to assume among the *powers* of the *earth* the separate and equal *station* to which the *laws* of *nature* and of *nature's God* entitle them, a decent *respect* to the *opinions* of *mankind* requires that they should declare the *causes* which impel them to the *separation.*

Words are put into classes according to **morphological** and **syntactical criteria** (= tests). We will explain what we mean by these technical terms in the following frames. Here is the morphological criterion for nouns.

The words *events, opinions,* and *causes* in the Sample Text above are all the **class of word** that we call nouns. A noun is a class of word that operates like other words we call nouns. Here is what we mean by "operate like": what *one letter* do the three nouns *events,*

opinions, and *causes* have in common? _____

▶ □ ◀

A: The letter *s* (which is a suffix often added to nouns).

2 Most English nouns can have this suffix {**s**} added to the end of the word to show "more-than-one." We say "one event" but "two events." In the same way, we say "one opinion"

but "two _____."

▶ □ ◀

A: Opinions.

3 What, therefore, is one way to identify the words *opinions, causes,* and *events* as

nouns? _____

▶ □ ◀

A: They all have the suffix {s}. (This is the morphological criterion.)

4 What suffix does the word *causes* have to show contrast between one and more-than-

one? _____

▶ □ ◀

A: {s}

5   What class of word is *event/events?* _____

▶ □ ◀

   A: Noun.

6   The form *event* without the {s}, meaning one event, is called **singular number;** the form *events*, meaning more-than-one, is called **plural number.** Which number is the word *opinions*, singular number or plural? _____

▶ □ ◀

   A: Plural.

7   What number is *course?* _____

▶ □ ◀

   A: Singular.

8   What number is *event?* _____

▶ □ ◀

   A: Singular.

9–10   You know that *event* is a noun because it has a morphological contrast between the _____ and _____ forms of the word.

▶ □ ◀

   A: Singular; plural.

11   What class of word is the word *truth?* _____

▶ □ ◀

   A: Self-test item. (No answer given; as in Unit One, if you cannot answer, it means you have not learned what was presented in frames 1–10.)

12   When we describe a noun as singular or plural we refer to the _____ of the word.

▶ □ ◀

   A: Number

NICE-TO-KNOW ■ Verbs also have a suffix {s} to show number, as in "One boy *sits,*" but "Two boys *sit.*" The {s} in a verb, however, shows singular number, as in "One boy *sits.*"

13–14 So, the first criterion (test) in identifying an English noun is **morphological.** What morpheme often identifies a noun? The morpheme {_____} to show _____.

▶ ◻◻◻ ◀

A: {s}; plural. (Not all English nouns have the singular / plural contrast, however. An example is *news*, which is singular, as in "The news is good.")

NICE-TO-KNOW ■ In speech this {s} for plural has three allomorphs. If you pronounce aloud the words *events, opinions,* and *courses,* you will notice that *events* ends in the sound / s /, *opinions* ends in the sound / z /, and *causes* ends in the sound / iz /. These three allomorphs for {s} have been described as "a hiss, a buzz, and a grunt-buzz."

15 English nouns are also distinguished by a **syntactical** criterion, that is, word order. Nouns occupy certain **slots** (or positions) in a sentence. For example, most English nouns may be preceded by such function words as *the, a, many, that,* and *these.* These are called **noun markers** because they are found with the class of word we call _____.

▶ ◻◻◻ ◀

A: Nouns.

16 Which of these noun markers seems to be the most common one? _____

▶ ◻◻◻ ◀

A: The.

17 To repeat, the first criterion of an English noun is morphological. The second criterion is syntactical. What is this second criterion? _____
_____

▶ ◻◻◻ ◀

A: Most English nouns can be preceded by a noun marker.

18–20 Here is the second sentence of the Declaration of Independence, which follows the sentence you studied in the last sequence. Read it through. We will then ask you to identify the nouns.

> We hold these truths to be self-evident: That all men are created equal; that they are endowed by their Creator with certain inalienable rights; that among these are life, liberty, and the pursuit of happiness.

You have already identified *truths* as a noun on a morphological criterion because it has a contrast between the _____ and _____ forms of the word. What is the noun marker that precedes it? _____

▶ ◻◻◻ ◀

A: Singular; plural. These.

21–23 There are seven other nouns besides *truths* in the paragraph above. Identify three of them. _____, _____, _____.

▶ □ ◀

A: (Any three) Men, Creator, rights, life, liberty, pursuit, happiness. (It may not be clear to you why *men* should be included in this list. We will explain in a moment.)

24 There are two words in the list of nouns from the Sample Text that need special explanation. Is *men* a noun? _____ (yes / no)

▶ □ ◀

A: Yes.

25 What number is *men*, singular or plural? _____

▶ □ ◀

A: Plural.

26 Can we insert *men* in place of *trees* in the sentence "We saw these trees"? _____ (yes / no)

▶ □ ◀

A: Yes.

27 What is the signal for plural in the pair *man / men?* (in your own words) _____
_____

▶ □ ◀

A: The change from *a* in *man* to *e* in *men*.

28 That is, instead of **mans* as a plural of *man* we find the form _____.

▶ □ ◀

A: Men. (The asterisk before **mans* means that the form does not exist.)

NICE-TO-KNOW ■ Nouns have another morphological contrast that we are not going to discuss in any detail because it is not essential for dictionary skills. This contrast is seen in the form *man's,* as in "The man's hat blew off," and *men's,* as in "The men's hats blew off." This is called the possessive.

29 Here is a second word in the Sample Text which needs explanation. The plural of *life* is not * *lifes;* what is it? _____

▶ □□ ◀

    A: Lives.

30 In other words, when *life* becomes plural, the base {**life**} changes to an allomorph. What is the allomorph of *life* in the plural? _____

▶ □□ ◀

    A: {live}, as in "two lives."

31 We see this same kind of allomorph in a few other words. For example, we say "one knife" but "two _____."

▶ □□ ◀

    A: Knives.

32 Can you think of any other English noun which shows this variation that we see in *life* / *lives* and *knife* / *knives?* _____ / _____.

▶ □□ ◀

    A: Common ones are *half* / *halves, self* / *selves, wife* / *wives, leaf* / *leaves.* Some words have two plural forms, like *scarf*, whose plural can be either *scarfs* or *scarves.*

33 It should also be pointed out that a few nouns either do not have a plural (like *information*) or they have a plural that is rare (like *happiness*). In such a case we have to rely solely on the syntactical slots that the words occupy in order to identify them as nouns. Can *information* go in the slot that X occupies, as in "The X seems useful"? _____ (yes / no)

▶ □□ ◀

    A: Yes.

34 In spite of words that have no plural or a rare plural, like *information* and *happiness*, the fact remains that most English nouns have an {**s**} morpheme that shows _____.

▶ □□ ◀

    A: Self-test item.

35–38 Nouns are identified in dictionaries by the abbreviation **n.** On the opposite page are seven entries from the *American Heritage Dictionary*. List the four nouns:

_____, _____, _____, _____.

Gre·co (grĕk′ō, grā′kō), **El.** Original name, Kyriakos Theo-
tokopoulos. 1548?–1614? Spanish painter born in Crete.
Gre·co-Ro·man (grĕ′kō-rō′mən, grĕk′ō-) *adj.* Also **Grae·co-
Ro·man.** Of, relating to, or pertaining to both Greece and
Rome: *Greco-Roman mythology.* [Greco-, from Latin *Graecus,*
GREEK.]
gree[1] (grē) *n. Scottish.* **1.** Superiority or victory. **2.** The prize or
reward for victory. [Middle English, rank, from Old French
gre, from Latin *gradus,* GRADE.]
gree[2] (grē) *n. Obsolete.* Good will; favor. [Middle English,
from Old French *gre,* from Late Latin *grātum,* from Latin
grātus. pleasing, thankful. See **gwere-**[1] in Appendix.*]
Greece (grēs). *Greek* **Hel·las** (hĕl′əs). *Modern Greek* **El·las**
(ĕ-läs′). *Abbr.* **Gr.** A republic, 50,147 square miles in area, of
southeastern Europe, in the southern Balkan Peninsula. Population, 8,736,000. Capital, Athens. [Latin *Graecia,* from
Graecus, GREEK.]
greed (grēd) *n.* A rapacious desire for more than one needs or
deserves, as of food, wealth, or power; avarice. [Back-forma-
tion from GREEDY.]
greed·y (grē′dĕ) *adj.* **-ier, -iest. 1.** Excessively desirous of acquiring or possessing something, especially in quantity; covetous; avaricious. **2.** Wanting to eat or drink more than one can
reasonably consume; gluttonous; voracious. [Middle English
gredy, Old English *grǣdig.* See **gher-**[6] in Appendix.*] —**greed′-
i·ly** *adv.* —**greed′i·ness** *n.*

▶ □□□ ◀

A: Gree¹, gree², greed, greediness.

> **NICE-TO-KNOW** ■ Many people (including the authors of this program) would call *El Greco* and *Greece* nouns. They
> are often called ''proper nouns,'' and they are names of people, places, and so forth.
> The abbreviation **adj.** in the entry *greedy* stands for **adjective,** the next class of word we will examine. The abbre-
> viation **adv.** in the entry *greedy* stands for **adverb,** another class of word.

39–40 Give the *morphological* definition of an English noun: an English noun (usually) has a

morpheme {_____} to show _____.

▶ □□□ ◀

A: {s}; plural.

41 Give the *syntactical* definition of an English noun: an English noun may be preceded by

the type of function word we call a _____.

▶ □□□ ◀

A: Noun marker.

> **NICE-TO-KNOW** ■ The noun marker does not have to come directly before a noun. We can say, for example, ''The
> good dog is asleep,'' where *the* precedes the noun phrase ''good dog.'' (''Phrase'' = group of words.)

A Second Class of Word: English Adjectives
(Frames 42–103)

■ We will now identify a second class of word according to morphological and syntactical criteria. As a Sample Text we will use the Preamble to the Constitution of the United States. The
words which belong to this new class of word are printed in boldface type. They are called
adjectives.

> We, the people of the **United** States, in order to form a more **perfect** union, establish justice, insure **domestic** tranquility, provide for the **common** defense, promote the **general** welfare and secure the blessings of liberty to ourselves and our posterity, do ordain and establish this constitution for the **United** States of America.

42 First the morphological criterion. An adjective like *big* has two morphemes to show "more" and "most." That is, we say "This dog is certainly *big*, but the second one is much *bigger*, and the third one is the _____ of all."

▶ □ ◀

    A: Biggest.

43 The morphemes {er} and {est}, as in *bigger* and *biggest*, which show "more" and "most," are found with short adjectives; longer adjectives take the function words *more* and *most*. For example, we do not say "This rose is **beautifuller* than that one," but rather "This rose is _____ than that one."

▶ □ ◀

    A: More beautiful. (The asterisk in **beautifuller* means that the form does not exist.)

44 Which word in the Sample Text preceding frame 42 occurs with the function word *more?* _____

▶ □ ◀

    A: Perfect.

45 Try the *more / most* test on the words in the Sample Text that are in boldface. Can we say "more common" and "most common"? _____ (yes / no)

▶ □ ◀

    A: Yes.

46 What class of word, therefore, is *common?* _____

▶ □ ◀

    A: Adjective.

47 Can we say "more America" and "most America"? _____ (yes / no)

▶ □ ◀

    A: No.

48 What class of word is *America*, noun or adjective? _____

A: Noun.

I   NICE-TO-KNOW ■ *America* is a *proper noun;* see Nice-to-Know p. 45.

49–52 Apply the *more / most* or {**er**} / {**est**} test to the following six words. Each can be used either as a noun or as an adjective: *excellent, long, number, part, movable, wide.* Circle the four words that are adjectives.

A: Excellent, long, movable, wide.

NICE-TO-KNOW ■ The word *United* in the Sample Text is a special kind of adjective formed on the verb *unite.* Such an adjective is called a past participle, abbreviated in dictionaries to *pp.* There is also a present participle, abbreviated to *prp.* as in the phrase "the *uniting* force."

53 As with other content words, the class called *adjective* has both morphological and syntactical criteria. The syntactical criteria for adjectives are more complicated than those for nouns. An adjective can come between a noun marker and the noun, as we see in the phrase "the good boy." Which of these words is an adjective and can be written between

"these" and "apples"? *Eat / event / more / spotty:* _____

A: Spotty, as in "These spotty apples," but not "These more apples."

54 A second syntactical criterion is that most adjectives also fit in a second slot; they can follow the word *seem,* as in "These apples seem spotty." Which of these words can be

inserted after *seem* in "These dogs seem _____"? *Bark / loyal / quickly / running.*

A: Loyal.

55–57 Which three words in the list below can fit into both adjective slots? *War, timely, scandal, historical, delightful:* "The _____ novel is a bestseller"; "The novel seems

_____."

_____ , _____ , _____

A: Timely, historical, delightful.

58–59 Which words in this list can fit into both adjective slots? *Confusing, insult, wordy, revision:* "The _____ language made us unhappy"; "The language seems _____."

_____ , _____

▶ □ ◀

   A: Confusing, wordy.

60–61 We will now review both nouns and adjectives. There are *two* tests that can be used to identify most English nouns. The first criterion is morphological. What contrast in form do *most* (but not all) nouns have? There are two ways to answer this; one is by using a symbol, the other is by giving the meaning of the symbol. (a) Most nouns have the morpheme {_____}, (b) most nouns have a contrast between _____ and _____ forms.

▶ □ ◀

   A: {s}; singular; plural.

62–63 The second requirement is syntactical; most nouns fit into the slot after a noun marker. Which words in this list can fit into this slot? *Welfare, union, establish, promote.*

_____ , _____

▶ □ ◀

   A: Welfare, union.

64 What are the morphological criteria for adjectives? That is, what changes in form do many English adjectives have? _____

_____

▶ □ ◀

   A: The morphemes {er} and {est} can be added to show "more" and "most."

65 What do we say in place of the nonexistent form *domesticer?* _____

▶ □ ◀

   A: More domestic.

66–67 According to syntactical criteria, what two slots can most adjectives fill? _____

_____

▶ □ ◀

   A: Between noun marker and noun, as in "the easy lesson," and after *seems* in "The lesson seems easy."

48

68-70 Identify the class of word of the italicized words: "The *people* of the United States do ordain this constitution." _____ "The constitution is *clear* on this matter." _____ ". . . insure *domestic* tranquility. . . ." _____

▶ □ ◀

A: People: noun. Clear: adjective. Domestic: adjective.

71 What class of word is *domestic* in the sentence "She worked as a *domestic* for two years to pay her tuition"? _____

▶ □ ◀

A: Noun.

72-73 What class of word is the word *general* in the phrase "promote the *general* welfare"? _____. What class of word is *general* in the sentence "The *general* did not agree on the strategy"? _____

▶ □ ◀

A: Adjective; noun.

74-75 What class of word is *common* in "provide for the *common* defense"? _____. What class of word is *common* in the sentence "We ate our lunch sitting on the *common*"? _____

▶ □ ◀

A: Adjective; noun. (*Common* is a term used for "park" in certain regions of the country.)

76-77 Observe the word *red* in these contrasting sentences:

      (a) The *red* sunset slowly faded away.
      (b) The sunset was *red* last night, but it is even *redder* tonight.
      (c) The *red* of the sunset was striking.
      (d) The *red* of the leaves is like the *reds* of the sunset.

In which sentence does the word *red* show by morphological criteria that it is a noun? _____. In which sentence does the word *red* show by morphological criteria that it is an adjective? _____.

▶ □ ◀

A: d (red / reds)
     b (red / redder).

78–79 What morphemes does the adjective *red* have? _____ and _____

▶ □ ◀

  A: Redder; reddest (or {er} and {est}).

80–81 Give two examples, from frame 76–77, of *red* used as an adjective. "_____"
and "_____"

▶ □ ◀

  A: "The *red* sunset"; and "The sunset was *red*" or "it is even *redder*."

82 What morpheme marks *red* as a noun? {_____}

▶ □ ◀

  A: {s}

83 Give an example, from frame 76–77, of *red* used as a noun. _____
_____

▶ □ ◀

  A: "The red" (that is, after a noun marker, "*The* red of the sunset" or "*The* red of the leaves").

84 Adjectives **modify** nouns. *Modify* means "limit," "describe," or "restrict." If we advertise to say that we want to hire a typist, we would do well to specify "skilled," "beginning," and so forth. By *modifying* "typist" and saying "experienced typist" we have _____ or _____ the number of qualified applicants.

▶ □ ◀

  A: Restricted or limited.

85–86 In discussing the phrase "skilled typist" we say that "skilled" is the **modifier** and "typist" is the **head** of the phrase. In the phrase "red sunset," which word is the modifier?
_____ Which is the head? _____

▶ □ ◀

  A: Red. Sunset.

87–88 Adjectives are identified in dictionaries by the abbreviation **adj.** On the opposite page are the same entries from the *American Heritage Dictionary* given earlier. List the two words identified as adjectives: _____ and _____.

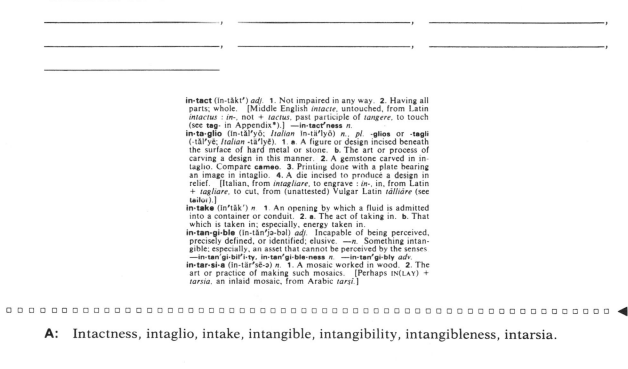

Gre·co (grĕk′ō, grā′kō), **El.** Original name, Kyriakos Theo-tokopoulos. 1548?-1614? Spanish painter born in Crete.
Gre·co-Ro·man (grē′kō-rō′mən, grĕk′ō-) *adj.* Also **Grae·co-Ro·man.** Of, relating to, or pertaining to both Greece and Rome: *Greco-Roman mythology.* [*Greco-,* from Latin *Graecus,* GREEK.]
gree[1] (grē) *n. Scottish.* **1.** Superiority or victory. **2.** The prize or reward for victory. [Middle English, rank, from Old French *gre,* from Latin *gradus,* GRADE.]
gree[2] (grē) *n. Obsolete.* Good will; favor. [Middle English, from Old French *gre,* from Late Latin *grātum,* from Latin *grātus.* pleasing, thankful. See **gwere-**[1] in Appendix.*]
Greece (grēs). *Greek* **Hel·las** (hĕl′əs). *Modern Greek* **El·las** (ĕ-làs′). *Abbr.* **Gr.** A republic, 50,147 square miles in area, of southeastern Europe, in the southern Balkan Peninsula. Population, 8,736,000. Capital, Athens. [Latin *Graecia,* from *Graecus,* GREEK.]
greed (grēd) *n.* A rapacious desire for more than one needs or deserves, as of food, wealth, or power; avarice. [Back-formation from GREEDY.]
greed·y (grē′dē) *adj.* **-ier, -iest. 1.** Excessively desirous of acquiring or possessing something, especially in quantity; covetous; avaricious. **2.** Wanting to eat or drink more than one can reasonably consume; gluttonous; voracious. [Middle English *gredy,* Old English *grǣdig.* See **gher-**[6] in Appendix.*] —**greed′·i·ly** *adv.* —**greed′i·ness** *n.*

□ □ □ □ □ ◀ □ ◀

A: Greco-Roman, greedy.

89–95 Here are some more entries from the *American Heritage Dictionary.* List the seven words identified as nouns:

_____ , _____ , _____ ,

_____ , _____ , _____ ,

_____

in·tact (ĭn-tăkt′) *adj.* **1.** Not impaired in any way. **2.** Having all parts; whole. [Middle English *intacte,* untouched, from Latin *intactus : in-,* not + *tactus,* past participle of *tangere,* to touch (see **tag-** in Appendix*).] —**in·tact′ness** *n.*
in·ta·glio (ĭn-tăl′yō; *Italian* ĭn-tä′lyō) *n., pl.* **-glios** or **-tagli** (-tăl′yē; *Italian* -tä′lyē). **1. a.** A figure or design incised beneath the surface of hard metal or stone. **b.** The art or process of carving a design in this manner. **2.** A gemstone carved in intaglio. Compare **cameo. 3.** Printing done with a plate bearing an image in intaglio. **4.** A die incised to produce a design in relief. [Italian, from *intagliare,* to engrave : *in-,* in, from Latin + *tagliare,* to cut, from (unattested) Vulgar Latin *tálliāre* (see **tailor**).]
in·take (ĭn′tāk′) *n.* **1.** An opening by which a fluid is admitted into a container or conduit. **2. a.** The act of taking in. **b.** That which is taken in; especially, energy taken in.
in·tan·gi·ble (ĭn-tăn′jə-bəl) *adj.* Incapable of being perceived, precisely defined, or identified; elusive. —*n.* Something intangible; especially, an asset that cannot be perceived by the senses —**in·tan′gi·bil′i·ty, in·tan′gi·ble·ness** *n.* —**in·tan′gi·bly** *adv.*
in·tar·si·a (ĭn-tär′sē-ə) *n.* **1.** A mosaic worked in wood. **2.** The art or practice of making such mosaics. [Perhaps IN(LAY) + *tarsia,* an inlaid mosaic, from Arabic *tarsi.*]

□ ◀

A: Intactness, intaglio, intake, intangible, intangibility, intangibleness, intarsia.

96 Some words which are borrowed into English have two plural forms. The word *intaglio* has one plural formed in the English way. Copy this regular form from the dictionary entry above. What is this form? _____

□ ◀

A: Intaglios.

97 The word *intaglio* comes from Italian and also has the Italian plural form as a variant. Copy this variant form from the dictionary entry. _____

▶ ▫▫▫ ◀

   A: Intagli.

98 *Intake* has a regular plural; the dictionary therefore does not bother to list it. What is this regular plural of *intake*? _____

▶ ▫▫▫ ◀

   A: Intakes.

99–100 List the two words identified as adjectives in the entries in frame 89–95:

   _____ and _____.

▶ ▫▫▫ ◀

   A: Intact, intangible.

101 Of these two entries, which can be either a noun or an adjective? _____

▶ ▫▫▫ ◀

   A: Intangible.

102 What class of word is *intangible* in "John's knowledge of mushrooms was an *intangible* we had not counted on"? _____

▶ ▫▫▫ ◀

   A: Noun.

103 What class of word is *intangible* in "John's knowledge of mushrooms was an intangible advantage we had not counted on"? _____

▶ ▫▫▫ ◀

   A: Adjective.

Nouns Used as Modifiers of Other Nouns
(Frames 104–126)

■ The fact that nouns can modify other nouns, as in "the race track," has led many people to confuse nouns with adjectives. We will apply the morphological and syntactical criteria for such phrases in this section.

104–105 Compare the sentences:

(a) The *black* horse was exciting to watch.
(b) The *horse race* was exciting to watch.
(c) The *race horse* was exciting to watch.

In "The black horse," which word is the modifier? _____ Which word is the

head? _____

▶ □ ◀

A: Black. Horse.

106 What class of word is *black* in "the black horse"? _____

▶ □ ◀

A: Adjective.

107–108 What are the two types of criteria that can be used to test for class of word?

_____ and _____

▶ □ ◀

A: Morphological and syntactical.

109 Which word is the modifier in the phrase "the horse race" from sentence (b) in frame
104–105? _____

▶ □ ◀

A: Horse.

110 But is *horse* an adjective? First of all, on morphological criteria, can we say "this animal
seems horser than that"? _____ (yes / no)

▶ □ ◀

A: No (nor can we say *horsest).

111 Therefore, *horse* is not an adjective by morphological criteria. Let's apply the syntactical
criteria. Does *horse* fill the slots for adjectives? First, can we say "the horse race"?
_____ (yes / no)

▶ □ ◀

A: Yes.

112   So *horse* fills one syntactical slot. Does it fill the second slot? Can we say "The race seems horse"? _____ (yes / no)

▶ □ ◀

   A: No.

113   Is *horse* in "horse race" an adjective? _____ (yes / no)

▶ □ ◀

   A: No.

114   What class of word is it? _____

▶ □ ◀

   A: Noun.

115   In "the horse race" the word *horse* is a noun used as a **noun modifier.** That is, it is a noun in a modifier slot. In the sentence "The race horse was exciting to watch," what class of word is *race?* _____

▶ □ ◀

   A: Noun.

116   Which word in "the race horse" is the noun modifier? _____

▶ □ ◀

   A: Race.

117–126   Here are several **phrases** (= groups of words) with a modifier, which is either a noun or an adjective, and a noun head. Circle the modifier in each phrase and label it as a noun or adjective.

   (a) the little heir _____

   (b) the fish knife _____

   (c) a cucumber salad _____

   (d) a wonderful experience _____

   (e) the table top _____

   (f) a noun phrase _____

   (g) the swimming pool _____

   (h) an apple pie _____

   (i) my weak eye _____

   (j) the broken boxes _____

▶ □ ◀

A: (a) little; adjective   (f) noun; noun
    (b) fish; noun   (g) swimming; noun
    (c) cucumber; noun   (h) apple; noun
    (d) wonderful; adjective   (i) weak; adjective
    (e) table; noun   (j) broken; adjective

A Third Class of Word: English Verbs
(Frames 127–154)

■ Another common class of word that you need to understand in order to use a dictionary is the **verb.** The italicized words in the following sentences are verbs:

> The girls *hear* the dog.   The people *walk.*
> The girls *heard* the dog.   The people *walked* their dogs.

Verbs have a morphological contrast, as in the examples above. In the next sequence, we will first consider the morphological criteria.

127 The contrast between *hear* and *heard*, and between *walk* and *walked*, shows the _____ when the hearing and the walking happen.

▶ □ ◀

    A: Time.

128 This difference in form and in meaning in verbs is called **tense.** We say that *see* is in the **present tense** and *saw* is in the **past** _____.

▶ □ ◀

    A: Tense.

129–132 Examine this partial entry from *Webster's New World Dictionary.* The three forms printed in boldface type are other forms of the verb *see.*

see¹ (sē) *vt.* **saw, seen, see′ing** [ME. *seen* < OE. *seon* (< **sehwan*), akin to G. *sehen*, Goth. *saihwan* < IE. base **sekw-*, to observe, show, see, tell, whence L. *inseque*, tell: cf. SAY] **1.** *a)* to get knowledge or an awareness of through the eyes; perceive visually; look at; view *b)* to visualize as though present; picture **2.** *a)* to get a clear mental impression of; grasp by thinking; understand [to *see* the point of a joke] *b)* to accept as right, proper, or suitable [I can't *see* him as president] *c)* to consider to be; judge [*saw* it as his duty] **3.** *a)* to learn; discover; find out [*see* what they want] *b)* to learn by reading, as in a newspaper **4.** to have personal knowledge of; experience; witness [to have *seen* better days] **5.** to look over; inspect; examine [let me *see* that burn] **6.** to take care; make sure [*see* that he does it right] **7.** *a)* to escort; accompany; attend [to *see* someone home] *b)* to keep company with; be dating regularly **8.** *a)* to encounter; meet; come in contact with [have you *seen* John?] *b)* to recognize by sight **9.** *a)* to call on; visit *b)* to have an interview with; consult [*see* a lawyer] **10.** to admit to one's presence; receive [too ill to *see* anyone] **11.** to be a spectator at; view or attend [to *see* a show] **12.** *Card Games a)* to meet

Put one of the four forms *(see, saw, seen, seeing)* into the slot in which it will fit:

I have _____ this picture before.

They now _____ more clearly with new glasses.

Jane _____ the snake immediately.

He has been _____ a doctor for his back problem for a long time.

▶ □ ◀

A: Seen; see; saw; seeing.

133   There are perhaps forty verb phrases composed of these different forms of *see* and various function words like *can, would have,* and *may.* But to understand the dictionary it is sufficient to know that the contrast in form between *walk* and *walked* is one of the

_____ criteria that identifies a verb.

▶ □ ◀

A: Morphological.

NICE-TO-KNOW ■ Common verbs of one syllable frequently have irregular forms for their contrast in tense: for example, *run / ran, give / gave, shoot / shot.* Longer verbs usually have a regular form, the {ed} allomorph, to show past time, as in *cover / covered* and *perceive / perceived.*

134   English sentences are usually in one of two word-order patterns, subject-verb, as in "The dog barks," or subject-verb-object, as in "The frog grabbed the fly." This fixed position of the verb is therefore a *syntactical* criterion for identifying verbs.
   Verbs that have an **object** following the verb are called **transitive** verbs. These sentences have transitive verbs:

Anna *bought* a book.
My neighbor *collects* old cars.
The teacher *wrote* many comments on my paper.

What is the technical term for "book," "cars," and "comments" as they are used in these

sentences? _____

▶ □ ◀

A: Object.

135–138   Verbs that do not take an object are called **intransitive verbs.** Circle the verbs which are intransitive in the sentences below.

The old man next door died.   We often jog in the early morning.

A big dog bit the boy.   The owners of the house just left.

After the race, we swam.   We purchased our tickets early.

▶ □ ◀

A: Died; swam; jog; left.

139–140 It is a characteristic of English that many verbs can be either transitive or intransitive. Observe this contrasting pair:

(a) The ship *sank* the raft.   (b) The raft *sank* immediately.

Which verb is *transitive*, that is, has an object, (a) or (b)? _____ Which verb is *intransitive*, (a) or (b)? _____

▶ □ ◀

A: (a); (b).

141 Listed below are the dictionary entries for five verbs (from *Webster's New World Dictionary*). Indicate for each verb whether it occurs just as a transitive *(vt.)* verb, just as an intransitive verb *(vi.)*, or as either a transitive or an intransitive verb.

> **smirch** (smurch) *vt.* [ME. *smorchen*, prob. < OFr. *esmorcher*, to hurt] **1.** to make dirty or discolor, as by smearing or staining with grime **2.** to sully or dishonor (a reputation, good name, etc.) —*n.* **1.** a smudge; smear; stain **2.** a stain on reputation, etc.

Transitive, intransitive, or both? _____

▶ □ ◀

A: Transitive.

142
> **smirk** (smurk) *vi.* [ME. *smirken* < OE. *smearcian*, to SMILE] to smile in a conceited, knowing, or annoyingly complacent way —*n.* a smile of this kind —*SYN.* see SMILE —**smirk'er** *n.* —**smirk'ing·ly** *adv.*

Transitive, intransitive, or both? _____

▶ □ ◀

A: Intransitive.

143
> **sneer** (snir) *vi.* [ME. *sneren*, akin to Fris. *sneere*, to scorn, Dan. *snaere*, to grin like a dog: for IE. base see SNARL[1]] **1.** to smile derisively; show scorn or contempt as by curling the upper lip **2.** to express derision, scorn, or contempt in speech or writing —*vt.* **1.** to utter with a sneer or in a sneering manner **2.** to affect in a particular way by sneering *[to sneer down a proposal]* —*n.* **1.** an act of sneering **2.** a sneering expression, insinuation, etc. —*SYN.* see SCOFF —**sneer'er** *n.* —**sneer'ing·ly** *adv.*

Transitive, intransitive, or both? _____

▶ □ ◀

A: Both.

144
> **sneeze** (snēz) *vi.* **sneezed, sneez'ing** [ME. *snesen*, altered (prob. by confusion of initial *f* with *ʃ*, long *s*) < *ʃnesen* < OE. *fneosan*: for IE. base see PNEUMA] to exhale breath from the nose and mouth in a sudden, involuntary, explosive action, as a result of an irritation of the nasal mucous membrane —*n.* an act of sneezing —**not to be sneezed at** not to be considered lightly or disregarded —**sneez'er** *n.* —**sneez'y** *adj.*

Transitive, intransitive, or both? _____

▶ □ ◀

A: Intransitive.

145

> **sniff** (snif) *vi.* [ME. *sniffen*, akin to Dan. *snive*, of echoic orig.] **1.** to draw in air through the nose with enough force to be heard, as in clearing the nose or smelling something **2.** to express disdain, skepticism, etc. by sniffing —*vt.* **1.** to breathe in forcibly through the nose; draw in or inhale nasally **2.** to smell (a substance) by sniffing **3.** to detect, perceive, or get a suspicion of by or as by sniffing (often with *out*) —*n.* **1.** an act or sound of sniffing **2.** something sniffed —**sniff'er** *n.*

Transitive, intransitive, or both? _____

▶ □ ◀

A: Both.

146 Here are the dictionary entries for the word *grave*, taken from the *American Heritage Dictionary*:

> **grave¹** (grāv) *n.* **1.** An excavation for the interment of a corpse; burial place. **2.** Any place of burial or final disposition: *The sea was his grave.* **3.** The sign or marker of a burial place. **4.** The receptacle or resting place of anything dead in a figurative sense: *"She was dry and sandy with working in the graves of deceased languages"* (Dickens). **5.** Death or extinction. [Middle English *grave*, Old English *græf.* See ghrebh-² in Appendix.*]
> **grave²** (grāv; *also* grāv *for sense 6) adj.* **graver, gravest. 1.** Extremely serious; important; weighty: *a grave decision in a time of crisis.* **2.** Fraught with danger; critical: *a grave wound.* **3.** Grievous; dire: *a grave sin.* **4.** Dignified in conduct; sedate: *a grave procession.* **5.** Somber; dark. Said of colors. **6.** *Linguistics.* **a.** Written with or modified by the mark , as the *è* in *Sèvres.* **b.** Articulated toward the back of the oral cavity. —See Synonyms at **serious.** —*n.* (grāv, gräv). The grave accent, , indicating a pronounced *e* for the sake of meter in the usually nonsyllabic ending *-ed* in English poetry. [Old French, from Latin *gravis*, heavy, weighty. See gwer-² in Appendix.*] —**grave'ly** *adv.* —**grave'ness** *n.*
> **grave³** (grāv) *tr.v.* **graved, graven** (grā'vən), **graving, graves. 1.** To sculpt or carve; engrave: *"I wis'l I could grave my sonnets on an ivory tablet."* (Oscar Wilde) **2.** To stamp or impress deeply; fix permanently, as words or ideas. [Grave, graven; Middle English *graven, graven*, Old English *grafan, grafen.* See ghrebh-² in Appendix.*]
> **grave⁴** (grāv) *tr.v.* **graved, graving, graves.** To clean (the bottom of a wooden ship) by removing barnacles and other accretions, and coating with pitch. [Middle English *graven*, probably from Old French *greve, grave*, sand, GRAVEL.]
> **gra·ve⁵** (grä'vā) *adv. Music.* Slowly and solemnly. Used as a direction to the performer. —*adj.* Slow and solemn. [Italian, from Latin *gravis*, heavy, weighty, GRAVE.]

First of all, how many different words *grave* do the editors of this dictionary list?

_____

▶ □ ◀

A: Five.

147 What class of word is the first *grave*, marked with a superscript (raised) numeral 1?

_____

▶ □ ◀

A: Noun (abbreviated to *n.*).

148–149 What two classes of word can *grave*² be, according to this dictionary? _____

and _____

▶ □□□ ◀

A: Adjective and noun.

150 What class of word does the dictionary say *grave*³ is? _____

▶ □□□ ◀

A: Verb. (The abbreviation for "transitive," as well as for other terms, may vary in different dictionaries.)

151 Is *grave*³ a transitive or an intransitive verb? _____

▶ □□□ ◀

A: Transitive.

152 *Grave*⁴ is not a common word. What class of word is it, according to this entry?

_____

▶ □□□ ◀

A: Transitive verb.

153–154 What two classes of word is *grave*⁵? _____ and _____.

▶ □□□ ◀

A: Adverb and adjective.

The Fourth Class of Words: Adverbs
(Frames 155–176)

155–157 There are four classes of content words in English. You have already encountered three of them. What are they? _____, _____, and _____

▶ □□□ ◀

A: Nouns, adjectives, verbs.

158–160 The fourth and last class of content words in English that you will find in dictionaries is called an **adverb**, abbreviated as **adv.** First the morphological criteria. Some English adverbs are formed from adjectives by adding the suffix {ly}, as in "She sings *beautifully*," "They are *completely* sold out of umbrellas," or "David accepted the award *gratefully*."

The adjectives from which these three adverbs are formed are _____,

_____, _____.

▶ □ □ □ □ □ ■ □ □ □ □ □ □ □ ■ □ □ □ □ □ □ □ ■ □ □ □ □ □ ■ □ □ □ □ □ ■ □ □ □ □ □ □ □ ■ □ □ □ □ □ □ □ ■ □ □ □ □ ◀

    A: Beautiful, complete, grateful.

161–164 The syntax of adverbs is too complex to be presented here and is not necessary for understanding a dictionary. In general they answer such questions as "how?", "when?", or "where?" Circle the adverb, if any, in each sentence below.

           She looked at John intently.   Sue devoured the fruit.

           Tim returned yesterday.   Soon we will board the airplane.

           Lenny ate the apple greedily.

▶ □ □ □ □ □ ■ □ □ □ □ □ □ □ ■ □ □ □ □ □ □ □ ■ □ □ □ □ □ ■ □ □ □ □ □ ■ □ □ □ □ □ □ □ ■ □ □ □ □ □ □ □ ■ □ □ □ □ ◀

    A: Intently; yesterday; greedily; soon.

165–171 As you saw in the last frame, there are a variety of words that are adverbs but do not have an adverb {ly} suffix. These include such words as "yesterday," "soon," and "well." Circle the words below that can substitute for the adverb "well" in the sentence: "Diana drove the bus *well*." (sometimes, month, weekdays, often, daily, day, three hundred miles, home, homeward, city)

▶ □ □ □ □ □ ■ □ □ □ □ □ □ □ ■ □ □ □ □ □ □ □ ■ □ □ □ □ □ ■ □ □ □ □ □ ■ □ □ □ □ □ □ □ ■ □ □ □ □ □ □ □ ■ □ □ □ □ ◀

    A: Sometimes, weekdays, often, daily, three hundred miles, home, homeward.

172 Notice that adverbs have more freedom of position than nouns, adjectives, and verbs. Circle the sentence that has *soon* in an impossible slot.

    (a)   Soon we will board the airplane.

    (b)   We soon will board the airplane.

    (c)   We will soon board the airplane.

    (d)   We will board soon the airplane.

    (e)   We will board the soon airplane.

    (f)   We will board the airplane soon.

▶ □ □ □ □ □ ■ □ □ □ □ □ □ □ ■ □ □ □ □ □ □ □ ■ □ □ □ □ □ ■ □ □ □ □ □ ■ □ □ □ □ □ □ □ ■ □ □ □ □ □ □ □ ■ □ □ □ □ ◀

    A: "We will board the soon airplane" is not possible in normal language. ("We will board soon the airplane" is possible but highly improbable for a native speaker of English.)

173–176   Here are the dictionary entries for four adjectives from *Webster's New World Dictionary*. Copy the adverbs (identified by *adv.*) formed from the adjectives below.

ob·tru·sive (-troo′siv) *adj.* [< L. *obtrusus*, pp. of *obtrudere* + -IVE] **1.** inclined to obtrude **2.** obtruding itself; esp., calling attention to itself in a displeasing way —**ob·tru′-sive·ly** *adv.* —**ob·tru′sive·ness** *n.*

_____

off·hand (ôf′hand′) *adv.* without prior preparation or study; at once; extemporaneously —*adj.* **1.** said or done offhand; extemporary; unpremeditated **2.** casual, curt, informal, brusque, etc. Also **off′hand′ed** —**off′hand′ed·ly** *adv.* —**off′hand′ed·ness** *n.*

_____

grump·y (grum′pē) *adj.* **grump′i·er, grump′i·est** [prec. + -Y²] grouchy; peevish; bad-tempered: also **grump′ish** — **grump′i·ly** *adv.* —**grump′i·ness** *n.*

_____

com·i·cal (käm′i k′l) *adj.* **1.** causing amusement; humorous; funny; droll **2.** [Obs.] of or fit for comedy —*SYN.* see FUNNY —**com′i·cal′i·ty** (-kal′ə tē) *n.* —**com′i·cal·ly** *adv.*

_____

▶ □ ◀

    A: Obtrusively; offhandedly; grumpily; comically.

■ This concludes the programmed part of the unit. Use the list that follows to review the concepts presented in this unit. Following the list is a set of unprogrammed exercises. As in all units, the first of these provides additional practice in an important aspect of the unit, in this case the identification of word classes. No dictionary is necessary for this exercise, but we recommend it for all students. As in Unit One and all remaining units, the other three exercises are Words of Interesting Origin (dictionary required), Easily Confused Words (no dictionary required), and Latin Phrases (dictionary required). Together with your instructor, decide which exercises fit your needs and interests.

WORD LIST

■ Below is a list of the concepts which were introduced in this unit. Be sure that you can give examples of each of them. This unit presented no derivatives. The objective of the unit was to teach some concepts necessary to discuss words and use dictionaries.

adjective 1, 42	morphological criterion 1, 13	plural number 6
adverb 1, 155	noun 1	present tense 128
class of word 1	noun marker 15	singular number 6
criterion 1	noun modifier 115	slot 15
head 86	number 6	syntactical criterion 1, 15
intransitive verb 135	object 134	tense 128
modifier 85	past tense 128	transitive verb 134
modify 84	phrase 117	verb 1, 127

REVIEW EXERCISES

Purpose: To reinforce knowledge of classes of words.

Directions: Identify the class of word of each italicized word. (One word from each set appeared in Unit 1 or Unit 2.)

Class of Word

_____ 1. a. The teachers *assented* to the proposal.

_____ b. The teacher's *assent* is necessary for progress to be made.

_____ 2. a. The students will *convene* at 8 o'clock this evening.

_____ b. The scouts hold their *convention* every summer.

_____ c. Ms. Nelson did not use *conventional* methods in the classroom.

_____ 3. a. Dan's *respect* for his coach was great.

_____ b. The girls *respect* the coach for the high quality of coaching.

_____ c. Because of the boys' *respectful* behavior, there are no discipline problems in the class.

_____ 4. a. Mr. Perez and Ms. Price always *separate* the teams.

_____ b. The *separate* teams each have their own practice schedule.

_____ c. The *separateness* of the groups interfered with our ability to make plans.

_____ d. My mother and father arrived *separately* on the same day.

_____ 5. a. Dan will *station* himself at the door to guard it.

_____ b. Dan was tired of being at the same *station* for so long.

_____ c. Dan felt that remaining in a *stationary* position was unnecessary.

Directions: Use each of these words in a sentence: (1) greed, (2) greedily, (3) greedy, (4) greediness. Label the class of word of each of these words in the sentence.

Class of Word   Sentence

_____ 1. _____

_____

_____ 2. _____

_____

_____ 3. _____

_____

_____ 4. _____

_____

WORDS OF INTERESTING ORIGIN

Directions: Find in your dictionary the origins of the italicized words. Then write down (a) the language of origin, (b) the etymological meaning (= early meaning), and (c) the modern meaning.

1. The ancient *alchemists* tried to turn other metals into gold.

    Language of origin: _____

    Etymological meaning: _____

    Modern meaning: _____

2. As the ball dropped through the hoop, absolute *pandemonium* broke loose in the gymnasium.

    Language of origin: _____

    Etymological meaning: _____

    Modern meaning: _____

3. "You are acting like a *lunatic*," shouted Mr. Boggs.

    Language of origin: _____

    Etymological meaning: _____

    Modern meaning: _____

4. "My, this *punch* is delicious," said Mrs. Blauvelt. "I must have the recipe."

   Language of origin: _____

   Etymological meaning: _____

   Modern meaning: _____

5. "Our team has been *decimated* by injuries this season," said the new coach.

   Language of origin: _____

   Etymological meaning: _____

   Modern meaning: _____

EASILY CONFUSED WORDS

Use a dictionary as needed.

1. ***Stationary / stationery.*** Both words are derived from Latin *stare* meaning "stand." *Stationary* is an adjective meaning "standing without moving," as in "Although we watched carefully, the guard remained *stationary* for one hour," or "The price of gold has been *stationary* for a week".

   Stationery, however, is a noun and means writing materials like paper and envelopes, as in "If I am going to write all those Christmas letters, I will need some *stationery*." A stationery shop is run by a stationer, that is, a person doing business in a fixed store, as opposed to a peddler who moves around. To keep the spelling clear, just try the mnemonic device (= trick to help remember) that *stationary* with an *a* is an adjective.

2. ***Conservatism / conservation.*** Both words are derived from Latin *conservare*, meaning "to keep without change." *Conservatism* is the belief that on the whole it is best not to make changes, as opposed to *progressivism*, the belief that change is necessary in order to improve our system of life. Frequently, however, individuals are conservative in some ways (let us say in financial matters) but progressive in some other respects, like race relations. *Conservation*, on the other hand, is the preservation of such things as our natural resources.

3. ***Rout / route.*** Both words are derived from Latin *rupta* (= broken). *Rout* means a "crushing defeat," as in "Although we played them on even terms for the first half, the second half was a *rout*, with our players dazed and bewildered." A *rout* is a retreat but it further means a disorderly retreat. The word *route*, on the other hand, etymologically meant a "way that is rough and broken." Today it usually means either a highway of some sort, as in "To get to our cottage you follow *Route* 19 as far as Cross Corners—then ask for directions," or a regular course taken for delivery, as in "Billy's early morning newspaper *route* was hard on him but it was worse on his parents."

Use the six words in the sentences where each makes sense.

1. The Sierra Club has been one of the leading forces in many _____
   projects, such as the fight to block the building of a dam in the Grand Canyon.

2. Jim was almost fanatical about being on time with his paper _____.

3. Ellen was delighted with her operation of the _____ store.

4. Not even the loyalist papers could keep secret the fact that what the loyalists had called a victory was in fact a disgraceful _____.

5. Since the election was won by the party that favored easing pollution controls, many people considered it a triumph for _____.

6. In the middle of the mob Karen stood firm and _____, holding her flag on high.

LATIN PHRASES

First, try to get the meaning of each Latin phrase from the context of the sentences below, choosing a meaning from the list that follows. Write the number of the Latin phrase beside the definition that fits.

1. *Pro tempore*, as in "Sally was appointed president *pro tempore*." (*Pro tempore* is often abbreviated to *pro tem*.)

2. *Ex officio*, as in "The Dean is chairman of the Executive Committee *ex officio*."

3. *Magnum opus*, as in "This book was to be Janet's *magnum opus*."

4. *Persona non grata*, as in "After only four months in his job as ambassador, the country to which Tim had been assigned designated him as a *persona non grata*."

5. *Ex cathedra*, as in "The Pope made it quite clear that he was speaking *ex cathedra* on this issue." (Note: *Cathedra* means "seat," especially the throne of a bishop. From *cathedra* comes the word *cathedral*.)

_____ temporarily		_____ increase in effort	
_____ unofficial		_____ by reason of one's office	
_____ ungrateful person		_____ great work	
_____ from the seat of authority		_____ unacceptable person	
_____ without sufficient time		_____ outside the church	

Use a dictionary to find the word-for-word translation and the modern meaning for each phrase.

	Word-by-Word Translation	Modern Meaning
pro tempore	_____	_____
ex officio	_____	_____
magnum opus	_____	_____
persona non grata	_____	_____
ex cathedra	_____	_____

UNIT THREE
Analysis of a Literary Text

Through the use of a Sample Text, this unit will introduce many words for you to learn or review. You will use several common suffixes; you will practice using words by pairing them with synonyms; and you will practice getting information from dictionary entries.

Edward Gibbon (1737–1794) was one of the most famous historians who ever wrote in English. His writing is not easy for some, because he has an extensive vocabulary. For that reason, his work is a useful basis for learning more about words.

CONTENTS

1–6	Introduction
7–24	A Common Noun Suffix
25–52	A Common Adjective Suffix
53–64	Substitution of Synonyms in the First Sample Text
65–129	Substitution of Synonyms in the Second Sample Text
130–179	Dictionaries as Tools

SAMPLE TEXTS IN THIS UNIT

Excerpts from Gibbon's *Decline and Fall of the Roman Empire*

Introduction
Frames 1–6

1   Gibbon's monumental work, *Decline and Fall of the Roman Empire*, was published in 1776–1783. His language may seem a little old-fashioned to you. Here is the first paragraph of the *Decline and Fall*, with the Greek and Latin derivatives in boldface. Read it through for content and then answer the questions.

In the **second century** of the **Christian aera,**[1] the **empire** of **Rome comprehended** the fairest **part** of the earth, and the most **civilized portion** of mankind. The **frontiers** of that **extensive monarchy** were guarded by **ancient renown** and **disciplined valour.**[2] The **gentle,** but powerful, **influence** of laws and **manners** had **gradually cemented** the **union** of the **provinces.** Their **peaceful inhabitants enjoyed** and **abused** the **advantages** of wealth and **luxury.** The **image** of a free **constitution** was **preserved** with **decent reverence.** The **Roman senate appeared** to **possess** the **sovereign authority,** and **devolved** on the **emperors** all the **executive** powers of **government.** During a happy **period** of more than four-score years, the **public administration** was **conducted** by the **virtue** and **abilities** of **Nerva,**[3] **Trajan,**[3] **Hadrian,**[3] and the two **Antonines.**[3] It is the **design** of this and of the two **succeeding chapters,** to **describe** the **prosperous condition** of their **empire;** and afterwards, from the death of **Marcus Antoninus,**[3] to **deduce** the most **important circumstances** of its **decline** and fall: a **revolution** which will ever be **remembered,** and is still felt by the **nations** of the earth.

---

[1] *Aera* is an older spelling of *era.*   [2] British spelling of *valor.*   [3] Roman emperors.

    Gibbon's style has been called *Latinate.* What do you think *Latinate* means? _____

_____

▶ □ ◀

    A: Having an excessive use of Latin derivatives. (This is one reason the work was chosen for study.)

2–3   Here is the opening sentence with the Anglo-Saxon words printed and the words borrowed from Greek and Latin represented by dashes:

In the --------- ---------- of the ------------ -------, the --------- of ------- -------------- the fairest ---- of the earth, and the most --------- ------- of mankind.

    The only Anglo-Saxon *content* words are two nouns and an adjective. What are the two

nouns? _____ and _____

▶ □ ◀

    A: Earth; mankind.

4   And what is the Anglo-Saxon adjective? _____

▶ □ ◀

    A: Fairest.

5 In the second sentence from Gibbon, "The frontiers of that extensive monarchy were guarded by ancient renown and disciplined valour," what kind of words are *the, of, that, were, by,* and *and?* Are they function words or content words?

_____

▶ □□ ◀

A: Function words.

6 From what language do you suppose these six function words come?

_____

▶ □□ ◀

A: Anglo-Saxon.

> **NICE-TO-KNOW** ■ Like content words, function words are divided into different classes, but it is not necessary to know them to do this program.
> You learned in the last unit that words such as *the, those, a(n),* and so forth are noun markers.
> *Were,* as in *were guarded,* is a **helping verb,** like *will* in "He *will guard* the house" and *has* in "He *has guarded* the house."
> *Of* and *by,* as in "the frontiers *of* that extensive monarchy were guarded *by* ancient renown," are called **prepositions** and are followed by noun phrases.
> The words *and* and *but* are **conjunctions,** connecting two equal things, like the nouns *renown* and *valour* or the adjectives *gentle* but *powerful.*

A Common Noun Suffix
(Frames 7–24)

■ Some words are taken into English from Greek and Latin without any change. Examples of this kind of borrowing in Unit One were *bonus, emphasis, per annum,* and *Creator.* But usually the English word has a change—sometimes small, sometimes large—from the Greek or Latin original. Here is an example of a small change in a borrowing from Latin.

7 In Latin the suffix {**io**} makes a noun out of a verb. In English this suffix has changed to {**ion**}, as in the word *competition.* What class of word is *compete,* as in "My sisters *compete* in the running events"? _____

▶ □□ ◀

A: Verb.

8 What class of word is *competition?* _____

▶ □□ ◀

A: Noun.

9 *Competition* means "the act of _____."

▶ □□□ ◀

  A: Competing.

10–12 In the Sample Text in frame 1 there are seven nouns with the same suffix that means "act or result of." Write three of these seven nouns. _____

_____, _____

▶ □□□ ◀

  A: (Any three) Portion, union, constitution, administration, condition, revolution, nations.

13 What class of word are all the {**ion**} words in the last frame? _____

▶ □□□ ◀

  A: Nouns.

14–16 You can now break *nations* into three morphemes, {_____}, {_____}, and {____}.

▶ □□□ ◀

  A: {nat}, {ion}, {s}.

17 What is the meaning of the suffix {**s**} in *nations?* (In your own words.)

_____

▶ □□□ ◀

  A: It shows that *nations* is plural in number.

18 The Latin word from which English *condition* is derived is *conditio;* and the Latin word from which English *nation* is derived is *natio.* What must the Latin original of *portion* have been? _____

▶ □□□ ◀

  A: *Portio.*

19 What English noun means "act of administrating"? _____

▶ □□□ ◀

  A: Administration.

20   What English noun means "state of being unified"? _____

▶ □ ◀

   A: Union.

21   When two teams are *contending* for the championship, we say that they are in *contention*. The prefix {**con**} means "together with." What is the base of the verb *contend*?

   {_____}

▶ □ ◀

   A: {tend}

22   And what is the base of the noun *contention*? {_____}

▶ □ ◀

   A: {tent}

23   The base {**tend**} means "stretch" or "exert oneself." What allomorph of {**tend**} occurs in the noun *contention*? {_____}

▶ □ ◀

   A: {tent}

24   What class of word does the suffix {**ion**} in the word *nation* indicate? _____

▶ □ ◀

   A: Self-test item.

A Common Adjective Suffix
(Frames 25–52)

25   Here is the quotation from Gibbon again:

> In the **second century** of the **Christian aera**, the **empire** of **Rome comprehended** the fairest **part** of the earth, and the most **civilized portion** of mankind. The **frontiers** of that **extensive monarchy** were guarded by **ancient renown** and **disciplined valour**. The **gentle**, but powerful, **influence** of laws and **manners** had **gradually cemented** the **union** of the **provinces**. Their **peaceful inhabitants enjoyed** and **abused** the **advantages** of wealth and **luxury**. The **image** of a free **constitution** was **preserved** with **decent reverence**. The **Roman senate appeared** to **possess** the **sovereign authority**, and **devolved** on the **emperors** all the **executive** powers of **government**. **During** a happy **period** of more than four-score years, the **public administration** was **conducted** by the **virtue** and **abilities** of **Nerva, Trajan, Hadrian**, and the two **Antonines**. It is the **design** of this and of the two **succeeding chapters**, to **describe** the **prosperous condition** of their **empire**; and afterwards, from the death of **Marcus Antoninus**, to **deduce** the most **important circumstances** of its **decline** and fall: a **revolution** which will ever be **remembered**, and is still felt by the **nations** of the earth.

In English the suffix {ive}, of Latin origin, is added to verb bases to form adjectives. In the quotation from Gibbon above there are two such adjectives with the suffix {ive}. First, how large does Gibbon say the monarchy was? He says it was _____.

▶ □ ◀

A: Extensive.

"extent oneself"

26–28 The Latin word meaning "stretch" has three allomorphs, {tend}, {tens}, and {tent}. Write three words using each of these allomorphs, beginning with the prefix {ex}.

_____, _____, _____.

▶ □ ◀

A: Extent, extensive, extend.

29 What class of word is *extend?* _____

▶ □ ◀

A: Verb.

30 What is the English adjective that means "stretched out"? _____.

▶ □ ◀

A: Extensive.

31 We saw in frame 26–28 that the Latin word for "stretch" has three allomorphs. Which allomorph appears in the base of the *verb* form? {_____}

▶ □ ◀

A: {tend}

32 Which allomorph of this same base appears in the *adjective* form? {_____}

▶ □ ◀

A: {tens}

33 Gibbon uses one other {ive} word in the sixth sentence of this same paragraph ("The Roman senate . . . ."). What sort of powers of the government does he say devolved on (= were given to) the emperors? _____

▶ □ ◀

A: Executive.

34 The legislative branch of the United States (Congress) makes our laws and the judicial branch interprets them. What third branch of the government *executes* these laws?

_____

▶ □ ◀

A: The executive branch.

| **NICE-TO-KNOW** ■ Of course some words ending in {ive} are also nouns, as in "Ms. Pruitt became an executive in the company."

35 What is the noun form of *execute* with the noun suffix {**ion**}? _____

▶ □ ◀

A: Execution.

36 Gibbon uses five verbs that can be changed into adjectives by adding the {**ive**} suffix. These often have variants for the bases, as you will now see.
      Gibbon says, "The empire of Rome *comprehended* the fairest part of the earth." A government that "comprehends" many large areas is *comprehensive*. The {**com**} is an allomorph of {**con**}. What is the base of the adjective *comprehensive*? {_____}

▶ □ ◀

A: {prehens}

37 What is the allomorph of the base {**prehens**} which appears in the verb *comprehend*?
      {_____}

▶ □ ◀

A: {prehend}

38 What is the noun with the suffix {**ion**} built on the {**prehens / prehend**} base?

_____

▶ □ ◀

A: Comprehension.

39 Gibbon says, "The Roman senate appeared to *possess* the sovereign authority." What adjective is formed on the verb *possess*? _____

▶ □ ◀

A: Possessive.

40 What noun means "result of possessing"? _____

▶ □□□ ◀

    A: Possession.

41 Do the noun *possession* and adjective *possessive* have the same form of the base or do they have variant forms? _____

▶ □□□ ◀

    A: Same.

42 Gibbon says that the public administration was *conducted* by the virtues and abilities of five emperors. The prefix in the verb *conduct* is {**con**}. What is the base? {_____}

▶ □□□ ◀

    A: {duct}

43 What is the adjective that is formed on an allomorph of {**duct**} with the suffix {**ive**} and will fit the context of this sentence? "Exercise that leads to good health is said to be _____ to your health."

▶ □□□ ◀

    A: Conducive.

44 What is the allomorph of {**duct**} used in the adjective in the last frame? {_____}

▶ □□□ ◀

    A: {duc}

45 Gibbon says that he intends to *describe* the prosperous condition of the Roman empire. The prefix in *describe* is {**de**}. What is the base? {_____}

▶ □□□ ◀

    A: {scribe}

46 When a person *describes* something, what does he give? _____

▶ □□□ ◀

    A: A description.

47–49 What are the prefix, the base, and the suffix of *description*? {_____}, {_____}, and {_____}.

▶ □□□ ◀

    A: {de}, {script}, {ion}.

50 What class of word is *descriptive?* _____

▶ □ ◀

  A: An adjective.

51 What is a variant form of the base {**script**}? {_____}

▶ □ ◀

  A: {scribe}

52 Gibbon says that the inhabitants of the Roman empire enjoyed and *abused* their advantages. What is an adjective form of the verb *abuse* with the suffix {**ive**}? _____

▶ □ ◀

  A: Abusive.

Substitution of Synonyms in the First Sample Text
(Frames 53–64)

■ A **synonym** is a word that means about the same thing as another word. Thus, *big* and *large* are synonyms. Opposites are called **antonyms**; *big* and *small* are antonyms.

53–54 *Smooth* and *rough* are _____ of each other; *rough* and *uneven* are _____.

▶ □ ◀

  A: Antonyms; synonyms.

55–64 Here are the first three sentences of the text from Gibbon again, with Greek and Latin derivatives printed in boldface type.

In the **second century** of the **Christian aera**, the **empire** of **Rome comprehended** the fairest **part** of the earth, and the most **civilized portion** of mankind. The **frontiers** of that **extensive monarchy** were guarded by **ancient renown** and **disciplined valour**. The **gentle**, but powerful, **influence** of laws and **manners** had **gradually cemented** the **union** of the **provinces.**

In the exercise below, we have replaced some of Gibbon's words in the first three sentences of the Sample Text. The synonyms that we put in place of the original words are in parentheses. Following the replacement is space for you to write the original word that Gibbon used. This exercise will help you learn the words in the Sample Text. At the bottom of the passage is a list of the words you will insert. While some students may remember the Gibbon original, most students will rely on the context for clues. Take, for example, the first task. What is (a) a synonym for "hundred years" that (b) fits into the slot in "In the second _____of the Christian aera," and (c) is included in the list below, and (d), most important, makes sense in this context?

In the second (hundred years / _____) of the Christian aera, the empire of Rome (included / _____) the fairest part of the earth, and the most (cultured / _____) portion of mankind. The (borders / _____) of that (wide / _____) monarchy were guarded by ancient (reputation / _____) and disciplined valour. The gentle, but powerful, (effect / _____) of laws and (customs / _____) had (little by little / _____) (strengthened / _____) the union of the provinces.

Here are the Latin derivatives you will use:

| cemented | civilized | extensive | gradually | manners |
| century | comprehended | frontiers | influence | renown |

▶ □ ◀

A: (In order of occurrence): century, comprehended, civilized, frontiers, extensive, renown, influence, manners, gradually, cemented.

NICE-TO-KNOW ■ The following words in the Sample Text are of Greek origin: *Christian, monarchy, period.* *Christian* is made up of {Christ} plus the suffix {ian}. *Monarchy* is made up of two bases, {mon} = one, and {arch} = rule, plus the suffix {y}. There are many similar words, like *patriarchy,* which means "rule by fathers." *Period* is made up of the morpheme {peri} = around and {od} = road. A *period* is therefore a "trip around" or a recurring cycle of time.

Substitution of Synonyms in the Second Sample Text
(Frames 65–129)

65 Here is the second paragraph of Gibbon's *Decline and Fall of the Roman Empire,* with Greek and Latin derivatives again shown in boldface type. Read the paragraph through and look up in your dictionary any words you do not understand.

The **principal conquests** of the **Romans** were **achieved** under the **republic;** and the **emperors,** for the most **part,** were **satisfied** with **preserving** those **dominions** which had been **acquired** by the **policy** of the **senate,** the **active emulation** of the **consuls,** and the **martial enthusiasm** of the **people.** The seven first **centuries** were filled with a **rapid succession** of **triumphs;** but it was **reserved** for **Augustus** to **relinquish** the **ambitious design** of **subduing** the whole earth, and to **introduce** a **spirit** of **moderation** into the **public councils. Inclined** to **peace** by his **temper** and **situation,** it was easy for him to discover that **Rome,** in her **present exalted situation,** had much less to hope than to fear from the chance of **arms;** and that, in the **prosecution** of **remote** wars, the undertaking became every day more **difficult,** the **event** more **doubtful,** and the **possession** more **precarious** and less **beneficial.** The **experience** of **Augustus** added weight to these **salutary reflections,** and **effectually convinced** him that, by the **prudent vigour** of his **counsels,** it would be easy to **secure** every

concession which the **safety** or **dignity** of **Rome** might **require** from the most **formidable barbarians.** Instead of **exposing** his **person** and his **legions** to the arrows of the **Parthians,** he **obtained,** by an **honourable** treaty, the **restitution** of the standards and prisoners which had been taken in the **defeat** of **Crassus.**

Many Latin words have been borrowed into English with little change. For example, look at the first sentence in the Sample Text. What English word is derived from Latin *principalis?* _____

A: Principal.

66–68   Latin *Romanus* becomes English "_____."

Latin *respublica* becomes English "_____."

Latin *imperator* becomes English "_____."

A: Roman; republic; emperor.

69–71   Latin *pars* becomes English "_____."

Latin *dominio* becomes English "_____."

Latin *acquiro* becomes English "_____."

A: Part, dominion; acquire.

72–74   Latin *senatus* becomes English "_____."

Latin *activus* becomes English "_____."

Latin *aemulatio* becomes English "_____."

A: Senate, active, emulation (Latin *ae* becomes English *e*).

75–77   Latin *consul* becomes English "_____."

Latin *martialis* becomes English "_____."

Latin *populus* becomes English "_____."

A: Consul; martial; people (the difference in spelling between Latin *populus* and English *people* is rather large).

77

78 Here are the English words you just practiced, in the order they occurred: *principal, Roman, republic, emperor, part, dominion, acquire, senate, active, emulation, consul, martial, people.*

There is a word in this list that has a suffix which means "a person who does something." First, what word, used here as a synonym for "ruler," has this new suffix?

_____

▶ □ ◀

A: Emperor.

79 What is the suffix of *emperor* that means "person who does something"? {_____}

▶ □ ◀

A: {or}

80 What is the noun in this list that is a synonym for "territory" or "rule over territory"?

_____

▶ □ ◀

A: Dominion.

81 What noun means "rivalry" in this context? _____

▶ □ ◀

A: Emulation.

82 What suffix do these last two nouns have? {_____}

▶ □ ◀

A: {ion}

83–84 What class of word is *martial*? _____ What class of word is *active*?

_____

▶ □ ◀

A: Adjective; adjective.

85 In addition, there are two other words in the Sample Text (frame 65) derived from Greek. One is derived from the Greek word *politeia*. What is the form of this word in English?

_____

▶ □ ◀

A: Policy.

86   The second is Greek *enthousiasmos*. What did this word become in English?

_____

▶ □ ◀

A: Enthusiasm.

87–96   Below is the first sentence of the second paragraph of the Gibbon text. As before, we have replaced some of Gibbon's words from the Sample Text in frame 65 with synonyms. Replace these synonyms with the Greek and Latin derivatives that Gibbon used.

The (chief / _____) conquests of the Romans were achieved under the republic; and the (rulers / _____), for the most part, were (content / _____) with (saving / _____) those (lands / _____) which had been (obtained / _____) by the policy of the senate, the active (ambition / _____) of the (chief magistrates / _____), and the (warlike / _____) (eagerness / _____) of the people.

Here are the words you will use:

acquired	dominions	emulation	martial	principal
consuls	emperors	enthusiasm	preserving	satisfied

▶ □ ◀

A: (In order of occurrence): principal, emperors, satisfied, preserving, dominions, acquired, emulation, consuls, martial, enthusiasm.

97–106   Continue to replace the synonyms with Gibbon's words for the second sentence of the Sample Text:

The seven first (hundred years / _____) were filled with a (quick / _____) (sequence / _____) of (victories / _____); but it was (left / _____) for Augustus to (abandon / _____) the ambitious (plan / _____) of (overcoming / _____) the whole earth, and to (bring forward / _____) a spirit of moderation into the public (meetings / _____).

Here are the words you will use:

centuries	design	rapid	reserved	succession
councils	introduce	relinquish	subduing	triumphs

▶ □ ◀

A: (In order of occurrence): centuries, rapid, succession, triumphs, reserved, relinquish, design, subduing, introduce, councils.

107–116   Replace the words in parentheses with Gibbon's words which occur in the third sentence of the Sample Text.

(Tending / _____) to peace by his (disposition / _____) and situation, it was easy for him to discover that Rome, in her present (lofty / _____) (state / _____), had much less to hope than to fear from the chance of arms; and that, in the (waging / _____) of (distant / _____) wars, the undertaking became every day more difficult, the (outcome / _____) more doubtful, and the (ownership / _____) more (dangerous / _____) and less (advantageous / _____).

Here are the words you will use:

beneficial	*exalted*	*possession*	*prosecution*	*situation*
event	*inclined*	*precarious*	*remote*	*temper*

▶ □ ◀

A: (In order of occurrence): inclined, temper, exalted, situation, prosecution, remote, event, possession, precarious, beneficial. (The meaning of *event* in this context is an example of how the common modern meaning of a word may not coincide with an earlier meaning.)

117–124   Continue as before: replace the synonyms with Gibbon's words from the fourth sentence of the Sample Text.

The experience of Augustus added weight to these (healthy / _____) (thoughts / _____), and (successfully / _____) convinced him that, by the (cautious / _____) vigour of his (plans / _____), it would be easy to (get / _____) every (yielding / _____) which the safety or dignity of Rome might require from the most (dangerous / _____) barbarians.

Here are the words you will use:

concession	*effectually*	*prudent*	*salutary*
counsels	*formidable*	*reflections*	*secure*

▶ □ ◀

A: (In order of occurrence): salutary, reflections, effectually, prudent, counsels, secure, concession, formidable.

125–129   Continue to replace the words in parentheses; these are from the last sentence of the Sample Text.

Instead of (presenting / _____) his (body / _____) and his (soldiers / _____) to the arrows of the Parthians, he (got / _____), by an honourable treaty, the (return / _____) of the standards and prisoners which had been taken in the defeat of Crassus.

Here are the words you will use:

exposing   legions   obtained   person   restitution

▶ □ ◀

    A: (In order of occurrence): exposing, person, legions, obtained, restitution.

Dictionaries as Tools
(Frames 130–179)

■ Read through the third paragraph of Gibbon's *Decline and Fall*, given below. Then proceed to do the frames that follow.

His **generals,** in the early **part** of his **reign, attempted** the **reduction** of **Aethiopia** and **Arabia Felix.** They marched near a thousand **miles** to the south of the **tropic;** but the heat of the **climate** soon **repelled** the **invaders** and **protected** the unwarlike **natives** of those **sequestered** regions. The northern **countries** of **Europe scarcely deserved** the **expense** and **labour** of **conquest.** The **forests** and morasses of Germany were filled with a hardy **race** of **barbarians,** who **despised** life when it was **separated** from freedom; and though, on the first attack, they seemed to yield to the weight of the **Roman** power, they soon, by a **signal act** of **despair,** regained their **independence,** and reminded **Augustus** of the **vicissitude** of **fortune.** On the death of that **emperor** his **testament** was **publicly** read in the **senate.** He bequeathed, **as a valuable legacy** to his **successors,** the **advice** of **confining** the **empire** within those **limits** which **nature** seemed to have **placed** as its **permanent** bulwarks and **boundaries;** on the west the **Atlantic Ocean;** the Rhine and Danube on the north; the Euphrates on the east; and towards the south the sandy **deserts** of **Arabia** and **Africa.**

---

130 When you look up a word in the dictionary you should, if possible, already have a *general* idea from the context of what the word means. Here is an example. In the first sentence of the Sample Text above, we read that the generals of the Roman emperor Augustus attempted the *reduction* of Aethiopia and Arabia Felix. We then find out in the second sentence that "the heat of the climate soon repelled the invaders." Now, what the Roman army was trying to do was to _____ (conquer / explore / help / surrender to) Aethiopia and Arabia Felix.

▶ □ ◀

    A: Conquer.

NICE-TO-KNOW ■ *Aethiopia* is an old-fashioned spelling of *Ethiopia*, just as *aera* was an older spelling of *era*. *Arabia Felix* means "Fertile Arabia," now called Yemen.

81

131 Now look below at the dictionary entry for *reduction* (from *Webster's New World Dictionary*). How many meanings are given for *reduction*? _____

> **re·duc·tion** (ri duk′shən) *n.* [LME. *reduccion* < MFr. *reduction* < L. *reductio* < *reductus*, pp. of *reducere*] **1.** a reducing or being reduced **2.** anything made or brought about by reducing, as a smaller copy, lowered price, etc. **3.** the amount by which anything is reduced —**re·duc′- tion·al** *adj.*

▶ □ ◀

A: Three.

132 In this dictionary entry, what one verb is used (in two different forms) to explain these three meanings? _____

▶ □ ◀

A: Reduce (in the forms "reducing" and "reduced").

133 So, if you want to find out the meaning of *reduction* from the dictionary, what do you have to look up next? _____

_____

▶ □ ◀

A: You must look up the verb "reduce."

134–135 How many major meanings are listed under the verb *reduce*? _____

> **re·duce** (ri dōōs′, -dyōōs′) *vt.* **-duced′, -duc′ing** [ME. *re-ducen* < L. *reducere*, to lead back < *re-*, back + *ducere*, to lead: see DUCT] **1.** *a)* to lessen in any way, as in size, weight, amount, value, price, etc.; diminish *b)* to put into a simpler or more concentrated form **2.** to bring into a certain order; systematize **3.** to break up into constituent elements by analysis **4.** *a)* to put into a different form [to *reduce* a talk to writing] *b)* to change to a different physical form, as by melting, crushing, grinding, etc. **5.** to lower, as in rank or position; demote; downgrade **6.** *a)* to bring to order, attention, obedience, etc., as by persuasion or force *b)* to subdue or conquer (a city or fort) by siege or attack **7.** *a)* to bring into difficult or wretched circumstances [a people *reduced* to poverty] *b)* to compel by need to do something [*reduced* to stealing] **8.** *a)* to weaken in bodily strength; make thin [*reduced* to skin and bones] *b)* to thin (paint, etc.), as with oil **9.** *Arith.* to change in denomination or form without changing in value [to *reduce* fractions to their lowest terms] **10.** *Chem.* *a)* to decrease the positive valence of (an element or ion) *b)* to increase the number of electrons of (an atom, element, or ion) *c)* to remove the oxygen from; deoxidize *d)* to combine with hydrogen *e)* to bring into the metallic state by removing nonmetallic elements **11.** *Phonology* to give an unstressed quality to (a vowel) **12.** *Photog.* to weaken the density of (a negative) **13.** *Surgery* to restore (a broken bone, displaced organ, etc.) to normal position or condition —*vi.* **1.** to become reduced **2.** to lose weight, as by dieting —*SYN.* see DECREASE —**re·duc′i·bil′i·ty** *n.* —**re·duc′i·ble** *adj.* —**re·duc′i·bly** *adv.*

▶ □ ◀

A: 15 (13 major transitive meanings, with several meanings for most of these, and 2 intransitive meanings). Which one of these meanings under the verb *reduce* does the noun *reduction* have in "His generals . . . attempted the *reduction* of Aethiopia" from the Sample Text? Number of the dictionary entry: _____.

A: 6b.

136 Since you already had a general idea of the meaning of *reduction* from the context of Gibbon, it should have been easy to let your eye skim the entry until you found the meaning you had thought was correct. But think of the time it would take to read through all the meanings if you did not already (in your own words) _____

_____

► □ ◄

    A: Have a general idea of the meaning from the context.

137 Let us return to the dictionary entry for *reduction* in frame 131. First, what does "(ri duk′ shən)" tell, in your own words? _____

_____

► □ ◄

    A: It tells us how to pronounce the word. (The meaning of pronunciation symbols is given at the bottom of every right-hand page of most dictionaries. You can easily learn to use these pronunciation guides by yourself, and we will do nothing more with them in the program. Different dictionaries use slightly different sets of symbols.)

138 The next item in the entry *reduction* is the letter **n.** What does this abbreviation stand for? _____

► □ ◄

    A: Noun.

139 The next item in the entry *reduction* is of great importance in this course. What does it give us? (In your own words) _____

_____

► □ ◄

    A: The etymology of the word *reduction*.

140 It is characteristic of dictionaries to economize on space by using abbreviations. We will ask you to interpret the abbreviations and symbols in the square brackets. If we tell you that the L in LME means "late," what do you think LME means? _____

_____

► □ ◄

    A: Late Middle English. (M is also used in some dictionaries as an abbreviation for *medieval*. If in doubt about abbreviations, consult your dictionary.)

141   What was the form of the modern word *reduction* in Late Middle English? _____

> re·duc·tion (ri duk′shən) *n.* [LME. *reduccion* < MFr. *reduction* < L. *reductio* < *reductus*, pp. of *reducere*] **1.** a reducing or being reduced **2.** anything made or brought about by reducing, as a smaller copy, lowered price, etc. **3.** the amount by which anything is reduced —**re·duc′-tion·al** *adj.*

▶ □ ◀

   A: *Reduccion.*

142   What language was the word *reduccion?* _____

▶ □ ◀

   A: Late Middle English.

143   What do you think the abbreviation MFr stands for? _____

▶ □ ◀

   A: Middle French.

144   Continue to read the entry. What was the Middle French form of the word *reduction?*
   _____

▶ □ ◀

   A: *Reduction.*

145   From what language did Middle French get the word *reduction?* _____

▶ □ ◀

   A: Latin.

146   What was the Latin form of the modern English word *reduction?* _____

▶ □ ◀

   A: *Reductio.*

147   Latin *reductio* in turn was formed on *reductus*, the past participle of *reducere*. What is
   the abbreviation for "past participle"? _____

▶ □ ◀

   A: pp.

148 At the very end of the entry is the word *reductional* followed by **adj.** What does the abbreviation **adj.** mean? _____

▶ □ ◀

A: Adjective.

149 What is the suffix that makes *reductional* an adjective? {_____}

▶ □ ◀

A: {al}

150 To proceed with the Sample Text: Gibbon says, "They marched near a thousand miles to the south of the tropic." Look at the dictionary entry for *tropic* (from *Webster's New World Dictionary*).

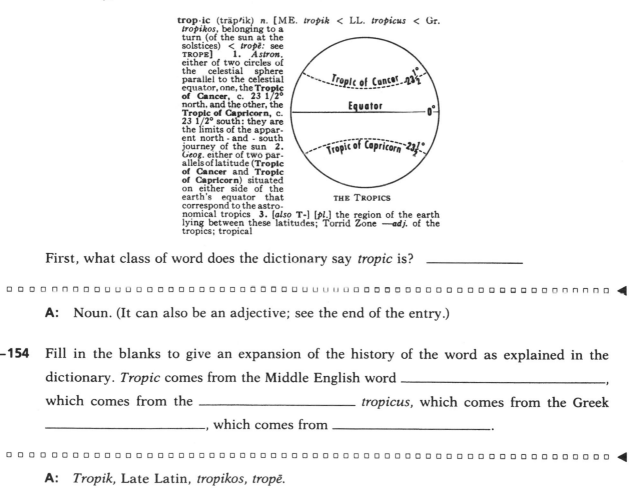

THE TROPICS

First, what class of word does the dictionary say *tropic* is? _____

▶ □ □ □ □ □ ⊓ ⊓ □ □ □ ⊔ ⊔ □ □ □ □ □ □ □ □ □ □ □ □ ⊔ ⊔ ⊔ ⊔ ⊔ □ □ □ □ □ □ □ □ □ □ □ □ □ ⊓ ⊓ ⊓ ⊓ □ ◀

A: Noun. (It can also be an adjective; see the end of the entry.)

151–154 Fill in the blanks to give an expansion of the history of the word as explained in the dictionary. *Tropic* comes from the Middle English word _____, which comes from the _____ *tropicus*, which comes from the Greek _____, which comes from _____.

▶ □ ◀

A: *Tropik*, Late Latin, *tropikos*, *tropē*.

155 The dictionary then tells you that for further information about the base {**trop**} you should look under the entry _____.

▶ □ ◀

A: TROPE. (But in this case it is not necessary for you to look it up.)

156 The base {**trop**} means "turn." In your own words, explain what it is that turns that gives the English word *tropic* its present meaning. _____

_____

▶ □ ◀

A: *Tropic* is the place where the sun appears to stop moving toward one pole and turns back to the other pole.

157 In our Sample Text, Gibbon speaks of the *barbarians* who live in Germany. Look at the entry for *barbarian* below, from *Webster's New World Dictionary*, and study it. At the beginning of the entry, what class of word does the dictionary say that *barbarian* is?

_____

bar·bar·i·an (bär ber′ē ən) *n.* [< L. *barbarus,* BARBAROUS]
1. orig., an alien or foreigner: in the ancient world applied esp. to non-Greeks, non-Romans, or non-Christians **2.** a member of a people or group with a civilization regarded as primitive, savage, etc. **3.** *a)* a person who lacks culture *b)* a coarse or unmannerly person; boor **4.** a savage, cruel person; brute —*adj.* of or like a barbarian; esp., *a)* uncivilized; crude *b)* savage; cruel; barbarous —**bar·bar′i·an·ism** *n.*
SYN.—**barbarian** basically refers to a civilization regarded as primitive, usually without further connotation [the Anglo-Saxons were a *barbarian* people]; **barbaric** suggests the crudeness and lack of restraint regarded as characteristic of primitive peoples [*barbaric* splendor]; **barbarous** connotes the cruelty and brutality regarded as characteristic of primitive peoples [*barbarous* warfare]; **savage** implies a more primitive civilization than **barbarian** and connotes even greater fierceness and cruelty [a *savage* inquisition] —**ANT.** **civilized**

▶ □ ◀

A: Noun.

158 Near the end of the entry you find that *barbarian* can also be another class of word. What can it also be? _____

▶ □ ◀

A: An adjective.

159 In this entry you are told that English *barbarian* comes from *barbarus*. What language is *barbarus*? _____

▶ □ ◀

A: Latin.

160 Elsewhere in this dictionary you are told that Latin *barbarus* comes from Greek *barbaros*, which came, presumably, from an earlier form **barbar*, which was what non-Greek languages sounded like to the Greeks. So an early meaning of Greek *barbaros* was "non-Greek."Now, where do you think it says this in the dictionary? _____

_____

▶ □ ◀

A: In the entry for *barbarous*.

161 Is it reasonable to expect someone to be able to find this etymological information under *barbarous* when he is looking up *barbarian*? _____ (yes / no)

▶ ▫ ◀

A: Yes.

162 It is reasonable because the dictionary gives guidance for finding more information. What was the signal to look up *barbarous?* _____

_____

▶ ▫ ◀

A: The word BARBAROUS printed in small capitals, as you saw earlier in TROPE under *tropic.* These small capitals mean, "Look me up."

163 In the entry for *barbarian*, what does the abbreviation **SYN.** mean? _____

▶ ▫ ◀

A: Synonyms.

164–166 In this part of the entry the editors explain the difference between *barbarian* and three synonyms. What are these synonyms? _____, _____, and _____

▶ ▫ ◀

A: Barbaric, barbarous, savage.

167 What does the abbreviation **ANT.** mean? _____

▶ ▫ ◀

A: Antonym.

168 What antonym does this dictionary give for *barbarian*? _____

▶ ▫ ◀

A: Civilized.

169 Considering that the Greeks used *barbarian* to refer to people whose speech was unintelligible to them and sounded like "bar-bar-bar," what would another antonym of *barbarian* be? _____

▶ ▫ ◀

A: Greek.

170 Here is a word that most of you will not know. In our Sample Text Gibbon says that the Emperor Augustus was reminded by the German barbarians "of the vicissitude of fortune." From its context, what does *vicissitude* mean? _____ (change / help / hindrance / impartiality)

▶ □ ◀

A: No answer; we are going to ask you to check this with a dictionary in the next frame.

171 From the dictionary entry below *(Webster's New World)*, what do you find that *vicissitude* means?

> **vi·cis·si·tude** (vi sis′ə to͞od′, -tyo͞od′) *n.* [Fr. < L. *vicissitudo* < *vicis*, a turn, change: see VICAR] **1.** *a)* a condition of constant change or alternation, as a natural process; mutability [the *vicissitude* of the sea] *b)* regular succession or alternation, as of night and day **2.** [*pl.*] unpredictable changes or variations that keep occurring in life, fortune, etc.; shifting circumstances; ups and downs —**SYN.** see DIFFICULTY —**vi·cis·si·tu′di·nar′y, vi·cis′si·tu′di·nous** *adj.*

_____

▶ □ ◀

A: Change.

172 Finally, we will compare the entries of three dictionaries for the word *legacy*—as in the sentence, "He bequeathed a valuable *legacy* to his successors"—in order to show you how to get more information.

Webster's New World Dictionary

> **leg·a·cy** (leg′ə sē) *n.,* *pl.* **-cies** [ME. *legacie* < OFr. < ML. *legatia* < L. *legatus*: see LEGATE] **1.** money or property left to someone by a will; bequest **2.** anything handed down from, or as from, an ancestor

American Heritage Dictionary

> **leg·a·cy** (lĕg′ə-sē) *n.,* *pl.* **-cies.** **1.** Money or property bequeathed to someone by will. **2.** Something handed down from an ancestor or predecessor, or from the past. [Middle English *legacie,* from Old French, from Medieval Latin *lēgantia,* from Latin *lēgāre,* to depute, commission, bequeath. See *leg-* in Appendix.*]

Webster's New Collegiate Dictionary

> **leg·a·cy** \′leg-ə-sē\ *n,* *pl* **-cies** [ME *legacie* office of a legate, bequest, fr. MF or ML; MF, office of a legate, fr. ML *legatia,* fr. L *legatus* — more at LEGATE] (15c) **1** : a gift by will esp. of money or other personal property : BEQUEST **2** : something received from an ancestor or predecessor or from the past ⟨the ∼ of the ancient philosophers⟩

Answer these questions with the help of the dictionary entries, where necessary.

The plural of *legacy* is not **legacys;* what is it? _____

▶ □ ◀

A: Legacies.

173 What abbreviation in all three entries means "The irregular plural of the word is *lega-cies*"? _____

▶ □ ◀

   A: *pl.* **-cies**

174 How many different meanings does each of the three different dictionaries list? _____

▶ □ ◀

   A: Two (unlike some entries we examined earlier, where there was considerable divergence).

175 Translate the etymological information (contained in square brackets) into your own words, spelling out the abbreviations and symbols. From *Webster's New World:*

   _____

   _____

▶ □ ◀

   A: Middle English *legacie*, derived from Old French, which is derived from Medieval Latin *legatia*, derived from Latin *legatus;* for more information see under the word LEGATE.

176 What spelling does the *American Heritage* show for the Medieval Latin form?

   _____

▶ □ ◀

   A: *Lēgantia.*

177 What spelling does *Webster's New World* show for the Medieval Latin form?

   _____

▶ □ ◀

   A: *Legatia.*

178 And what spelling of this form does the *Webster's New Collegiate Dictionary* give?

   _____

▶ □ ◀

   A: *Legatia.*

I   NICE-TO-KNOW ■ The Latin forms listed as *legatus* and *lēgāre* are different forms of the same Latin word.

179 Finally, in the *Webster's New Collegiate Dictionary* entry, we see ⟨the ~ of the ancient philosophers⟩. The angular brackets mean that what is enclosed is an example of the word in context. Can you figure out what the tilde (the symbol ~) means here? _____

_____

▶ ▫▫▫ ◀

A: It stands for "legacy"; that is, we are to read "the *legacy* of the ancient philosophers."

WORD LIST

The following concepts were introduced. Make sure you understand them and can give examples.

antonym 53   synonym 54

Here is a list of the words discussed in this unit. Use a dictionary if you need to.

abuse 52	emulation 74	possession 40
abusive 52	enthusiasm 86	possessive 39
acquire 71	event 107–116	precarious 107–116
active 73	exalt 107–116	preserve 87–96
administration 10	execute 35	principal 65
barbarian 157	execution 35	prosecution 107–116
beneficial 107–116	executive 34	prudent 117–124
cement 55–64	expose 125–129	rapid 97–106
century 55–64	extend 26	reduce 132
civilize 55–64	extensive 25	reduction 131
compete 7	extent 26	reflection 117–124
competition 7	fairest 4	relinquish 97–106
comprehend 36	formidable 117–124	remote 107–116
comprehension 38	frontier 55–64	renown 55–64
comprehensive 36	gradually 55–64	republic 67
concession 117–124	inclined 107–116	reserve 97–106
condition 10	influence 55–64	restitution 125–129
conducive 43	introduce 97–106	revolution 10
conduct 42	Latinate 1	Roman 66
constitution 10	legacy 172	salutary 117–124
consul 75	legion 125–129	satisfy 87–96
contention 23	mankind 3	secure 117–124
council 97–106	manners 55–64	senate 72
counsel 117–124	martial 76	situation 107–116
describe 45	nation 10	subdue 97–106
description 46	obtain 125–129	succession 97–106
descriptive 50	part 69	temper 107–116
design 97–106	people 77	triumph 97–106
dominion 70	person 125–129	tropic 150
earth 2	policy 85	union 10
effectually 117–124	portion 10	vicissitude 170
emperor 68	possess 39	

REVIEW EXERCISES

Purposes: To review some words learned in Unit Three and contrast them with some words close to them in spelling or form; to review some common suffixes. You will need a dictionary.

Directions: Explain the meaning of each italicized word as it is used in the sentence.

1. a. Maria's *emulation* of her sister's swimming ability was obvious to their mother.

   _____

   b. Linda's *adulation* of her teacher was obvious to all her classmates.

   _____

2. a. Many people appreciated the efforts of the *consul*.

   _____

   b. Many people appreciated the efforts of the *council*.

   _____

   c. Many people appreciated the efforts of the *counsel*.

   _____

   d. Many people appreciated the *counsel* they received.

   _____

3. a. The *salutary* effect of the dry weather on his health was noticeable.

   _____

   b. The *salutatory* comments of Ms. Smith were most gracious.

   _____

4. a. Mike is *apprehensive* about the upcoming exams because of his poor academic record.

   _____

   b. The teacher was *reprehensive* toward the students for their misbehavior.

   _____

5. a. A language student studies the *inflections* of the words in that language.

   _____

   b. The *deflection* of the hockey puck in the final shot saved the game.

   _____

Directions: Supply in each of these sentences the word *principal* or *principle*. (Use the plural form if necessary.)

6. The bank sent a statement of the interest on the _____.

7. Mr. White had been a _____with the ballet company for many years.

8. Ms. Rose, a woman of _____, was an ideal candidate for the office.

9. Ms. Johnson, a former school _____, was elected president.

10. The biology students were learning the _____ of cell division.

Directions: Below are listed some common words that can be combined with one or more of these suffixes: {**io** / **ion**}, {**ive**}, {**or**} and {**al**}. Form as many new words as you can. You may need to use an allomorph of the base. Check your dictionary if you are uncertain about the spelling or meaning, or just to make sure the new word exists.

Example. compete: competitor, competitive, competition

11. conduct _____

12. possess _____

13. person _____

14. influence _____

15. tropic _____

16. execute _____

17. administrate _____

WORDS OF INTERESTING ORIGIN

Directions: Find in your dictionary the origins of the italicized words. Then write down (a) the language of origin, (b) the etymological meaning (= early meaning), and (c) the modern meaning.

1. "Sometimes I wonder why I ever married an *idiot* like you," stormed Becky.

     Language of origin: _____

     Etymological meaning: _____

     Modern meaning: _____

2. My discovery of Uncle's diary was sheer *serendipity*. I was actually looking in the closet for my birth certificate.

     Language of origin: _____

     Etymological meaning: _____

     Modern meaning: _____

3. "Please don't bother me with such *trivial* questions," said Sue.

     Language of origin: _____

     Etymological meaning: _____

     Modern meaning: _____

4. "I can't stand that *sarcasm* of yours," sobbed Jane. "You discourage me every time I start feeling like a person."

     Language of origin: _____

     Etymological meaning: _____

     Modern meaning: _____

5. "They are *assassins* all right," shouted Kenneth. "Run for your life!"

Language of origin: _____

Etymological meaning: _____

Modern meaning: _____

EASILY CONFUSED WORDS

Use your dictionary as necessary.

1. **Raise / raze.**   This pair of words is most confusing. They are both verbs, are spelled differently, are pronounced alike, and have almost opposite meanings. If we *raise* something we build it, as in "They *raised* the skyscraper in six months," which means they built it. We can also say, "They *razed* the skyscraper in six months," which means they demolished it. The only common meaning of *raze* is to tear something down, but the verb *raise* has a number of meanings: we *raise* a laugh, *raise* a family, and *raise* money. We also *raise* a question, our voice, and our social standing.

2. **Prone / supine.**   These words both mean "lying down," but one is face down, the other face up. Here is how you can remember *prone:* "There are three positions in firing a rifle in the army: standing, kneeling, and *prone*." You would not fire a rifle lying on your back, so *prone* means "lying on one's stomach." *Supine* is lying face upward, as in "Since Bob was lying *supine*, unable to move, the glare of the sun in his eyes was unbearable."

3. **Martial / marital.**   *Martial* comes from the Latin name Mars, the Roman god of war. It means warlike, as in "The colonel's appearance was so *martial*, with two revolvers and two rifles plus cartridge belts, that the enemy would have run without a shot had they seen him." *Marital* comes from Latin {**marit**} meaning "married," as in "Twenty years of minor *marital* problems had not dimmed their affection for each other."

Use the six words in the sentences where each makes sense.

1. The roll of drums and the blare of the bugles always aroused my _____ spirit.

2. The authorities condemned our old clubhouse as a fire hazard and had it _____ to the ground.

3. Bruce staggered, fell on his back, and continued to lie there _____ without making a sound.

4. On the command "Hit the dirt!", we all threw ourselves _____ on the earth and covered our heads.

5. Since Gwen and her husband, Hank, both held jobs, they divided up the _____ chores like washing dishes and vacuuming.

6. In view of our increased costs we will have to _____ our prices.

LATIN PHRASES

First try to get the meaning of the Latin phrases from the context of the sentences below, choosing a meaning from the list that follows. Write the number of the Latin phrase beside the definition that fits.

1. *Modus operandi,* as in "We are helpless unless we can find out something about the *modus operandi* of this gang of thugs."

2. *Dramatis personae,* as in "The plot of the play was weak, but the talent of the *dramatis personae* made the production a success."

3. *Non sequitur,* as in "Albert's remarks were so full of *non sequiturs* that the conversation seemed pointless."

4. *Deus ex machina,* as in "The play was interesting until the last act, when it became apparent that the problem could be resolved only by a *deus ex machina.*"

5. *Summum bonum,* as in "My opponent seems to believe that the *summum bonum* of the country is to eliminate poverty—by starvation."

_____ a remark that doesn't fit with what went before

_____ an unconvincing character introduced in a play

_____ characters in a play

_____ method of working

_____ Don't follow (me).

_____ good total

_____ moderate operation

_____ tragic personalities

_____ God! Get out of that machine!

_____ greatest good

Use a dictionary to find the word-by-word translation and the modern meaning for each phrase.

	Word-by-Word Translation	Modern Meaning
modus operandi	_____	_____
dramatis personae	_____	_____
non sequitur	_____	_____
deus ex machina	_____	_____
summum bonum	_____	_____

UNIT FOUR

Derivatives from Greek

This unit will present to you many words borrowed from Greek. Most of them are probably unknown to you, but by paying attention to (1) the context in which these words occur and (2) the meaning of the prefixes, bases, and suffixes, you will in most cases be able to arrive at the meaning.

In the previous three units you have been asked to learn *all* the words listed at the end of the unit. That is, we were asking for mastery of all the material in the unit.

In this unit we will emphasize the processes by which words are formed. In order to do this we are going to give you some words that we are fairly sure many of you have never seen. We have therefore purposely used some words that are far from common. We have divided the word list at the end of the unit into two parts, first the words which you should learn, and second, the more unusual words, which your instructor may or may not assign for mastery.

CONTENTS

1–8	A Review of Latin Examples of Three-Part Words
9–49	Prefix, Base, and Suffix: Eleven Examples Derived from Greek
50–87	Words with Two Bases: Examples Derived from Greek
88–139	Unusual Words Derived from Greek
140–154	Optional Exercises

A Review of Latin Examples of Three-Part Words
(Frames 1–8)

1–2 Many Latin and Greek derivatives are composed of three parts: prefix, base, and suffix. You saw examples of this kind of three-morpheme word in the last unit. *Extensive* was such a word. What is the prefix of *extensive*, and what does it mean?

{_____} ; _____

▶ □ ◀

A: {ex}; out (out of).

3–4 What is the base of *extensive* and what does it mean?

{_____} ; _____

▶ □ ◀

A: {tens}; stretch (or stretched).

5 What is the suffix of *extensive*? {_____}

▶ □ ◀

A: {ive}

6 The meaning of {**ive**} is chiefly to show what class of word a word is. What class of word is *extensive*? _____

▶ □ ◀

A: Adjective.

7 What is the base of the verb *extend*? {_____}

▶ □ ◀

A: {tend}

8 We say that {**tend**} and {**tens**} are _____ s of the same morpheme.

▶ □ ◀

A: Allomorphs.

Prefix, Base, and Suffix: Eleven Examples Derived from Greek
(Frames 9–49)

■ In the next sequence of frames, use this **menu** (= table) of prefixes, suffixes, and bases to define the English words you will be given. Refer to this menu as necessary. Do not try to learn these morphemes in isolation.

PREFIXES:
{**dys**} = bad, poor, difficult
{**eu**} = well, good, easy

BASES:
{**enter**} = the inside, an intestine
{**gen**} = give birth to, be born
{**log**} = study, science, word
{**pept** / **peps**} = cook, digest
{**phon** / **phem**} = sound
{**pne**} = blow, breathe
{**thanas** / **thanat**} = die

SUFFIXES:
{**ia / a**} = condition of, act of
{**ic**} = pertaining to
{**ics**} = study of
{**ism**} = doctrine, condition of
{**istic**} forms an adjective
{**y**} = process of, condition of, act of

Using this menu of morphemes and observing the context, define the words below that are printed in italics. Notice that we have separated the morphemes for you.

9 *Dys-enter-y*, as in "From eating unwashed fruit Bill caught a case of *dysentery* and suffered diarrhea for a week, severe enough to be almost fatal." In your own words, what does

dysentery mean? _____

_____

▶ □ ◀

A: The condition of bad intestines; that is, a disorder of the lower intestine accompanied by violent diarrhea, sometimes fatal. (Naturally, no one would give this exact answer.)

10 *Eu-gen-ics*, as in "Some people believe that through the application of *eugenics* the physical and mental qualities of the human race could be much improved." Define *eugenics*

(in your own words). _____

_____

_____

▶ □ ◀

A: The study of good births; that is, the study of the improvement of the human race by such means as selection of parents with desirable genes, as is done with dogs and horses.

11 Is the {eu} in *eugenics* {**full**}, {**empty**}, or {**intens**} ? {_____}

▶ □ ◀

A: {full}

12 Which of these three kinds of morphemes is the base {**gen**} ? {_____}

▶ □ ◀

A: {full}

13 Which kind of morpheme is the suffix {ics}? Is it {full}? _____ (yes / no)

▶ □ ◀

A: Yes.

14 *Eú-log-y,* as in "At the funeral the minister spoke of the mayor in a stirring *eulogy* and praised his many services to the community." In your own words, what is a *eulogy?*

_____

▶ □ ◀

A: The act of speaking well; that is, an act of praising someone. (Remember that you may look back to the menu of prefixes, suffixes, and bases whenever you like.)

15 *Eu-péps-ia,* as in "Mr. Brown, after a full meal, was a glowing example of *eupepsia* at its finest." What is *eupepsia?* _____

▶ □ ◀

A: The condition of having good digestion.

16 *Dys-gén-ics,* as in "This small and isolated community, with several centuries of inbreeding, was a perfect field for the study of *dysgenics.*" Define *dysgenics.* _____

_____

▶ □ ◀

A: The study of bad births, that is, study of the factors leading to degeneration of descendants, particularly by inbreeding.

17 *Dys-péps-ia,* as in "We could not have come at a worse time with our gift of sausage and sauerkraut, for Uncle Tim was in the grip of his *dyspepsia* and, as he said with violence, all food was poison to him." What is *dyspepsia?* _____

_____

▶ □ ◀

A: The condition of having bad digestion.

18 What is the antonym of *dyspepsia?* _____

▶ □ ◀

A: Eupepsia.

19 The morphemes {dys} and {eu} are _____ of each other.

▶ □ ◀

A: Antonyms.

20 *Dys-log-istic,* as in "To everyone's surprise, the remarks of the minister at the funeral were brief and even *dyslogistic* in tone." Did the minister praise or criticize the dead person? _____

► □ ◄

A: Criticize.

21 *Eu-thanás-ia,* as in "Dr. Jones was attacked for her rash statements about *euthanasia* for the mentally defective." What is *euthanasia?* _____
_____

► □ ◄

A: The act of causing an easy and painless death (so as to end suffering).

22 *Eu-phon-y,* as in "The *euphony* of the children's voices singing in harmony charmed all who heard them." How did the children's voices sound? _____

► □ ◄

A: Pleasant.

23 *Dys-pné-a,* as in "Because of the extremely high altitude, they were all suffering in different degrees from *dyspnea.*" What difficulty were the climbers having? _____
_____

► □ ◄

A: Trouble breathing.

24 *Eu-phem-ism,* as in "So strong are the taboos against mentioning certain body functions that in 'polite society' one invariably uses some *euphemism* when wishing to answer the call of nature and may ask for the bathroom, when it is obvious that one is not intending to bathe." What is a *euphemism?* _____
_____

► □ ◄

A: The substitution of a pleasant or inoffensive term for an unpleasant or offensive one.

25–27 There were two purposes in presenting the words in this last sequence of frames. The first was to introduce new words into your vocabulary. Second, the words that were given illustrate borrowings (derivatives) from Greek words with three morphemes:
_____, _____, and _____.

► □ ◄

A: Prefixes, bases, suffixes.

28–32 In the next sequence of frames (28–38) you will be asked to *recognize* the eleven words you just practiced and will match them with explanations. Here are the words; review them if you need to.

dysentery	dyspepsia	eulogy	euphony
dysgenics	dyspnea	eupepsia	euthanasia
dyslogistic	eugenics	euphemism	

Below, match the definitions in the right-hand column with the words in the left-hand column by writing the correct letter in the space provided.

_____ 1. dysentery
_____ 2. dysgenics
_____ 3. dyslogistic
_____ 4. dyspepsia
_____ 5. dyspnea

a. study of factors in parents leading to degeneration of offspring
b. condition of having poor digestion
c. disorder of the lower intestine
d. difficulty breathing
e. pertaining to a speech or writing unfavorable to someone

▶ □ ◀

A: (In order 1–5) c, a, e, b, d.

33–38 Again, do the same task with the following words.

_____ 1. eugenics
_____ 2. eulogy
_____ 3. eupepsia
_____ 4. euphemism
_____ 5. euphony
_____ 6. euthanasia

a. study of desirable qualities in parents for producing good offspring
b. substitution of a pleasant word for an unpleasant one
c. a speech or writing favorable to someone
d. easy and painless death
e. quality of having pleasant sounds
f. good digestion

▶ □ ◀

A: (In order 1–6) a, c, f, b, e, d.

39 You will now be asked to *produce* these same eleven words. Substitute the Greek borrowings for synonymous words or phrases in parentheses. Here is a list of the words again.

dysentery	dyspepsia	eulogy	euphony
dysgenics	dyspnea	eupepsia	euthanasia
dyslogistic	eugenics	euphemism	

From the chapel came the (pleasant sound) of the young boys' voices. _____
(Look back at the menu if necessary.)

▶ □ ◀

A: Euphony.

40 The governor himself gave a (speech of praise) at the funeral. _____

▶ □ ◀

A: Eulogy.

41 The account of his life in the local paper was surprisingly (unfavorable) in tone.

_____

▶ □□ ◀

 A: Dyslogistic.

42 My uncle was unfortunately suffering from (poor digestion). _____

▶ □□ ◀

 A: Dyspepsia.

43 Our entire camp was stricken with a severe case of (intestinal disorders).

_____

▶ □□ ◀

 A: Dysentery.

44 He worked all his life to legalize (an easy death) for those who are incurably ill and wish to die. _____

▶ □□ ◀

 A: Euthanasia.

45 My grandfather considered all diets as fads and with his usual (good digestion) had second helpings of everything. _____

▶ □□ ◀

 A: Eupepsia.

46 The radiant health of the children, who had inherited Tom and Martha's good looks and vigor, convinced many of the value of (planning marriage to ensure good children).

_____

▶ □□ ◀

 A: Eugenics.

47 "I know I'm suffering from (difficulty in breathing)," said John, puffing hard. "I can't even pronounce the darn word." _____

▶ □□ ◀

 A: Dyspnea.

48 We all know that *darn* is a (polite substitution) for *damn*. _____

◻◻

A: Euphemism.

49 The behavior of the three Parker children at dinner was enough to make one wish to contribute to a fund to promote (the study of factors that lead to parents producing inferior children). _____

◻◻

A: Dysgenics.

Words with Two Bases: Examples Derived from Greek
(Frames 50–87)

50 The Greek derivative *pátri-arch-y*, which means "rule by the fathers" (that is, by the older men), is an example of a word made up of two bases and a suffix. What is the base in this word that means "father"? {_____}

◻◻

A: {patri}

51 What is the base that means "rule"? {_____}

◻◻

A: {arch}

52 And what is the suffix that makes the word a noun? {_____}

◻◻

A: {y}

53 Who exert the power in a patriarchy? _____

◻◻

A: The fathers (that is, the older men).

54 Greek {**mon**} = one. In a *món-arch-y*, how many people rule? _____

◻◻

A: One.

55 Two common bases from Greek are the antonyms {**phil**} and {**phob**}. We see the base {**phob**} plus noun-suffix {**ia**} in the word *phób-ia*, as in "He never goes anywhere in an airplane because he has a *phobia* about flying." What does *phobia* seem to mean? _____

▶ □ ◀

A: Fear.

56 Often it is normal for a person to be afraid of something, like falling or drowning. What kind of fear is a *phobia?* _____

▶ □ ◀

A: An excessive (unnatural, unusual, or morbid) fear of something.

57 The base {**phob**} is found in many compounds. For example, an *Ànglo-phobe* (with the variant {**phobe**} instead of {**phob**}) is one who has a morbid _____ of people from England.

▶ □ ∪ ∪ ∪ ∪ □ □ □ □ ◀

A: Fear.

58 The morpheme {**anglo**} is an _____ of {**englo**}.

▶ □ ◀

A: Allomorph.

59 In your own words, what is a *Russophobe?* _____

_____

▶ ∪ ∪ ∪ ∪ ∥ □ ◀

A: One who has a (morbid) fear of Russian people.

60 The morpheme {**phil / phile**} is the antonym of {**phob**}. Define, in your own words, a *Russophile.* _____

_____

▶ □ ◀

A: One who has an extreme liking for Russians (or things Russian).

61 So familiar are {**phil**} and {**phob**} that we can even construct new words with confidence that they will be understood, at least by well-educated people. Here is an example. The Greek base {**biblio**} occurs in *bibliò-graph-y*, which is a list of the _____ and other resources that pertain to a given subject.

▶ □ ◀

A: Books.

62 Therefore, what is a *biblio-phile?* _____

▶ □□ ◀

    A: One who is fond of books.

63 We might coin a new word and describe someone as being a *biblio-phobe.* What would characterize such a person? _____

▶ □□ ◀

    A: He would have a (morbid) fear of books.

64 In ancient Greek the *agora* was an open space in the center of a town or city where people met for various purposes, especially for business and politics. The English word *agora-phob-ia* might have meant "fear of business" or "fear of politics," but it does not. Instead, *agoraphobia* means "the condition of not wanting to leave one's house because of a morbid fear of _____ spaces."

▶ □□ ◀

    A: Open (or big).

65–66 The allomorphs {**phil / phile**} have another allomorph, {**philo**}. The allomorph {**philo**} is found in the words *philo-log-y* and *philo-soph-y,* while the allomorph {**phil**} occurs in *phil-harmon-ic* and *phil-anthrop-ist.* From these examples, which allomorph is used before elements beginning with a vowel or *h,* {**phil**} or {**philo**} ? {_____} Which allomorph is used before a consonant other than *h* ? {_____}

▶ □□ ◀

    A: {phil} (as in philanthropist); {philo} (as in philosophy).

67 *Anthropo-log-y* is a broad field; what does an *anthropologist* study? _____

▶ □□ ◀

    A: Man (particularly primitive man).

68 From the meaning of {**phil**}, {**anthrop / anthropo**} = man, and {**ist**} = one who does something, what would you assume that the meaning of the word *phil-anthrop-ist* is?

_____

▶ □□ ◀

    A: One who loves mankind.

69 *Philanthropist* did originally have this meaning of "lover of mankind," but the word today is used in a much more restricted meaning. It now means one who has access to money and shows his love of mankind by _____

_____

▶ □□□ ◀

    A: Giving money to worthy causes.

70 The word *philanthropist* illustrates the fact that to understand a word it is not always enough to know the meaning of the different _____.

▶ □□□ ◀

    A: Morphemes.

71 From the sum of the meanings of the morphemes, a *philharmonic* organization would seem to be one which _____ harmony, that is, music.

▶ □□□ ◀

    A: Loves.

72 The word *philharmonic* is used in a more restricted sense, however, than just "loving music." What kind of music does a philharmonic orchestra usually play?

    _____

▶ □□□ ◀

    A: Classical.

73 Another common base is {**log**}, which we saw earlier in the word *eulogy*. It has a different meaning in *bio-log-y*, *theo-log-y*, and *anthropo-log-y*. Since *anthropology* is the study of man, what is *biology*? _____

▶ □□□ ◀

    A: The study of life (of all sorts).

74 What is *theology*? _____

▶ □□□ ◀

    A: The study of God.

75 *Astro-log-y* in Greek and Roman times was the study of the stars and planets. What is the modern term for the scientific study of such bodies? _____

▶ □□□ ◀

    A: Astronomy.

76 *Astrology* has acquired a restricted meaning today. Now, it means the study of the stars in order to _____.

▶ □□□ ◀

    A: Predict the future.

77 Here is the base {**log**} used in a different way. *Philo-log-y* would seem to mean "study of love" but it rather means "love of _____."

▶ □□□ ◀

    A: Study.

78 But *philology* has a restricted and specialized meaning. It would be ridiculous to describe as *philology* the activity of a six-year-old who loves to read, to go to school, and to do his homework. Here is a sentence that may help you understand today's special meaning: "After decades of reading Latin and Greek authors, as well as studying half a dozen modern European languages and cultures, he finally established his position as a leading *philologist*." In your own words, what is *philology*? _____

_____

▶ □□□ ◀

    A: The study of languages and culture, usually those of Europe and particularly the ancient ones.

79 The meaning of {**soph**} is "wisdom." What does *philo-soph-y* mean? _____

_____

▶ □□□ ◀

    A: The love of wisdom (not "wisdom of love" as one might reasonably expect).

80 But *philosophy* also has a meaning that is more than the apparent sum of its morphemes. Observe the context in which it is used here: "His *philosophy* of life was simple: to get all he could and to give as little as possible." In your own words, what does *philosophy* mean in this sentence? _____

_____

▶ □□□ ◀

    A: Belief in how one should conduct one's life.

81 Here is a different meaning of *philosophy*, as in "The influence of Greek *philosophy* upon European thinking was profound." In your own words, what does *philosophy* mean here? _____

▶ □□□ ◀

A: A system of thought and knowledge, as for example one devised by Aristotle. (The field is too broad for a satisfactory short definition.)

82 {**Hellene**} = Greek. What feeling toward Greece did the English poet Lord Byron have that made him a *phil-héllene?* _____

▶ ▯▯ ◀

A: Love of Greece (he died there in 1824, fighting for her independence).

83 It is obvious from some of these examples that knowledge of the meaning of the morphemes is not always enough to tell what a word means; one must sometimes also see the word in its _____.

▶ ▯▯ ◀

A: Context.

84 Here is another example of the specialized meaning of certain words that could not be guessed without seeing the word in context. Consider the word *hydrophobia*. The base {**hydro**} also occurs in the word *hydrodynamic*. What is the source of *hydrodynamic* power? _____

▶ ▯▯ ◀

A: Water.

85 And the other base of *hydrodynamic* is the morpheme {**dynam**}. What does {**dynam**} mean? _____

▶ ▯▯ ◀

A: Power.

86 From the sum of its morphemes, what does a person fear who is suffering from *hydrophobia?* _____

▶ ▯▯ ◀

A: Water.

87 The word *hydrophobia*, however, is a term used to describe a symptom of the disease of rabies. Describe this symptom in your own words. _____

_____

▶ ▯▯ ◀

A: The victim cannot swallow water or other liquids.

Unusual Words Derived from Greek
(Frames 88–139)

■ Here is a menu of 14 Greek bases that you will use in the next 29 frames.

{acro} = height, point	{graph} = write	{ornitho} = bird
{crac} = rule	{helio} = sun	{phag} = eat
{dermato} = skin	{man} = madness	{pyro} = fire
{entomo} = insect	{ochlo} = mob	{theo} = god
{etymo} = real meaning	{ophio} = snake	

Some of the words to be discussed are ones that you may not have seen before. Since most of them are uncommon, your instructor may not require you to memorize all the words in this sequence of frames. The purpose is for you to see how unknown words may be analyzed from the morphemes and context. Sometimes you will be able to figure out the meaning from the context; sometimes you will have to look back to this menu. Here is the first problem.

88 *Acro-phób-ia*, as in "George had always concealed his *acrophobia* by never going to the mountains on his vacation." What was George's problem? _____

▶ □ ◀

A: He was afraid of heights.

89 The suffix {ia} shows that *eupepsia* and *acrophobia* are in the class of words we call a

_____ .

▶ □ ◀

A: Noun.

90 *Dermató-phag-ous*, as in "Unfortunately that scab mite we discovered in your physical examination is *dermatophagous*." What would this mite do to the patient's skin?

_____

▶ □ ◀

A: Eat it.

91 *Pýro-phile*, as in "Our dog Rover was a dedicated *pyrophile;* he would lie with his nose in the fireplace until the whole room smelled of scorched fur." What did Rover enjoy?

_____

▶ □ ◀

A: The fire in the fireplace.

92 *Helio-phil-ia,* as in "Every spring college students descend upon Florida for their spring rites of *heliophilia.*" What are the students looking for in Florida? _____

▶ □□□ ◀

   A: Sunshine (answers like liquor and sex not acceptable).

93 *Entomo-log-ist,* as in "Like many *entomologists,* this distinguished scientist was known to his students as 'Bugsy.'" What branch of science did Bugsy teach? _____
_____

▶ □□□ ◀

   A: The study of insects.

94 *Etymo-log-y,* as in "This course relies heavily on *etymology* to help the student understand words." What is the meaning of the base {etymo}? _____

▶ □□□ ◀

   A: Real meaning.

95 Certain early Greek scholars believed that the earliest meaning of a word was the real meaning. But the meaning of *etymology* today is the study of the _____
_____.

▶ □□□ ◀

   A: Origin of words.

96 Notice the difference between *etymologist* and *entomologist.* *Entomology* is the study of _____.

▶ □□□ ◀

   A: Insects.

97 *Ophio-phobe,* as in "We can hardly blame Eve if after her experience in Eden she became an *ophiophobe* and passed this feeling on to her daughters." What had Eve learned to fear? _____

▶ □□□ ◀

   A: Snakes.

98 *Ornitho-phob-ia,* as in "Ever since seeing Hitchcock's film *The Birds,* I have had *ornithophobia*—I can't even feed a pigeon." What is the person afraid of? _____

▶ □□□ ◀

   A: Birds.

{acro} = height, point	{graph} = write	{ornitho} = bird
{crac} = rule	{helio} = sun	{phag} = eat
{dermato} = skin	{man} = madness	{pyro} = fire
{entomo} = insect	{ochlo} = mob	{theo} = god
{etymo} = real meaning	{ophio} = snake	

99   *Ochlo-crac-y*, as in " 'There is no respect for elected officials anymore,' shouted the mayor. 'There is no true democracy in our city, only an *ochlocracy*.' " According to the mayor, who ran the city? _____

▶ □ ◀

    A: The mob (that is, the uneducated people).

100   *Dermato-log-ist*, as in the old joke, "A *dermatologist* has an ideal profession. His patients never die—and they never get cured." What part of the body does a *dermatologist* treat? _____

▶ □ ◀

    A: The skin.

101   *Anglo-man-ia*, as in "On his return from Europe, Ted had a severe form of *Anglomania*." Which people did Ted admire beyond all reason? _____

▶ □ ◀

    A: The English.

102   *Theo-phobe*, as in "The old man's hatred and fear of religious sects was unbelievable; he was, in fact, the only true *theophobe* I have ever met." What was the old man's problem? _____

▶ □ ◀

    A: He was afraid of God.

103   *Ochlo-phob-ia*, as in "I can tell you from my personal experience: the Ohio State game, with over 106,000 fans crowding into Michigan Stadium, is no place for someone with *ochlophobia*." What would a person with this condition find unpleasant about the game? _____

▶ □ ◀

    A: The crowd.

104   *Biblio-man-ia*, as in "*Bibliomania* was hardly the name for it: old Mr. Budge kept everything printed, even telephone directories whose cast of characters had died a quarter of a century ago." What was Mr. Budge's hobby? _____

▶ □ ◀

A: Collecting books.

105 *Pyro-graph-y,* as in "In the early years of this century all the young people decorated wooden picture frames and leather goods by means of *pyrography."* What is *pyrography?*

_____

▶ □ ◀

A: The art of burning designs with heated tools.

106 *Theo-phile,* as in "Although my father-in-law attended church regularly and paid his offerings without grumbling, he could hardly be classified as an ardent *theophile."* Define

theophile: _____

▶ ∪ ∪ ∪ □ □ □ □ □ □ □ □ □ □ □ □ □ □ □ □ □ □ □ ∩ ∩ ∩ ∩ □ ◀

A: One who loves God (the word can also mean "one who is loved by God").

107 *Anthropo-phag-y,* as in "*Anthropophagy* seems usually to be a religious ceremony, not a savage barbecue, as is often represented." What do *anthropophagous* people eat?

_____

▶ □ □ □ □ □ □ □ □ □ □ □ □ □ ∪ ∪ ∪ □ □ □ □ □ □ □ □ □ □ □ □ □ □ □ ∩ ∩ □ □ □ □ □ □ □ □ □ □ □ □ □ □ ◀

A: Other people.

108 *Ophio-log-ist,* as in "The gully into which I had fallen would have been a paradise for an *ophiologist,* but as for me, I scrambled out from that chorus of rattles and hisses as fast as I could." What was there in the gully that frightened the speaker? _____

▶ □ □ □ □ □ □ □ □ □ □ □ □ □ □ □ □ □ ∪ □ □ □ □ □ □ □ □ □ □ □ □ □ ∩ □ ∪ □ □ □ □ □ □ □ □ □ □ □ ◀

A: Snakes.

109 What is the suffix in the word in the last frame that means "a person who does something"? {_____}

▶ □ ◀

A: {ist}

110 *Theo-crac-y,* as in "In this science-fiction story the planet Glorm is ruled by a *theocracy* which is reactionary on all social questions." In the story, what class of people ruled Glorm? _____

▶ □ ◀

A: Priests (acting as the servants of their god).

{acro} = height, point	{graph} = write	{ornitho} = bird
{crac} = rule	{helio} = sun	{phag} = eat
{dermato} = skin	{man} = madness	{pyro} = fire
{entomo} = insect	{ochlo} = mob	{theo} = god
{etymo} = real meaning	{ophio} = snake	

---

111 *Ornithó-log-ist*, as in "During the migration season our cottage was a headquarters for all our friends who were *ornithologists*." What interested these friends at the cottage? _____

▶ □□□ ◀

A: Birds.

112 *Entomó-phag-ous*, as in "We put up a birdhouse to encourage martins to nest on our property because of their *entomophagous* habits." What do martins do that is useful to man? _____

▶ □□□ ◀

A: They eat bugs.

113 The *American Heritage Dictionary* defines a certain word as follows: "The origin and historical development of a word, as evidenced by study of its basic elements, earliest known use, and change in form and meaning; semantic derivatives and evolution." What is the word? _____

▶ □□□ ◀

A: Etymology.

114 *Pyro-mán-iac*, as in " 'Don't let that *pyromaniac* into my workshop!' screamed Manuel." What was Manuel afraid would happen? _____

▶ □□□ ◀

A: The person would set fire to his shop.

115 *Ophió-phag-ous*, as in "Since the captured bird was *ophiophagous*, it would not touch the hamburger we had bought for it." What did this bird usually eat? _____

▶ □□□ ◀

A: Snakes.

116 What class of word does {ous} show that *ophiophagous* is? _____

▶ □□□ ◀

A: Adjective.

117 Here is a menu of 12 of the 23 words you just practiced. We will now ask you to use each of them in the next 12 frames. Refer to this menu as necessary.

acrophobia	*dermatologist*	*ochlophobia*
Anglomania	*entomophagous*	*ophiophagous*
anthropophagy	*etymology*	*pyromaniac*
bibliomania	*heliophilia*	*theophile*

What do we call a morbid fear of crowds? _____

▶ □ ◀

   A: Ochlophobia.

■ REMINDER: Since we are not trying to teach you words like *ochlophobia*, as much as we are trying to show you how these words are constructed, it is important that you do this sequence properly. The "easy" way to answer these frames is just to pull down your card and read the answer. However, this "easy" way is not the efficient way to learn. The proper procedure (and the most efficient) is to look for the answer in the menu above if you cannot remember the word.

This sequence requires you only to *recognize* the word, not to *produce* it (though if you remember the word, all the better). Having recognized it in the menu, you should copy it carefully in the space provided.

118 What do we call the study of the meanings and the origin of words? (Use the menu as needed.) _____

▶ □ ◀

   A: Etymology.

119 What is a person called who has a desire to set fires? _____

▶ □ ◀

   A: Pyromaniac.

120 What is the term for an abnormal fear of heights? _____

▶ □ ◀

   A: Acrophobia.

121 Which term in the menu describes an extremely religious person? _____

▶ □ ◀

   A: Theophile.

122 What word is used to describe birds that live chiefly on insects? _____

▶ □□□ ◀

   A: Entomophagous.

123 What is an excessive fondness for books called? _____

▶ □□□ ◀

   A: Bibliomania.

124 What term describes a doctor who treats diseases of the skin? _____

▶ □□□ ◀

   A: Dermatologist.

125 Give a word from this list that is a synonym for "cannibalism." _____

▶ □□□ ◀

   A: Anthropophagy.

126 What mania does one have who is wild about the English? _____

▶ □□□ ◀

   A: Anglomania.

127 What term describes the urge to lie in the sun all day? _____

▶ □□□ ◀

   A: Heliophilia.

128 What adjective describes an animal that eats snakes? _____

▶ □□□ ◀

   A: Ophiophagous.

129 Here is a menu of the 11 remaining uncommon words you studied. You will be asked to copy them in the next 11 frames.

dermatophagous	*ophiophobe*	*pyrophile*
entomologist	*ornithologist*	*theocracy*
ochlocracy	*ornithophobia*	*theophobe*
ophiologist	*pyrography*	

Give the name for one who studies insects. _____

▶ ◻ ◀

A: Entomologist.

130 What is the name of a person who is afraid of God? _____ (Use the menu as you wish.)

▶ ◻ ◀

A: Theophobe.

131 What term means "rule by the mob"? _____

▶ ◻ ◀

A: Ochlocracy.

132 What is the name for a person who specializes in studying snakes? _____

▶ ◻ ◀

A: Ophiologist.

133 What is one called who is afraid of snakes? _____

▶ ◻ ◀

A: Ophiophobe.

134 What adjective describes an organism that feeds on skin? _____

▶ ◻ ◀

A: Dermatophagous.

135 What word means "fear of birds"? _____

▶ ◻ ◀

A: Ornithophobia.

136 What is the noun that means "the technique of burning designs into wood or leather objects"? _____

▶ ◻ ◀

A: Pyrography.

137   What do we call a scientist who specializes in the study of birds? _____

▶ □□ ◀

    A: Ornithologist.

138   What noun describes someone who loves to sit by an open fire? _____

▶ □□ ◀

    A: Pyrophile.

139   What term describes a government run by priests who claim to rule with divine authority? _____

▶ □□ ◀

    A: Theocracy.

Optional Exercises
(Frames 140–154)

140–147   Match the morphemes in the left-hand column with the definitions in the right-hand column and write the correct letter in the space. Here is the first half.

_____ {acro}, as in acrophobia	a. bird
_____ {anthropo}, as in anthropologist	b. eat
_____ {crac}, as in theocracy	c. God
_____ {ophio}, as in ophiophagous	d. real meaning
_____ {ornitho}, as in ornithologist	e. height
_____ {phag}, as in entomophagous	f. man
_____ {theo}, as in theology	g. rule
_____ {etymo}, as in etymology	h. snake

▶ □□ ◀

    A: e = {acro}; f = {anthropo}; g = {crac}; h = {ophio}; a = {ornitho}; b = {phag}; c = {theo}; d = {etymo}.

148–154   Here is the second half; follow the same directions.

_____ {**dermato**}, as in dermatologist

_____ {**graph**}, as in bibliography

_____ {**helio**}, as in heliophilia

_____ {**man**}, as in pyromaniac

_____ {**ochlo**}, as in ochlophobia

_____ {**pyro**}, as in pyrophilia

_____ {**entomo**}, as in entomology

a. fire
b. madness
c. mob
d. skin
e. sun
f. write
g. insect

▶ □ ◀

A: d = {**dermato**}; f = {**graph**}; e = {**helio**}; b = {**man**}; c = {**ochlo**}; a = {**pyro**};
g = {**entomo**}.

WORD LIST

Here is a list of the words discussed in this unit. Use a dictionary if you need to.

acrophobia 88	etymology 94	philanthropist 65
agoraphobia 64	eugenics 10	philharmonic 65
Anglomania 101	eulogy 14	philhellene 82
Anglophobe 57	eupepsia 15	philology 65
anthropology 67	euphemism 24	philosophy 65
astrology 75	euphony 22	phobia 55
bibliography 61	euthanasia 21	pyromaniac 114
bibliomania 104	extend 7	Russophile 60
bibliophile 62	extensive 1	Russophobe 59
biology 73	hydrodynamic 84	theocracy 110
dermatologist 100	hydrophobia 84	theology 73
dysentery 9	monarchy 54	theophile 106
dyspepsia 17	ornithologist 111	theophobe 102
entomologist 93	patriarchy 50	

OPTIONAL WORDS

anthropophagy 107	entomophagous 112	ophiophagous 115
bibliophobe 63	heliophilia 92	ophiophobe 97
dermatophagous 90	ochlocracy 99	ornithophobia 98
dysgenics 16	ochlophobia 103	pyrography 105
dyslogistic 20	ophiologist 108	pyrophile 91
dyspnea 23		

REVIEW EXERCISES

Purpose: To study new words using some morphemes introduced in this unit.

Directions: Guess at the general meaning of each italicized word. (You have already had several of them.) Then, with the aid of a dictionary, define them as they are used in these sentences.

1. A feeling of *euphoria* swept over the whole crowd.

   _____

2. The choice of words gave a *euphonious* tone to the passage.

   _____

3. The doctors suspected some type of kidney *dysfunction* in the patient.

   _____

4. Professor Smith was studying proposed treatments for *dyslexia.*

   _____

5. Researchers hope to learn more about the cure for muscular *dystrophy.*

   _____

6. We can compare the development of a *matriarchy* or a *patriarchy* in various tribes.

   _____

7. The shift from *monarchy* to *oligarchy* was accompanied by other political changes.

   _____

8. The *anthropocentric* views of the speaker were very controversial.

   _____

9. The teacher was particularly interested in *anthropogenesis*.

   _____

10. The anthropologist was studying *anthropomorphism* as it was practiced by the local tribes.

    _____

WORDS OF INTERESTING ORIGIN

Directions: Find in your dictionary the origins of the italicized words. Then write down (a) language of origin, (b) etymological meaning (= early meaning), and (c) modern meaning.

1. "What are you doing with all this *paraphernalia*, Mary?" I asked. "Are you getting married?"

   Language of origin: _____

   Etymological meaning: _____

   Modern meaning: _____

2. Japan is a country that has had great success in using *robots* in manufacturing.

   Language of origin: _____

   Etymological meaning: _____

   Modern meaning: _____

3. John has turned into a terrible *cynic* and will not give you the time of day without a sneer.

   Language of origin: _____

   Etymological meaning: _____

   Modern meaning: _____

4. With her new necklace and her low-cut dress, Amanda was the *cynosure* of all eyes.

   Language of origin: _____

   Etymological meaning: _____

   Modern meaning: _____

5. The ancient Romans did not use Roman numerals when they *calculated*, but worked with an abacus instead.

   Language of origin: _____

   Etymological meaning: _____

   Modern meaning: _____

EASILY CONFUSED WORDS

Use a dictionary as needed.

1. ***Complement / compliment.*** Both words are derived from Latin *complere*, meaning "fill up." The "full" idea is clear in *complement*, as in "Edgar cannot sail until he has a full *complement* of men for his crew, and he is still lacking a deck hand." When we say that two people *complement* each other, we mean that taken together they make a whole. The word *compliment*, however, refers to all the little things that one does to be polite or flattering, as in "Terry paid the older woman a number of *compliments*, which were well received by her, if not by her husband."

2. ***Connotation / denotation.*** These two words are both of Latin origin, from {**not**} = know. *Denotation* is the plain, direct meaning of a word as it is used by speakers of a language. *Connotation* refers to the emotional concepts that the word has for its users, as in "When Marvin referred to his apartment as 'my pad,' his father winced, for this word to him had the *connotation* of a dirty single room thick with the smoke from numerous cigarettes." A dictionary gives the *denotation* of words but seldom the *connotation*, which is generally personal.

3. ***Elementary / alimentary.*** Both words are from Latin. The suffix {**ary**} shows that the words are adjectives. *Elementary* is derived from the Latin noun *elementum*, which meant "first principle." The adjective *elementary* still means "of first principles" or "fundamental," as well as "simple," as in "Joanne was trying to learn the *elementary* principles of physics" and "The new textbook was at too *elementary* a level for the advanced students." *Alimentary* is made up of {**ali**} = eat, plus the suffixes {**ment**} and {**ary**}, and the word means "connected with food," as in "Our *alimentary* needs were planned for by a trained nutritionist—but the food was terrible just the same."

Use the six words in the sentences where each makes sense. You may need to change the form of the word—from a noun to a verb, for example.

1. The word "saloon" is interesting. Fifty years ago it _____ ed to many people the lowest sort of dive.

2. The _____ of the class has been reached and there can be no more additions.

3. Gene's assignment for biology was to report on the _____ canal.

4. "House" and "home" have the same _____ as a living space, but the connotations are very different.

5. "I do not find the _____ you pay me to be in good taste," said Katie with her most haughty air.

6. Sophie's knowledge of the field was _____, to be sure, but what she had studied she knew well.

LATIN PHRASES

First try to get the meaning of the Latin phrase from the context of the sentences below, choosing a meaning from the list that follows. Write the number of the Latin phrase beside the definition that fits.

1. *Post mortem*, as in "After we hold a *post mortem* we will probably know the reason for his death."

2. *Vice versa*, as in "It is therefore understood that we will contribute more to the United Fund if our profits go up and *vice versa;* that is, if the profits are less, so will our contributions be less."

3. *In toto*, as in "I would have to delay an opinion until I have read the book *in toto*, not just the first two chapters."

4. *Casus belli*, as in "The assassination of the Archduke was used by the Austrians as a *casus belli*."

5. *Per capita*, as in "It was calculated that the decline in real wages amounted to $500 *per capita* for the year."

_____	in the opposite way	_____	as a whole
_____	(care) after birth	_____	inclination to evil living
_____	for each person	_____	autopsy
_____	because of the head	_____	excuse for war
_____	in the whole sum (of money)	_____	beautiful opportunity

Use a dictionary to find the word-by-word translation and the modern meaning for each phrase.

	Word-by-Word Translation	Modern Meaning
post mortem	_____	_____
vice versa	_____	_____
in toto	_____	_____
casus belli	_____	_____
per capita	_____	_____

UNIT FIVE

Productive Greek Morphemes

There are about thirty prefixes of Greek origin; in this unit you will learn the nineteen most useful of these. They are highly productive (that is, they are found in many words), and a knowledge of them is absolutely essential if you wish to understand scientific vocabulary. By knowing these prefixes and using context, you can figure out at least the general meaning of many words previously unknown to you.

CONTENTS

1–19	The Greek Prefixes {**a**}, {**anti**}, {**epi**}, and {**syn**}
20–48	The Greek Prefixes {**ana**}, {**cata**}, {**dia**}, and {**peri**}
49–79	The Greek Prefixes {**ec**}, {**en**}, {**hyper**}, and {**hypo**}
80–117	Review of Greek Prefixes
118–148	The Greek Prefixes {**meta**}, {**palin**}, {**para**}, and {**pro**}
149–162	The Greek Prefixes {**amphi**}, {**apo**}, and {**exo**}
163–177	Review of Greek Suffixes

The Greek Prefixes {a}, {anti}, {epi}, and {syn}
(Frames 1–19)

1 Here are the first four prefixes with their allomorphs. (As you will see in the dictionary, there are other allomorphs of these prefixes, and other meanings.) Refer to this menu as necessary.

{a / an} = without, not	{epi / ep} = upon
{anti / ant} = against, opposite	{syn / sym} = with, same, together

These four prefixes can be combined with the base {onym} = name or meaning, to give the four words *an-ónym-ous*, *ánt-onym*, *ep-ónym-ous*, and *syn-ónym-ous*.

Whose name is signed to an *anonymous* letter? _____

▶ □□□ ◀

    A: No one's (that is, it is without a name).

2 Two words are *synonyms* if they have approximately the _____ meaning.

▶ □□□ ◀

    A: Same.

3 What makes two words *antonyms* of each other? _____
_____

▶ □□□ ◀

    A: They have approximately the opposite meaning.

4 In Latin and Greek history and legend, certain people are called *eponymous* heroes because they put their name on a city. To what famous city in Italy did the eponymous hero Romulus give his name? _____

▶ □□□ ◀

    A: Rome.

5 The words *rich* and *poor* are approximately opposite in meaning; what are they called? _____

▶ □□□ ◀

    A: Antonyms.

6 What are the words *rich* and *wealthy* called? _____

▶ □□□ ◀

    A: Synonyms.

7 Alexander founded the city of Alexandria. Since he gave his name to the city, what kind of hero is he? _____

▶ □ ◀

   A: Eponymous.

8 What do we call a story which has no author's name attached? _____

▶ □ ◀

   A: Anonymous.

9 The morpheme {ous} forms an adjective, as in *anonymous*. *Synonym* is a noun; what is the adjective form of this noun? _____

▶ □ ◀

   A: Synonymous.

10 From Greek {path} = feeling or emotion, we get *á-path-y*, *sým-path-y*, and *antí-path-y*. What class of word are these terms, since they end in the suffix {y}? _____

▶ □ ◀

   A: Nouns.

11 What emotion does someone have who shares feelings with someone else?

   _____

▶ □ ◀

   A: Sympathy.

12 What does someone feel who has feelings against another person? _____

▶ □ ◀

   A: Antipathy.

13 What does someone show who is without any emotion at all? _____

▶ □ ◀

   A: Apathy.

14–17 Give one meaning for each of the four prefixes you just practiced.

   {**epi** / **ep**} = _____ ; {**syn** / **sym**} = _____ ;
   {**a** / **an**} = _____ ; {**anti** / **ant**} = _____ .

▶ □ ◀

   A: On, upon; with, together; without; against, opposite.

18–19 If you compare the words *anonymous* and *apathy* you see that the Greek prefix meaning "without" takes the form {an} before _____ (consonants / vowels) and the form {a} before _____ (consonants / vowels).

▶ □ ◀

A: Vowels; consonants.

The Greek Prefixes {ana}, {cata}, {dia}, and {peri}
(Frames 20–48)

20 Refer to this menu as necessary as you use the four following prefixes.

{**ana**} = up, back, again	{**dia**} = through, between
{**cata**} = down	{**peri**} = around, near

Greek {**ba**} = go, as in *ana-ba-tic*. (The morpheme {**tic**} indicates an adjective.) In which direction do *anabatic* winds go? Do they blow up or down the slope of a mountain? _____

▶ □ ◀

A: Up.

21 In what direction is a *cata-ba-tic* fever going, up or down? _____

▶ □ ◀

A: Down.

22 You can answer this by just observing the prefixes: what Greek word is the antonym of *catabatic?* _____

▶ □ ◀

A: Anabatic.

23 In 401 B.C. a Greek named Xenophon joined a group of mercenary soldiers who were marching against the Persian king. He wrote an account of his adventures and called it the *Anabasis*. From this name, did he and his friends start at the sea coast and march *up*, or did they start inland and march *down* to the sea? _____

▶ □ ◀

A: Up.

24 The base {**drom**} = run or swim. In which direction do *ana-drom-ous* fish swim in order to spawn? _____

▶ □ ◀

A: Up (or upstream).

25 Then what do *cáta-drom-ous* fish do in order to spawn? _____

▶ □ ◀

    A: Swim down(stream).

26 Greek {**meter**} = measure. The *diá-meter* of a circle is the measurement of the distance _____ a circle.

▶ □ ◀

    A: Through.

27 The *perí-meter* of the circle is the distance _____ the circle.

▶ □ ◀

    A: Around.

28 What is the prefix of Greek origin that means "through"? {_____}

▶ □ ◀

    A: {dia}

29 What is the prefix of Greek origin that means "around"? {_____}

▶ □ ◀

    A: {peri}

30 What do we call a fever that is in the process of dropping? _____

▶ □ ◀

    A: Catabatic.

31 What adjective describes a freshwater fish that swims downstream to salt water to spawn? _____

▶ □ ◀

    A: Catadromous.

32 What kind of fish is one like the salmon, that swims upstream? _____

▶ □ ◀

    A: Anadromous.

129

33 Greek {**scope**} = look, see. The prefix {**peri**} tells us in what direction one can look through a *péri-scope*. In what direction can one see? _____

▶ □□ ◀

    A: Around (or, all around).

34 What is the distance around a circle called? _____

▶ □□ ◀

    A: The perimeter.

35 What is the noun that means "distance through the center of a circle"? _____

▶ □□ ◀

    A: Diameter.

36 Greek {**therm**} = heat. In treatments by *dia-therm-y*, heat goes _____ body tissue.

▶ □□ ◀

    A: Through.

37 Greek {**meta**} = change. *Metá-bol-ism* refers to the changes that take place in the body. *Aná-bol-ism* is used when these changes are constructive and _____ _____ the body.

▶ □□ ◀

    A: Build up.

38 *Catabolism*, however, is the term used to describe changes that _____ _____ the body.

▶ □□ ◀

    A: Tear down.

39 What is the constructive phase of metabolism called? _____

▶ □□ ◀

    A: Anabolism.

40 What do we call the destructive phase of metabolism? _____

▶ □□ ◀

    A: Catabolism.

41 What is the type of telescope that permits us to look all around? (Hint: it is used on submarines.) _____

▶ □ ◀

A: Periscope.

42 Here is another {**drom**} word. *Dia-drom-ous* fish migrate _____ fresh and salt water.

▶ □ ◀

A: Between.

43–46 Give one meaning for each of the four prefixes you just practiced. {**cata**} = _____; {**peri**} = _____; {**ana**} = _____; {**dia**} = _____.

▶ □ ◀

A: Down; around, near; up, back, again; through.

47 Two prefixes often confused are {**a / an**} and {**ana**}. Which prefix means "without" or "not," {**a / an**} or {**ana**}? {_____}

▶ □ ◀

A: {a / an}

48 Which of these two prefixes means "up"? {_____}

▶ □ ◀

A: {ana}

The Greek Prefixes {ec}, {en}, {hyper}, and {hypo}
(Frames 49–79)

49

{**ec / ex**} = out	{**hyper**} = above, excessive, too much
{**en / em**} = in, within	{**hypo**} = under, too little

How much acid in the gastric juices does a person have who suffers from *hyper-acidi-ty?*

_____

▶ □ ◀

A: Too much.

50 How much acid does one have who has *hypo-acidi-ty?* _____

▶ □ ◀

  A: Too little.

51 How much heat is in the body of one who is suffering from *hypo-thérm-ia?* _____
_____

▶ □ ◀

  A: Too little.

52 There is a condition called *hyper-thérm-ia.* What is the temperature of a patient with this condition? _____

▶ □ ◀

  A: Too high.

53 Greek {**ec / ex**} = out, and {**en / em**} = in, within. These prefixes are opposite in meaning and are therefore called _____.

▶ □ ◀

  A: Antonyms.

54 Greek {**top**} = place. Is an organ which is *en-tóp-ic* in its proper location? _____
(yes / no)

▶ □ ◀

  A: Yes.

55 Where is an organ of the body situated if it is *ec-tóp-ic?* _____
_____

▶ □ ◀

  A: Outside its normal place.

56 Greek {**hydr**} = water. What does an *en-hýdr-ous* crystal have in it? _____

▶ □ ◀

  A: Water.

57 What characterizes a crystal that is described as *an-hýdr-ous?* _____

_____

▶ □□ ◀

    A: It has no water in it.

58 In the Bible the book of *Éx-od-us* describes the journey of the Jews _____ Egypt.

▶ □□ ◀

    A: From (out of).

59–62 Give one meaning of each of the four prefixes you have just practiced:

    {ec / ex} = _____; {en / em} = _____;

    {hyper} = _____; {hypo} = _____.

▶ □□ ◀

    A: Out; in, within; above, excessive; under, too little.

63 Now use the following words in the next sequence:

anhydrous	*entopic*	*hyperthermia*
ectopic	*exodus*	*hypoacidity*
enhydrous	*hyperacidity*	*hypothermia*

Try, however, to do this sequence without the menu.

What is the name of the condition meaning "too much acid"? _____

▶ □□ ◀

    A: Hyperacidity.

64 What is the antonym of *hyperacidity?* _____

▶ □□ ◀

    A: Hypoacidity.

65 What word means that the body temperature is too high? _____

▶ □□ ◀

    A: Hyperthermia.

66 What is the term for a dangerously low temperature of the body? _____

▶ □□ ◀

    A: Hypothermia.

67 What adjective describes an organ that is abnormally located? _____

▶ □ ◀

  A: Ectopic.

68 What adjective is used to refer to an organ found in the normal position? _____

▶ □ ◀

  A: Entopic.

69 What noun means "the act of leaving a place"? _____

▶ □ ◀

  A: Exodus.

70 What is the antonym of *enhydrous?* _____

▶ □ ◀

  A: Anhydrous.

71 From Greek {**esthes** / **aesthet**} = feeling or sensation, come *esthés-ia, an-esthés-ia, hypo-esthés-ia,* and *hyper-esthés-ia.* How much reaction to sensation does a person have who is under *anesthesia?* _____

▶ □ ◀

  A: None.

72 In your own words, what is *hyperesthesia?* _____
_____

▶ □ ◀

  A: An excessively high level of sensitivity.

73 How much sensation does someone have who has the condition called *hypoesthesia?*
_____

▶ □ ◀

  A: Little.

74 In your own words, how do people described as *aesthetes* (also spelled *esthetes*) feel about artistic matters? _____

▶ □□□ ◀

   A: They are sensitive to them.

75 Now produce the words used in these last frames. First, what do doctors call a lack of sensation induced by drugs? _____

▶ □□□□∪∪□□ ◀

   A: Anesthesia.

76 What is the word for appreciation of artistic works? _____

▶ ∪∪∪∪□□□□□□□∪□□□□□□□□□□□□□□□□□□□□□□□□□□□□□□□□□□ ◀

   A: Aesthetics.

77 What is the name for the condition of having excessive sensitivity?

   _____

▶ □□□□□□□□□□□□□□□□□□□□□□□□□□□□□□□□□□□□□□□∪∪□□□□ ◀

   A: Hyperesthesia.

78 What is the condition of having too little feeling? _____

▶ □□□□□□□□□□□□□□□□□□□□□□□□□∪□□□□□□□□□□□□□□□□□□□ ◀

   A: Hypoesthesia.

79 The base {**aesthet**} occurs without a prefix in the word *aesthete*, referring to a person who is interested in the study of beauty in such fields as art, music, and nature. Define *aesthetics* (also spelled *esthetics*). _____

▶ □□□ ◀

   A: The study of beauty.

Review of Greek Prefixes
(Frames 80–117)

■ So far we have had 12 prefixes of Greek origin. We will now review them.

80–85 Match the English meanings with the prefixes. Do the whole exercise before checking your answers.

{ana} = _____   a. in, within
                                    b. against, opposite
{anti / ant} = _____   c. upon, on
                                    d. under, deficient
{en / em} = _____   e. with, together, same
                                    f. up, back, again
{epi / ep} = _____

{hypo} = _____

{syn / sym} = _____

□ □

A: (In order from top to bottom) f, b, a, c, d, e.

86–91 Again, do the same task with the following prefixes.

{a / an} = _____   a. out
                                    b. without, not
{cata} = _____   c. through
                                    d. down
{dia} = _____   e. above, excessive
                                    f. around, near
{ec / ex} = _____

{hyper} = _____

{peri} = _____

□ □

A: (In order from top to bottom) b, d, c, a, e, f.

You will now be given more examples of these same 12 prefixes with new bases. You will be asked to reason out the meanings of words that may be new to you by observing the morphemes and the context.

92 Greek {**derm**} = skin, as in *hypo-dérm-ic* and *en-dérm-ic*. Where is medicine injected that is administered by a *hypodermic* process? _____ the _____.

□ □

A: Under the skin.

93 What do we call medicine that is to be rubbed on the skin and absorbed by the body? _____ (Look back to frame 82 if necessary.)

□ □

A: Endermic.

94 The morpheme meaning "blood" is {**hema**}. The / h / is dropped under certain conditions, and so is the final / a /, leaving {**em**}, as in *an-ém-ia*. *Anemia*, a word first used in 1836, is not an accurate word etymologically. How much blood should be in the body of someone suffering from anemia if the inventor of the word had been accurate in his choice of prefix? _____

□ □

A: None.

95 A person with anemia does not suffer from *no* blood; how much blood does he have?

_____

▶ □ ◀

A: He has enough blood, but it is deficient in red corpuscles and/or hemoglobin.

96 The next four frames are of great importance. It is an unfortunate feature of language (or it seems unfortunate to the student) that the meaning of words is not always the sum of their morphemes. Students in courses like this are sometimes grossly misled by statements to the effect that if they learn a certain number of bases, suffixes, and prefixes, they will not have to use a dictionary. This is simply not true.

Here is an example:

Since {**ly**} = break, it would seem that *aná-ly-sis* would mean "act of breaking up" and *catá-ly-sis* would seem to be an antonym of *analysis* and mean "act of _____

_____."

▶ □ ◀

A: Breaking down.

97 But in English "break up" and "break down" are *not* antonyms. A car "breaks down" on the highway but we say that ship caught on a reef and pounded by waves "breaks

_____."

▶ □ ◀

A: Up. (A ship that breaks down has trouble with its motor.)

98 In your own words, define *analysis*, as in "After *analysis* of the problem there was no more difficulty, since he had laid out all the pieces for us to examine." _____

_____

▶ □ ◀

A: The act of breaking up (or breaking down) something into smaller pieces for examination.

NICE-TO-KNOW ■ *Catalysis* means speeding up or slowing down a chemical process by adding some extra ingredient that causes a chemical reaction but itself does not undergo a chemical change.

99 Greek {**the**} = put. The antonym of *analysis* is *sýn-the-sis*. If *analysis* is the act of taking things apart, what is *synthesis*? _____

▶ □ ◀

A: The act of putting things together.

100 Greek {**chron / chrono**} = time, as in *chronó-meter*. What does a *chronometer* do? _____
_____

▶ □ ◀

   A: It measures time.

101 *Syn-chrón-ic, dia-chrón-ic:* There are two ways of studying language. One way is *syn-chronic*, to study it as it exists at a given time, without regard for the historical development. The second way is *diachronic*, to study language down through the years, noting the changes that have taken place. Is the approach to language in this course *synchronic*

   or *diachronic?* _____

▶ □ ◀

   A: Diachronic.

102 In a *diachronic* approach, do we or do we not consider the historical development of the

   English language? _____

▶ □ ◀

   A: We do.

103 When two people *synchronize* their watches, what do they do (in your own words)?
_____

▶ □ ◀

   A: Set them to the same time.

104 Greek {**kine**} > English {**cine**} = move. What word using this morpheme describes pictures

   that seem to move? _____

▶ □ ◀

   A: Cinema.

105 *Kiné-sics: Kinesics* is the study of the _____ of the body.

▶ □ ◀

   A: Movements.

106 *Hyper-kiné-sia:* What would be the symptoms of someone who was afflicted with *hyperkinesia?* _____

▶ □ ◀

   A: Abnormally increased body movements.

107 *Hypo-kine-sia:* In your own words, define *hypokinesia.* _____
_____

▶ □ ◀

    A: Abnormally decreased body movements.

108 Remember that there are two prefixes which look somewhat alike. One is {**ana**}, as in *anadromous,* used to describe salmon. What does {**ana**} mean? _____

▶ □ ◀

    A: "Up" in *anadromous* (but it can also mean "back" and "again").

109 The other is {**a / an**}, as in *anesthesia.* What does this {**a / an**} mean? _____

▶ □ ◀

    A: Without, not.

110 *Ana-bio-sis:* There are insects that under certain conditions go into suspended animation and then come to life. This process is called *anabiosis.* What does the prefix {**ana**} mean?
_____

▶ □ ◀

    A: Again or back.

111 *Epi-derm-is:* The skin has two layers. Considering the meaning of the prefix {**epi**}, which layer of skin is the *epidermis,* the inner or outer? _____

▶ □ ◀

    A: Outer.

112 In the last unit we had the words *eugenics* and *dysgenics.* What did the base {**gen**} mean?
_____

▶ □ ◀

    A: Be born, give birth to.

113 *Hypo-gene, epi-gene:* Certain rocks, like granite, are called *hypogene.* Where were such rocks formed, *under* the surface or *on* the surface of the earth? _____

▶ □ ◀

    A: Under the surface.

114 What term is used in geology to describe rocks that are formed *on* (or *near*) the earth's surface? _____

▶ □ ◀

A: Epigene.

115 *Anti-bio-tic:* What does an *antibiotic* drug do to bacteria (in your own words)?

_____

▶ □ ◀

A: It destroys them.

116 *Em-path-y, sym-path-y, a-path-y, anti-path-y:* From the meaning of the prefix, which of these means the projection of one's personality *into* the personality of another in order to gain understanding? _____

▶ □ ◀

A: Empathy. (*Empathy* and *sympathy* are close in meaning.)

117 Greek {**odont**} = tooth. *Peri-odont-ist:* What part of the mouth does a *periodontist* specialize in? _____

▶ □ ◀

A: The area surrounding the teeth (bone and tissue).

The Greek Prefixes {meta}, {palin}, {para}, and {pro}
(Frames 118–148)

118 The next four prefixes of Greek origin common in English are as follows:

{**meta** / **met**} = after, among, changing, as in *meta-morpho-sis* and *meta-chromat-ism*
{**palin** / **pali**} = back, again, as in *palin-drome* and *palin-gene-sis*
{**para** / **par**} = side by side, abnormal, subordinate, as in *par-allel* and *para-psycho-log-y*
{**pro**} = in front of, before, as in *pro-logue* and *pro-gno-sis*

Refer to this menu as necessary in the sequence that follows. Choose your answers from the eight words given above.

An *epilogue* is spoken at the end of a play. There is a similar word with the base {**logue**} that means the introduction to a play. What is it? _____

▶ □ ◀

A: Prologue.

I **NICE-TO-KNOW** ■ These words are also spelled *epilog* and *prolog.*

119 In geometry, what do we call two lines that extend in the same direction and are always the same distance apart, but never meet? _____ (Choose from the eight words in frame 118.)

▶ □□ ◀

    A: Parallel.

120 Greek {**chromat**} = color. Some objects change color when they change temperature. What is such a property called? _____

▶ □□ ◀

    A: Metachromatism.

121 What word in the menu means "act of being born again"? _____

▶ □□ ◀

    A: Palingenesis.

122 Which of the eight words means a change in form, as occurs in myths and fairy stories?

_____

▶ □□ ◀

    A: Metamorphosis (also used of such creatures as butterflies).

123 Which word of the eight means a prediction or forecast? _____

▶ □□ ◀

    A: Prognosis.

124 Which word denotes the study of abnormal phenomena like mental telepathy?

_____

▶ □□ ◀

    A: Parapsychology.

125 Words can be fun to play with. There are certain names that read the same backwards as they do forwards, like *Anna* or *Otto.* Whole sentences may also read the same backwards as forwards; an example is "Name no one man." What word in the menu describes such a trick sentence? _____

▶ □□ ◀

    A: Palindrome.

126 Here is another palindrome: "Madam, I'm Adam." What are the first five letters from left to right? __ __ __ __ __

▶ ◻ ◀

    A: M A D A M.

127 And what are the first five letters if read from the end, going right to left? __ __ __ __ __

▶ ◻ ◀

    A: M A D A M.

128 Here is another palindrome: "Able was I ere I saw Elba." To what famous French general does this refer? _____

▶ ◻ ◀

    A: Napoleon (who was exiled to the island of Elba in 1814).

129 Does "Name no one man" read the same backwards as forwards? _____ (yes / no)

▶ ◻ ◀

    A: Yes.

130 "A man, a plan, a canal, Panama!" is another example of a _____.

▶ ◻ ◀

    A: Palindrome.

I NICE-TO-KNOW ■ The longest known palindrome is 5,000 words long (!).

131 Here follow ten frames testing your knowledge of these last four prefixes: {**para**}, {**meta**}, {**palin**}, and {**pro**}.

Para-méd-ic, as in "Since Tom had had one year in medical school, he was made a *para-medic* when he was drafted into the army." Describe Tom's job (in your own words).

_____

_____

▶ ◻ ◀

    A: He performed some medical tasks under the direction of qualified medical doctors. (Here, {para} has the meaning "subordinate.")

132 *Met-ónym-y,* as in "The saying 'The pen is mightier than the sword' is an example of *metonymy."* Writers use pens; in this sentence *pen* is used in place of *writer.* Who does *sword* stand for? _____

▶ □□□ ◀

A: Soldiers.

133 What morpheme in *metonymy* means "replace" or "change"? {_____}

▶ □□□ ◀

A: {met}

134 What morpheme in *metonymy* shows it is a noun? {____}

▶ □□□ ◀

A: {y}

135 What morpheme in *metonymy* means "name" or "meaning"? {_____}

▶ □□□ ◀

A: {onym}

136–137 Look at the words *metamorphosis* and *metonymy.* What form does the Greek prefix meaning "changing" have before vowels? {_____} What form does it have before consonants? {_____}

▶ □□□ ◀

A: {met}; {meta}.

138 Sometimes we will say, "The State Department announced today . . ." when we do not mean that the Department spoke, since a department does not have vocal chords. We have changed "Secretary of State" (or "spokesman," or the like) to another name. What do we call such a change in name? _____

▶ □□□ ◀

A: Metonymy.

139 *Pálin-ode,* as in "James paid dearly for his ill-tempered words to Eliza, and the least of the penalties was an elaborate *palinode* she demanded from him, in which he retracted everything he had said."

Poets often write short poems to those they love; these short poems are sometimes called *odes.* Sometimes an ode will be angry in tone and will criticize the loved one. The poet may subsequently repent and write a *palinode* in which he _____ _____ what he said before.

▶ □□□ ◀

A: Takes back.

140 What is the morpheme in *palinode* that means "back"? {_____}

▶ □ ◀

A: {palin}.

141 Greek {**phylac**} = guard, protect. Compare *pro-phylác-tic*, as in "Dr. Mercer devoted most of his attention as a dentist to making the public aware of *prophylactic* measures in dental hygiene." The prefix {**pro**} shows that the measures are taken _____ (before / after) dental decay begins.

▶ □ ◀

A: Before.

142 By way of review, what is the noun that is used to describe a person in the army who performs some medical tasks? _____

▶ □ ◀

A: Paramedic.

143 What noun describes a poem that apologizes for a previous poem which was unpleasant? _____

▶ □ ◀

A: Palinode.

144 What adjective means "guarding against something in advance"? _____

▶ □ ◀

A: Prophylactic.

145–148 Give *one* meaning for each of the four prefixes you have just practiced:

{**para** / **par**} = _____; {**palin** / **pali**} = _____;

{**pro**} = _____; {**meta** / **met**} = _____.

▶ □ ◀

A: Side by side, abnormal, subordinate; back, again; in front of, before; after, among, changing.

The Greek Prefixes {amphi}, {apo}, and {exo}
(Frames 149–162)

149 The last three most common prefixes of Greek origin are as follows:

{**amphi**} = around, both, as in *amphi-bi-ous* and *amphi-theater*
{**apo / ap / aph**} = away from, without, as in *apo-state* and *ap-anthrop-ia*
{**exo**} = outside, as in *exo-skele-ton* and *exo-bio-log-y*

Use one of these six words in each of the next six frames. Refer to this menu as necessary.

Our bodies have a skeleton, a framework of bone to support the tissues and support the organs. This skeleton is inside the body. What name do we give to such a supporting structure when it occurs *outside* the body, as is true of such animals as lobsters and clams? _____

▶ □ ◀

    A: Exoskeleton.

150 What noun means "condition of wishing to live *apart* from the rest of mankind"? _____
_____

▶ □ ◀

    A: Apanthropia.

151 A frog can live both in the water and on land. What adjective do we use to refer to animals that can live in two different environments? _____

▶ □ ◀

    A: Amphibious.

152 The Roman emperor Julian (born A.D. 332) departed from the Christian faith and returned to the ancient religion of Greece and Rome. What name did the Church Fathers give him for taking this position, standing *apart* from the accepted practice?
_____

▶ □ ◀

    A: The Apostate.

153 What name is given to the science that investigates the possibility of life *outside* the earth? _____

▶ □ ◀

    A: Exobiology.

154 A theater was traditionally built in the form of a semicircle. What name do we give to the oval building that looks as if two theaters had been joined together? _____

▶ □ ◀

    A: Amphitheater.

155 Here are more examples of prefixes. *Exo-dont-ist,* as in "John and his wife Betty were proud of his profession as an *exodontist,* but his next door neighbor called him 'Dr. Fang-snatcher.'" What did the doctor specialize in? _____

▶ □ ◀

    A: Tooth extraction.

156 Greek {**helion / elion**} = sun; {**ge / gee**} = earth, as in *Apo-gee, peri-gee, aph-elion, peri-helion.* The antonyms *aphelion* and *perihelion* are used in astronomy. One describes the condition when a planet, like the earth, is as *far away from* the sun as possible. The other is the condition when the planet is as *close to* the sun as possible. From the meaning of the prefix, which term means "away from the sun"? _____

▶ □ ◀

    A: Aphelion.

157 What term means that a planet is as close to the sun as it ever gets? _____

▶ □ ◀

    A: Perihelion.

158 The terms *apogee* and *perigee* are used to describe the orbit of the moon around the earth. Which of the two terms means that the moon is farthest away from the earth?

_____

▶ □ ◀

    A: Apogee.

159 Which term describes the condition when the moon is as close to the earth as is ever gets? _____

▶ □ ◀

    A: Perigee.

160 What prefix in this last sequence means "away from," "without"? {_____}

▶ □ ◀

    A: {apo}

161 Which prefix means "double" or "both"? {_____}

▶ □ ◀

    A: {amphi}

162 Which prefix means "outside"? {_____}

▶ □ ◀

   A: {exo}

Review of Greek Suffixes
(Frames 163–177)

163–165 So far in this unit we have had many words with three morphemes, as in *exodontist*. What are these three morphemes called? _____, _____, _____

▶ □ ◀

   A: Prefix, base, suffix.

166 A common suffix {ous} occurred in several words in this unit, as in *anonymous*. What class of word is *anonymous?* _____

▶ □ ◀

   A: Adjective.

167 The main meaning of {ous} is to show what class of word a term is. What class of word is *catadromous?* _____

▶ □ ◀

   A: Adjective.

168 Other suffixes identify words as nouns. A common suffix is {ia}, which occurred in the noun that means "lack of sensation" or often "treatment used to induce lack of sensation, as during an operation." What is this noun? _____

▶ □ ◀

   A: Anesthesia.

169 Another common suffix that shows that a word is a noun is {y}. It occurs in the word that means "hostile feeling against." What is the word? _____

▶ □ ◀

   A: Antipathy.

170 A third suffix that makes a word a noun is {sis}. What word means "prediction" and ends in {sis} ? _____

▶ □ ◀

   A: Prognosis.

171 The ending {ist}, as in *exodontist*, has more meaning than just "this is a noun." An *exodontist* is a _____ _____ extracts teeth.

▶ □ ◀

   A: Person who.

172 What noun ending in {ist}, with the variant {st}, means "a person who analyzes"?

_____

▶ □ ◀

   A: Analyst.

173 What do we call a person who administers anesthesia? _____

▶ □ ◀

   A: Anesthetist.

174 The suffix {ic} can form an adjective. What class of word is *comic* in the sentence "Billy loves to read *comic* books"? _____

▶ □ ◀

   A: Adjective.

175 What class of word is *comic* in "Pedro is a natural-born *comic*"? _____

▶ □ ◀

   A: Noun.

176 Greek {athlet} = contest, athlete. What class of word is *athletic* in "No group of people ever engaged in *athletic* contests with more enthusiasm than the Greeks"?

_____

▶ □ ◀

   A: Adjective.

177 What class of word is *athletics* in "He excelled in *athletics*"? _____

▶ □ ◀

   A: Noun.

WORD LIST

Here is a list of the words discussed in this unit. Use a dictionary if you need to.

aesthete (esthete) 74
aesthetics (esthetics) 79
amphibious 149
amphitheater 149
analysis 96
analyst 172
anemia 94
anesthesia 71
anesthetist 173
anonymous 1
antibiotic 115
antipathy 10
antonym 1
apathy 10
apostate 149
athletic 176
athletics 177
chronometer 100
cinema 104
comic 174

diachronic 101
diameter 26
diathermy 36
cctopic 55
entopic 54
epidermis 111
epilogue 118
eponymous 1
exodus 58
exoskeleton 149
hyperacidity 49
hyperesthesia 71
hyperthermia 52
hypoacidity 50
hypodermic 92
hypoesthesia 71
hypothermia 51
kinesics 105
metabolism 37

metamorphosis 118
metonymy 132
palindrome 118
palinode 139
parallel 118
paramedic 131
parapsychology 118
perimeter 27
periodontist 117
periscope 33
prognosis 118
prologue 118
prophylactic 141
sympathy 10
synchronic 101
synchronize 103
synonym 2
synonymous 1
synthesis 99

OPTIONAL WORDS

anabatic 20
anabiosis 110
anabolism 37
anadromous 24
anhydrous 57
apanthropia 150
aphelion 156
apogee 156
catabatic 21

catabolism 38
catadromous 25
diadromous 42
endermic 93
enhydrous 56
epigene 113
esthesia 71
exobiology 149

exodontist 155
hyperkinesia 106
hypogene 113
hypokinesia 107
metachromatism 118
palingenesis 118
perigee 156
perihelion 156

REVIEW EXERCISES

Purpose: To review Greek prefixes and learn new words.

Directions:
With the aid of a dictionary find one word beginning with each of the following prefixes. Choose a word that you can use correctly.
Write the word and at least one meaning.
Write the meaning that the prefix has in your word.
Use the word in a sentence.

1. {a / an}_____

_____

_____

2. {ana}_____

_____

_____

3. {anti / ant}_____

_____

_____

4. {amphi}_____

_____

_____

5. {apo / ap / aph}_____

_____

_____

6. {cata}_____

_____

_____

7. {dia}_____

_____

_____

8. {ec / ex}_____

_____

_____

9. {em / en}_____

_____

_____

10. {epi / ep}_____

_____

_____

11. {exo}_____

_____

_____

12. {hyper}_____

_____

_____

13. {hypo}_____

_____

_____

14. {meta / met}_____

_____

_____

15. {palin / pali}_____

_____

_____

16. {para / par}_____

_____

_____

17. {peri}_____

_____

_____

18. {pro} (Greek prefix)_____

_____

_____

19. {sym / syn}_____

_____

_____

Purpose: To review the meanings of three prefixes that are easily confused.

Directions: With the aid of your dictionary identify the prefix and its meaning in each of these words. Enter this meaning in the appropriate column. Give the meaning of the word.

Optional: Use each word in a sentence whose content reinforces the meaning of the word.

	{a / an}	{ana}	{anti / ant}	Meaning of Word
EXAMPLE: *anarchy*	*without*			*complete absence of government*
anecdote				
antidote				
anagram				
antagonize				
aseptic				
anesthetic				
anachronism				
antithesis				
analogous				
asexual				
analgesic				

WORDS OF INTERESTING ORIGIN

Many words are derived from the names of people. This is true of medicine, where diseases are often named after the scientist who investigated them. For example, leprosy is now commonly known as Hansen's disease.

In this exercise, first read the brief biographical notes on ten eponymous persons. Then fit into the correct slot one of the ten words below that fits the context.

Thomas *Bowdler* (1754–1825) edited a heavily censored version of Shakespeare.

Captain C. C. *Boycott* was on the other side of the question of land reform from his neighbors in Ireland in 1880. They refused to have any dealings with him.

Ambrose *Burnside* was a general for the Union in the War Between the States.

J. I. *Guillotin* (1738–1814) was a French physician who lived during the French Revolution; he proposed the use of a machine that would execute prisoners more humanely.

Samuel *Maverick* (1803–1870) was a Texas rancher who did not bother to brand his cattle.

John *McAdam* (1756–1836) was a Scots engineer who invented a type of road surface where small stones are bound together with something like tar.

Jean *Nicot*, French ambassador to Portugal in 1560, imported a drug from the New World.

Sir *Robert* Peel (1788–1850) reorganized the police force in Great Britain.

Pyrrhus (died 272 B.C.) was King of Epirus in Greece. He invaded Italy and fought two successful battles against the Romans but suffered heavy losses.

St. *Valentine* was supposed to be a saint who died in the third century A.D. His name is connected with lovers and sweethearts.

Use these eponymous words to answer the questions below.

bobbies	boycott	macadam	nicotine	Pyrrhic
bowdlerizing	guillotine	maverick	sideburns	valentine

1. Today the idea of _____ an author like Shakespeare seems absurd.

2. "I don't know how much longer I can undergo this _____ by the union members," said Mr. Grubbs.

3. In this age of superhighways and cement, our country roads are still largely

    _____.

4. When the Senator first ran for office he ran without support from either party, and he has

    been a _____ ever since.

5. In 1792 an instrument designed to kill criminals painlessly was introduced in France, the

    dreaded _____.

6. We defeated State handily, but since our quarterback and his favorite receiver were both

    injured in the game, we must consider it a _____ victory.

7. When Al remembered the date, he rushed to the store and bought the first _____ he saw. He should have read the message inside it; Gail never forgave him.

8. "I don't like long hair," said Julie, "and I don't like a moustache, but a nice flourishing pair of _____ really appeals to me."

9. The cigarette companies try to emphasize the low amount of _____ in their products.

10. The famous British policemen are called _____ in honor of their early chief.

EASILY CONFUSED WORDS

Use a dictionary as needed.

1. **Parameter / perimeter.** This is an odd pair. Both contain the Greek morpheme {**meter**} = measure. The prefix {**peri**} means "around," and the meaning of the word is clear in "Around the *perimeter* of the estate was a six-foot stone wall." A recent book* lists different and highly technical meanings for the word *parameter* in such fields as mathematics, astronomy, crystallography, music, medicine, and statistics. All these meanings are too technical to be discussed here. The word is now most commonly used as nothing more than a grand and showy substitute for "boundary, limit, framework, or condition," as in "It is hoped that this course will enlarge the *parameters* of the students."

2. **Stanza / verse.** It is well to distinguish between these two and use *verse* for a single line, as in "Observe the repetition of sounds in the tenth *verse*," meaning the tenth line from the beginning; and to use *stanza* for a group of four or more verses. *Stanza* is from Middle Latin, meaning "a place where one stops." *Verse* is from Latin {**vers**} = turn; etymologically speaking, a verse is where one turns to the beginning of the next line.

3. **Statue / statute.** *Statue* is derived from Latin *stare* (= *stand*) and means the form of a person or animal made out of stone or other material, as in "The best known *statue* in America is probably the Statue of Liberty." *Statute* is from Latin *statuere* = set up. A *statute* is therefore a rule or regulation set up by a legislative body, as in "If we look long enough in this material we will surely find a *statute* that will get us acquitted."

Use the six words in the sentences where each makes sense.

1. One word I never want to hear is _____ in place of *perimeter*.

2. "Fortunately for you," said the judge, "the _____ of limitations prevents your neighbor from getting what you owe him."

3. "What an imposing _____ of Lincoln," cried Jean.

4. The fourth stanza contains the thirteenth _____.

*Philip Howard, *New Words for Old* (New York: Oxford University Press, 1977).

5. "It is obvious," said Mike with insulting slowness, "that since the area is a square measuring 40 on a side the _____ must be 160 feet.

6. Let us all join in singing the first, second, and fourth _____ of Hymn 96.

LATIN PHRASES

First try to get the meanings of the Latin phrases from the context of the sentences below, choosing a meaning from the list that follows. Write the number of the Latin phrase beside the definition that fits.

1. *Terra firma*, as in "After a week at sea in a 28-foot sloop, it was a pleasure to set foot again on *terra firma*."

2. *Rara avis*, as in "In that community a person who went jogging in the early morning was a *rara avis* and regarded as eccentric by all."

3. *Anno Domini*, as in "It was early in February, A.D. 1856."

4. *Vade mecum*, as in "As its name suggests, this little pocket dictionary has been my *vade mecum* whenever I go to Greece."

5. *Sui generis*, as in "You may not like Professor Small personally, but you will have to admit that he is *sui generis* and a great asset to the college."

_____ something usually carried by someone for constant use

_____ consistent fear

_____ in the year of (the birth of) our Lord

_____ unique

_____ occasional advice

_____ in the years before (the birth of) our Lord

_____ solid land

_____ trifling amount of money

_____ type of pig

_____ strange bird

Use a dictionary to find the word-by-word translation and the modern meaning for each phrase.

	Word-by-Word Translation	Modern Meaning
terra firma		
rara avis		
anno Domini		
vade mecum		
sui generis		

UNIT SIX

The Most Useful Latin Prefixes

In the preceding unit you studied common prefixes borrowed from Greek. In this unit you will meet a number of new prefixes borrowed from Latin.

Again we remind you that for simplicity we sometimes present only one or two meanings for a prefix, or other morpheme, whereas there may be several other meanings also. The exercises at the end of the unit are designed to acquaint you with some of the additional meanings.

CONTENTS

1–13	Review
14–26	Four Latin Prefixes and Five Latin Bases
27–61	Allomorphs of Latin Prefixes
62–69	Combinations of the Base {gress} with Both Old and New Prefixes
70–82	Combinations of the Base {ced / cede / ceed / cess} with Both Old and New Prefixes
83–104	Review of {empty}, {full}, and {intens} Morphemes
105–126	Review of Eight Prefixes
127–140	Combinations of the Base {fer} with Old and New Prefixes
141–170	Combinations of the base {pose / pone / posit } with Old and New Prefixes
171–186	Four More Latin Prefixes
187–204	Two Latin Prefixes Meaning "Not"
205–219	Four New Latin Prefixes

Review
(Frames 1–13)

1 In the last unit you learned that there are three common kinds of morphemes found in English words derived from Greek and Latin, namely prefix, base, and suffix. An example of such a word which is constructed of Greek morphemes is *hypothermia*, as in "Jim was suffering so severely from *hypothermia* that his body temperature was down to 90°." What is the prefix in *hypothermia*? {_____}

▶ □ ◀

   A: {hypo}

2 What does the prefix {**hypo**} mean? _____

▶ □ ◀

   A: Too little.

3–4 What is the base of *hypothermia* and what does it mean? {_____} = _____

▶ □ ◀

   A: {therm}; heat.

5 And what is the suffix of *hypothermia*? {_____}

▶ □ ◀

   A: {ia}

6 What information does {**ia**} give? (In your own words.) _____
   _____

▶ □ ◀

   A: Its chief use is to tell us that hypothermia is a noun.

7 {**puls** / **pulse** / **pel**} = push. English has the same kinds of three-morpheme words borrowed from Latin. An example is the word *re-púls-ion*, as in "As Tim entered the dirty office, with its smell of stale cigar smoke, he felt such *repulsion* that it was difficult to remember his purpose in going there." What is the prefix of *repulsion*? {_____}

▶ □ ◀

   A: {re}

8–9 In *repulsion* what is the base? {_____} What is the suffix? {_____}

▶ □□□ ◀

    A: {puls}; {ion}.

10–11 Give the meanings: {**re**} = _____; {**puls**} = _____.

▶ □□□ ◀

    A: Back; drive, push.

12 The function of {**ion**} is partly to show the class of word. What class of word is *repulsion?*
_____

▶ □□□ ◀

    A: Noun.

13 What is the *main* function of the suffixes of English words? _____
_____

▶ □□□ ◀

    A: To show what class of word a word is.

Four Latin Prefixes and Five Latin Bases
(Frames 14–26)

14 The following four useful prefixes are taken from Latin.

        {**ab**} = from   {**ex / e**} = out
        {**ad**} = toward, to, forward   {**in**} = in, into

In the next 13 frames you will combine these prefixes with the following bases:

        {**duce / duct**} = lead, take   {**it**} = go
        {**err**} = wander   {**ject**} = throw
        {**hes / here**} = stick   {**tract**} = draw, pull

"The cruel baron forcibly *ab-duct-ed* the young princess from her father's castle." Considering the context, in what direction relative to the castle did the baron take the princess? _____

▶ □□□ ◀

    A: (Away) from the castle.

15 "He covered the cut on his foot with a piece of *ad-hés-ive* tape." What does something do which *adheres?* _____

▶ □ ◀

A: It sticks to something else.

16 {**here**} is an _____ of {**hes**}.

▶ □ ◀

A: Allomorph.

17 "Bill had led such a sheltered life that it was a great shock to him when he was *in-dúct-ed.*" In which direction was Bill led, *into* or *out of* the military service? _____

▶ □ ◀

A: Into.

18 In what direction does an *éx-it* take you? _____

▶ □ ◀

A: Out.

19 In the sentence "He forcibly abducted the princess," what is the suffix of the verb *ab-ducted?* _____

▶ □ ◀

A: {ed}

20 In your own words, what is the meaning of this suffix {**ed**} here? _____
_____

▶ □ ◀

A: It forms the past tense (shows past time).

21 In the word *adhesive*, what is the suffix? {_____}

▶ □ ◀

A: {ive}

22 In your own words, what is the meaning of the suffix {**ive**}? _____
_____

▶ □ ◀

A: It shows that *adhesive* is an adjective.

23 Here are the same four prefixes used with different bases to form different words:

aberrant   adduce   inject   eject

Refer to this menu as necessary. In the next four frames, choose from these four words the best replacement for the synonyms in parentheses. Use the information given by the prefixes.

"The doctor (introduced) the medicine into Tom's arm with a hypodermic needle." What is a synonym of *introduced?* _____

▶ □ ◀

    A: Injected.

24 "Such (unusual) behavior on Judge Robinson's part could only be explained by a total breakdown." What is a synonym for *unusual?* _____

▶ □ ◀

    A: Aberrant.

25 "The students were (thrown out) from the restaurant because of their noisy behavior." Give a synonym for *thrown out:* _____

▶ □ ◀

    A: Ejected.

26 "Imagine Peter's surprise when the prosecution (brought forward as proof) the account book that Peter thought had been burned!" What is a synonym for *brought forward?*

_____

▶ □ ◀

    A: Adduced.

Allomorphs of Latin Prefixes
(Frames 27–61)

27 You have already seen that most Greek prefixes have allomorphs. For example, the Greek prefix that means "in" has two forms, {en} and {em}. In the word used (in Unit Five, frame 54) for an organ in its proper place, was the spelling *entopic* or *emtopic?* _____

▶ □ ◀

    A: Entopic.

28 When {en / em} is prefixed to {pathy}, do we say *enpathy* or *empathy*? _____

▶ □□□□□□□□□□□□□□□□□□□□□□□□□□□□□□∪□□□□□□∩□□□□□□□□□□□□□□□□□ ◀

    A: Empathy.

29 This kind of change in the prefix, which is determined by the initial sound of the base, is more common in Latin than in Greek. Here are some examples.

{**tain**} = hold. If a congressman holds off from voting, we do not say that he *abtained from voting, but we use the allomorph {**abs**} and say, "He _____ from voting."

▶ □□ ◀

    A: Abstained.

30 The asterisk (star) in *abtained means that this form (in your own words)

_____ .

▶ □□ ◀

    A: Is an imaginary form, invented to prove a point.

31 {**tract**} = draw. If we *draw away* from a document the important information, what do we do to the information? _____

▶ □□ ◀

    A: Abstract it.

32 What is the allomorph of {ab} that occurred in the last few frames? {_____}

▶ □□ ◀

    A: {abs}

33 What sound did both of these last two bases begin with? / ____ /

▶ □□ ◀

    A: / t /

I NICE-TO-KNOW ■ The slashes in / t / indicate that we are talking about sounds—that is, **phonemes.**

34 The rule is that before / t /, the prefix {ab} becomes the allomorph {_____}.

▶ □□ ◀

    A: {abs}

35–36 What were the two examples of this {abs} allomorph that you just saw? _____
and _____

▶ □ ◀

    A: Abstract; abstain.

37 You have seen the prefix {in}, meaning "in" or "into," in the words *inject* and *induct*. But when we prefix {in} to {pel}, we find that the result is not **inpel* but _____.

▶ □ ◀

    A: Impel.

38 What do we get when we add the prefix {ex} to the base {pel}? _____

▶ □ ◀

    A: Expel.

39 What do we get if we add the prefix {in} to {pulse}? _____

▶ □ ◀

    A: Impulse.

40 {bibe} = drink. When we drink something in, we do not **inbibe* it, but rather we _____ it.

▶ □ ◀

    A: Imbibe.

41 The prefix {ex} has three allomorphs distributed as follows:

{ex}, used most of the time, as in *exit* (frame 18)
{ef}, always used before / f / and only before / f /, as in *effusive* (frame 43)
{e}, used in a few words such as *eject* (frame 25)

In other words, you _____ (can / cannot) always predict whether the form will be {e} or {ex}.

▶ □ ◀

    A: Cannot.

42 What is the most common form of the Latin prefix meaning "out"? {_____}

▶ □ ◀

    A: {ex}

43 {**fus**} = pour, gush. "Our former teacher, Mr. Oates, was so *ef-fús-ive* in his praise, so lavish in his compliments, that we thought he had mistaken us for two other students."

In your own words, how did Mr. Oates act? _____

_____

▶ □□ ◀

   A: Words of praise poured (or gushed) out of him.

44 {**viscer**} = intestines. "Unfortunately no one had told us that the first step after shooting a deer is to *e-vìscer-ate* it." What does *eviscerate* mean? _____

_____

▶ □□ ◀

   A: Take the intestines out.

┃ **NICE-TO-KNOW** ■ The suffix {ate} in *eviscerate* shows that this is a verb.

45 {**mit / miss**} = send, let go. "The volcano *e-mìtt-ed* a lot of poisonous gases as well as ash." What did the volcano do to these gases and ash? _____

▶ □□ ◀

   A: Sent them out (or, let them out).

46 {**ad**} = toward, to, forward. This prefix has many allomorphs. The form {**ad**} occurs before / d /, vowels, and / h /, as in *adduce, adapt,* and *adhesive.* You had *adduce* in frame 26. In your own words, what did it mean? _____

▶ □□ ◀

   A: Bring forward.

47 You also had *adhesive* in this unit. In your own words, what does *adhere* (the verb) mean?

_____

▶ □□ ◀

   A: To stick to something.

48 {**apt**} = fit, fasten. "Mike *ad-ápt-ed* his style of living to his reduced income." In your own words, what did Mike do? _____

_____

▶ □□ ◀

   A: Fitted his style of living to the changed situation.

49   When we come to other bases, those beginning with the sounds / c / , / f / , / g / , and the like, we find that the following changes take place in the prefix {**ad**} :

{**ad**} + cede = accede	{**ad**} + nounce = announce
{**ad**} + fluent = affluent	{**ad**} + petite = appetite
{**ad**} + gression = aggression	{**ad**} + sume = assume
{**ad**} + locate = allocate	{**ad**} + tract = attract

In your own words, make up a rule about the allomorphs of {**ad**} before bases beginning

with / c / , / f / , / g / , / l / , / n / , / p / , / s / , and / t / , as listed above. _____

_____

▶ □□ ◀

A: The / d / changes to the first sound of the base.

50   The technical term for the change of {**ad**} to {**ac**} before {**cede**}, and from {**ad**} to {**as**} before {**sume**}, is **assimilation**. The base {**similat**} means "like," as in the word *similar*. The word

assimilation is itself an example of assimilation, since the prefix {**ad**} changes to {_____}
before {**similat**}.

▶ □□ ◀

A: {as}

51   Here are the eight bases you will now use:

{**ced** / **cede** / **ceed** / **cess**} = go, come	{**nounce**} = proclaim
{**flu**} = flow	{**petit**} = seek, desire
{**gress**} = step, move	{**sume**} = take
{**loc**} = place	{**tract**} = pull, drag

We will next use the eight words listed in frame 49 with the prefix {**ad**}.

"Al *as-súm-ed* the heavy responsibility of chairman." Where did Al put the responsibility?

_____

▶ □□ ◀

A: On himself (or, he took it to himself).

52   "George's *áp-petite* for sweets could not be easily satisfied." George had a strong feeling
_____ sweets.

▶ □□ ◀

A: Toward (or for).

53   "The brutal *ag-gréss-ion* of this large country against its defenseless neighbor shocked the
world." The larger country moved _____ its neighbor.

▶ □□ ◀

A: Toward (or against).

54 In military contexts, *aggression* is used of _____ (friendly / hostile / neutral) movements.

▶ □ ◀

A: Hostile.

55 "When Colette saw the stranger she felt a strange, overpowering *at-tráct-ion*." Colette was drawn _____ the visitor.

▶ □ ◀

A: To (or toward).

56 "The student body listened in silent horror as the new regulations were *an-nóunc-ed*." The speaker declared these regulations _____ the student body.

▶ □ ◀

A: To.

57 "The manager was apologetic and *ac-céd-ed* to my request for a refund without question." Did the manager agree or disagree with the request? _____

▶ □ ◀

A: Agree.

58 When a country becomes *áf-flu-ent*, does money flow into the country or out of it? _____

▶ □ ◀

A: Into.

59 When an administrator *ál-loc-ate-s* funds, does he hand them out to people or withdraw them? _____

▶ □ ◀

A: He hands them out.

60 What is the technical term for the change from {**ad**} to {**an**} before {**nounce**}? _____

▶ □ ◀

A: Assimilation.

61 In your experience with the program, how many meanings do the prefixes seem to have? _____ (just one / two at the most / usually two or more).

▶ □ ◀

A: Usually two or more.

Combinations of the Base {gress} with Both Old and New Prefixes
(Frames 62–69)

■ Here are four more Latin prefixes:

{**di** / **dis**} = away, away from   {**re**} = back, backwards, again
{**pro**} = forward   {**trans**} = across

62 If you read that the relationships between two countries have *re-gréss-ed*, in which direction have they gone? _____

▶ □ U □ ◀

A: Backwards.

63 "Backwards" here means that the conditions are _____ (better than / the same as / worse than) before.

▶ □ □ □ U U □ ◀

A: Worse than.

64 If relationships *pro-gréss*, in what direction do they move? _____

▶ □ ◀

A: Forward. (Note that the Greek prefix {**pro**} means for or in favor of.)

65 *Cón-gress* is a group of people who have come _____ in the same place.

▶ □ ◀

A: Together.

66 If you read a sign that said, "All *in-gress* prohibited," what would you know you could not do? _____

▶ □ ◀

A: Enter (or, go in).

67 "Although Professor Parks wrote out his lectures in detail, he invariably *di-gréss-ed* from his topic." What part of *digressed* means "away from"? {_____}

▶ □□ □ □□□□□□ □□□□□□ □□□□□□ □□□□□□ □□□□□□ □□□□□□ □□□□□□ □□□□□□ □□□ ◀

A: {di}

68 What does someone do who *trans-gréss-es* a law or custom? _____

_____

▶ □□ □ □□□□□□ □□□□□□ □□□□□□ □□□□□□ □□□□□□ □□□□□□ □□□□□□ □□□□□□ □□□ ◀

A: He oversteps it or breaks it.

69 When the famous showman P. T. Barnum set up his American Museum in New York, he wanted a way to get rid of people who had found the exhibition so interesting that they did not leave, thus preventing others from buying tickets. He therefore erected a sign that read "This Way to the Egress." The public followed this sign, thinking they were to see another marvel. What did they come to? _____

▶ □□ □ □□□□□□ □□□□□□ □□□□□□ □□□□□□ □□□□□□ □□□□□□ □□□□□□ □□□□□□ □□□ ◀

A: An exit (or, way out).

Combinations of the Base {ced / cede / ceed / cess}
with Both Old and New Prefixes
(Frames 70–82)

70 In the next sequence you will practice eight prefixes of Latin origin combined with the base {**ced** / **cede** / **ceed** / **cess**} = go, come. These prefixes are:

{**ante**} = before	{**pre**} = before
{**con**} = together with (or, it intensifies)	{**pro**} = forward
{**ex**} = out	{**re**} = back, backwards, again
{**inter**} = between	{**se**} = away, apart

In what direction does a man's hairline go when it *re-céde-s?* _____

▶ □□ □ □□□□□□ □□□□□□ □□□□□□ □□□□□□ □□□□□□ □□□□□□ □□□□□□ □□□□□□ □□□ ◀

A: Back.

71 When a meeting *proceeds*, does it go back, go forward, or stand still? _____

_____

▶ □□ □ □□□□□□ □□□□□□ □□□□□□ □□□□□□ □□□□□□ □□□□□□ □□□□□□ □□□□□□ □□□ ◀

A: It goes forward.

72   What is the allomorph of {**cede**} used in the last frame?   {_____}

▶ □ ◀

   A: {ceed}

73   What do we call it when people *proceed* to a place?   _____

▶ □ ◀

   A: A procession.

74   In what direction did the Southern states go relative to the Union when they *seceded?*
     _____

▶ □ ◀

   A: Away (or apart).

75   {**se**} = _____

▶ □ ◀

   A: Away (or apart).

76   If one *intercedes* in an argument, where does he place himself?   _____
     _____

▶ □ ◀

   A: Between the two arguing parties.

77   If a man *precedes* his wife in death, when does he die, before his wife, after his wife, or at
     the same time as his wife?   _____

▶ □ ◀

   A: Before his wife.

78   If a father examines the *antecedents* of his daughter's boyfriend, he is looking at what
     the boyfriend _____ (did in the past / is doing in the present / will do in the
     future).

▶ □ ◀

   A: Did in the past.

79 When someone *exceeds* the speed limit, what has he gone out of?   (In your own words)

_____

▶ □ ◀

    A: The boundaries of the permissible speed.

80 In all of these compounds the base has meant something like "go" or "come." However, this base is also used without any prefix, as in "After the war the defeated country was forced to *cede* all its colonies." Give a synonym for *cede* in that sentence: _____

_____

▶ □ ◀

    A: Give up, hand over, yield, etc.

81 That is, if you *cede* some territory you _____ (go toward / go away from / stay in) it.

▶ □ ◀

    A: Go away from.

82 The compound word *concede* means almost the same as the simple verb *cede*. There is a difference in some contexts, however; we *concede* a putt on a golf course, but we *cede* a territory to the victors. Is {**con**} in *concede* {**empty**} or {**full**}?   _____

▶ □ ◀

    A: {empty}

NICE-TO-KNOW ■ The word *concede* presents a difficulty. *Cede* is a stronger word than *concede* (at least, we *concede* small things and *cede* great ones), but there is nothing in {con} or {cede} to show this. In general, the Latin prefixes are more difficult to assign meanings to than the Greek ones. The reason is that Greek derivatives were usually adapted into English directly through Greek and often for technical terms, where the meaning became fixed. Latin derivatives, however, came into English sometimes directly from Latin but often through French or other languages. For this reason you will find the sections on Greek derivatives somewhat easier than those on Latin derivatives, since it is possible for us to set down more definite rules about the meanings of the Greek morphemes than the Latin ones.

Review of {empty}, {full}, and {intens} Morphemes
(Frames 83–104)

83 Since the simple verb *cede* means about the same as the compound verb **concede**, we say that the prefix {**con**} in *concede* is {**empty**}. What do we mean by {**empty**}?   _____

_____

▶ □ ◀

    A: It is an empty morpheme; that is, it has little or no meaning that we can identify.

84 As you know, a common meaning of {**con**} is "with" or "together with." For example, here is a word that you may not know, *com-méns-al,* as in "The dons of the college, with their tradition of *commensal* dining, enjoy both good food and good conversation." The word *commensal* is made up of the prefix {**com / con**} = with, the base {**mens**} = table, and the suffix {**al**}, which means that the word is an adjective. How does a *commensal* group dine? _____

▶ □□□ ◀

A: Together (or, at the same table).

85 Is the prefix in *commensal* {**empty**} or {**full**}? _____

▶ □□□ ◀

A: {full}

86 The prefix {**com / con / co**} is a {**full**} in the word *co-aúthor.* What does a *coauthor* do?

_____

▶ □□□ ◀

A: Works with another author.

87 Latin {**labor**} = work. What do *col-láborat-ors* do? _____

▶ □□□ ◀

A: They work together.

88 What allomorph of {**con**} did you see in the last frame? _____

▶ □□□ ◀

A: {col}

89 It is useful to see prefixes contrasted with one another by being used with the same base. For example, *impose* and *depose* are antonyms. The base {**pose**} = put, place. A group that *imposes* a king puts him _____ power over the people.

▶ □□□ ◀

A: In (or into).

90 If the group *deposes* him, what does it do? (Guess the meaning of the new prefix.) _____

_____

▶ □□□ ◀

A: Removes him from power.

91 Are the prefixes {in} and {de} in the words *impose* and *depose* {full} or {empty}? _____

▶ □ ◀

    A: {full}

92 The meaning of some {empty}s seems to be solely the desire to use a longer word. Here are some examples. There is a Latin verb *dicare*, which means "dedicate," "vow," or "consecrate." But there is no English word **dicate*. Instead we have borrowed a compound of *dicare*, namely *dedicare*. Why did English borrow the longer form with the prefix, that is, *dedicate?* _____

_____

▶ □ ◀

    A: It is hard to say why, except that *dedicate* may seem to sound grander than the verb **dicate*, which speakers of English might have used (but didn't).

93 There is a verb base in Latin {**linqu**} = leave. It is sometimes used by itself in Latin (*linquit* = he leaves [something]), but most of the time it is found with the prefix {**re**}, as in *relinquit* = he leaves (something) behind. Which form was taken into English, the simple verb or the compound? _____

▶ □ ◀

    A: The compound.

94 But where could someone leave something if not behind him? Is the {**re**} in *relinquish* {**full**} or {**empty**}? _____

▶ □ ◀

    A: {empty}

95 The whole question of prefixes, particularly the Latin prefixes, is complicated. We will now give you another chance to see just how complicated it is.
    Here is an entry on the prefix {**de**} from *Webster's New World Dictionary:*

> **de-** (di, də; *with some slight stress*, dē) [L., a prefix signifying separation, cessation, intensification, or contraction; also < Fr. *dé-* (< L. *de*) or OFr. *des-* (< L. *dis-*): see DIS-] *a prefix meaning:* **1.** away from, off [*depilate, derail*] **2.** down [*depress, decline*] **3.** wholly, entirely [*defunct*] **4.** reverse the action of; undo [*defrost, decode*]

How many separate meanings are listed: _____

▶ □ ◀

    A: Four.

96 The {**de**} in the word *depose* in frame 90 has the meaning that the *New World Dictionary* lists as number _____.

▶ □ ◀

    A: 1 (away from, off). Number 4 is also a possible answer.

97 What numbered meaning does this entry say that the {de} in *defrost* has? _____

▶ □□□ ◀

A: 4 (reverse the action of, undo).

98 Here is what *Webster's New Collegiate Dictionary* has about the entry {de}:

> **de-** *prefix* [ME, fr. OF *de-*, *des-*, partly fr. L *de-* from, down, away (fr. *de*, prep.) and partly fr. L *dis-*; L *de* akin to OIr *di* from, OE *tō* to — more at TO, DIS-] **1 a :** do the opposite of ⟨*de*vitalize⟩ ⟨*de*activate⟩ **b :** reverse of ⟨*de*-emphasis⟩ **2 a :** remove (a specified thing) from ⟨*de*louse⟩ ⟨*de*hydrogenate⟩ **b :** remove from (a specified thing) ⟨*de*throne⟩ **3 :** reduce ⟨*de*value⟩ **4 :** something derived from (a specified thing) ⟨*de*compound⟩ : derived from something (of a specified nature) ⟨*de*nominative⟩ **5 :** get off of (a specified thing) ⟨*de*train⟩ **6 :** having a molecule characterized by the removal of one or more atoms (of a specified element) ⟨*de*oxy-⟩

How many *main* meanings are given? _____

▶ □□ ◀

A.: Six.

99 Which meanings are subdivided?   Numbers _____ and _____

▶ □□ ◀

A: 1 and 2.

100 Here is the same prefix as explained in the *American Heritage Dictionary*:

> **de–.** Indicates: **1.** Reversal or undoing; for example, **deactivate**, **decode**. **2.** Removal; for example, **deaminate**, **delouse**. **3.** Degradation, reduction; for example, **declass**. **4.** Disparagement; for example, **demean**. *Note:* Many compounds other than those entered here may be formed with *de-*. In forming compounds, *de-* is normally joined with the following element without space or hyphen: *decarbonize*. However, if the second element begins with *e*, it is separated with a hyphen: *de-escalate*. It is also preferable to use the hyphen if the compound brings together three or more vowels: *de-aerate*. In the rare case that the second element begins with a capital letter, it is separated with a hyphen: *de-Americanize*. [In borrowed Latin and French compounds, Latin *dē-* (French *dé-*, Old French *des-*) indicates: 1. Down, downward, as in **declivity**, **deject**. 2. Away, away from, off, as in **decide**, **deprecate**. 3 Reversal, undoing, as in **decrease**, **destroy**. 4. Removal, riddance, as in **defoliate**, **decapitate**. 5. Completely, carefully, intensively, as in **denominate**, **declare**. 6. Pejorative sense, as in **deride**, **deceive**. Latin *dē-*, from *dē*, from. See **de-** in Appendix.*]

How many meanings are there in the first part of the entry? _____

▶ □□ ◀

A: Four.

101 How many meanings are there in the second half? _____

▶ □□ ◀

A: Six.

102 Now the question arises: which dictionary is correct? _____

▶ □□ ◀

A: They are all "correct." The editors have chosen to select and organize the material differently.

103 Which of the three entries do you find the clearest? _____

_____

▶ □□ ◀

A: There is no one answer; people differ, of course.

104 Which dictionary gives the *shortest* explanation? _____

▶ □□ ◀

A: *Webster's New World.*

Review of Eight Prefixes
(Frames 105–126)

105 Where does a person go when he *returns*? _____

▶ □□ ◀

A: Back.

106 If we *redivide* some property, what do we do? _____

▶ □□ ◀

A: Divide it again.

107 {**rupt**} = break. In the word *interrupt*, as in "Bill constantly *interrupted* the conversation,"
the prefix {**inter**} means "break _____."

▶ □□ ◀

A: Into the middle of, up, between.

108 The prefix {**ante**} we call a **live morpheme,** meaning that we can use it to coin new words
that we can be sure will be understood by a speaker of English. Suppose the President of
the United States was named Jones. What would the *ante-Jones* administration be?

_____

▶ □□ ◀

A: The one that came before the Jones administration.

109 One must be careful not to confuse the Latin prefix {**ante**} = before with the Greek prefix
{**anti**} = against. What would an *anti-Jones* senator be? _____

_____

▶ □□ ◀

A: One who was opposed to Jones personally or against his policies.

110 {**cure**} = care. In the sentence "Because of his successful investments Bob felt financially *secure*," what does {**se**} mean? _____

▶ □□ ◀

   A: Without.

111 {**pose**} = put, place. When a person *proposes* something, he puts his plan _____ the proper people.

▶ □□ ◀

   A: Before.

112 If something has been *predetermined*, when has it been decided? _____

▶ □□ ◀

   A: Before (or, ahead of time).

113 *Exit* and *egress* are synonyms. Do they have the same morpheme as a prefix? _____ (yes / no)

▶ □□ ◀

   A: Yes.

114 What do we call the forms {**e**} and {**ex**}, relative to each other? _____

▶ □□ ◀

   A: Allomorphs.

115 The prefix {**ex**} has another meaning. What is an *ex-convict*? _____
_____

▶ □□ ◀

   A: One who has moved out of the group of people known as convicts.

I NICE-TO-KNOW ■ The allomorph {**e**} is never used to mean "former"; only {**ex**} has this meaning.

116 What is the meaning of {**com**} in "Tim all by himself raised such a *commotion* that we were afraid the police would arrest us all"? (In your own words) _____
_____

▶ □□ ◀

   A: It makes the word "motion" stronger than just "motion."

117 What symbol do we use to show that a morpheme makes the meaning of a word stronger? {_____}

▶ □ ◀

A: {intens}

118 The prefix {**pro**} can also mean "in favor of"; when used in this way, it is a live morpheme. For example, what would characterize a person who is *pro-Jones*? _____
_____

▶ □ ◀

A: He would support Jones.

119–126 See if you can give *one* meaning to each of these eight prefixes:

{**ante**} = _____   {**pre**} = _____

{**con**} = _____   {**pro**} = _____

{**ex**} = _____   {**re**} = _____

{**inter**} = _____   {**se**} = _____

▶ □ ◀

A: {ante} = before; {con} = together, with, or {intens}; {ex} = out; {inter} = between; {pre} = before; {pro} = forward, in favor of; {re} = back, backwards, again; {se} = away, apart.

Combinations of the Base {fer} with Old and New Prefixes
(Frames 127–140)

127 In the next sequence you will use the base {**fer**} = carry with these nine prefixes, some of which are new to you:

{**circum**} = around, as in *circumference*
{**con**} = together, with, or {**intens**}, as in *conference*
{**de**} = down, as in *deference*
{**dis / dif**} = apart, as in *difference*
{**in**} = in, as in *infer*
{**ob / of**} = against, toward, as in *offer*
{**re**} = back, again, as in *refer*
{**trans**} = across, as in *transfer*
{**sub / suf**} = under, as in *suffering*

As you read this account of an adventure in an airport, put the appropriate compounds of {**fer**} listed in the menu above in the blanks. Rely on the context as well as the meanings of the prefixes.

Since we had to change airlines during our trip, we were concerned about moving our luggage across the airport. We were right to worry, for during this _____ our luggage disappeared.

▶ □ ◀

    A: Transfer.

128   An airline official sent us over to the lost baggage office. The person to whom he _____ us was sympathetic.

▶ □ ◀

    A: Referred.

129   You might conclude that with his help we quickly found our luggage, but if you _____ this, you would be quite wrong.

▶ □ ◀

    A: Inferred.

130   For a long time we talked with our new friend in lost baggage, but this _____ between us was useless.

▶ □ ◀

    A: Conference.

131   At first, we could not agree with the officials on what should be done, but these _____ finally became resolved.

▶ □ ◀

    A: Differences.

132   We agreed that in view of the inconvenience to which we had been subjected, they should grant any reasonable request. They did indeed show considerable respect and _____ toward us.

▶ □ ◀

    A: Deference.

133   They told us we could wait in a special VIP room until the next flight came in, which might contain our luggage. We accepted their _____ with gratitude.

▶ □ ◀

    A: Offer.

134 The luxury of the lounge did little to relieve our _____ as we spent three anxious hours.

▶ □□ ◀

A: Suffering.

135 At last we received word that the bags had arrived. But we were misdirected to the place where our property was, and were forced to walk around almost the entire _____ of the terminal until we were finally united with our suitcases.

▶ □□ ◀

A: Circumference.

136 When the people in the last sequence wanted to *transfer* their baggage, where did they wish to move it? _____

▶ □□ ◀

A: Across the airport.

137 When people *differ*, do they move together or apart or stay in the same place? _____

▶ □□ ◀

A: They move apart.

138 When you *suffer* something, you bear up _____ it.

▶ □□ ◀

A: Under.

139 When you *confer* with someone, you bring the two of you _____.

▶ □□ ◀

A: Together.

140 When you *refer* something, you send it _____ to someone else.

▶ □□ ◀

A: Back.

Combinations of the Base {pose / pone / posit}
with Old and New Prefixes
(Frames 141–170)

■ In the next sequence you will examine compounds of {pose / pone / posit} = put, place. We will also introduce two new prefixes:

{post} = after (of time), behind (of place), as in *postdate* or *posterior*
{super} = above, as in *Superman* and *superhuman*

141   When a musician *composes* music, he puts it all _____.

▶ □ ◀

   A: Together.

142   When a dentist *exposes* a nerve, he sets it _____ from the rest of the tooth.

▶ □ ◀

   A: Apart, away, out.

143   If a member of an audience *interposes* a question in a lecture, he puts it _____
_____ (at the beginning / in the middle / at the end) of the talk.

▶ □ ◀

   A: In the middle.

144   When a musician *transposes* a piece of music from the key of C to the key of F, he moves
it _____ the scale from C to F.

▶ □ ◀

   A: Across.

145   If a photographer *superimposes* two images, what does he do? _____
_____

▶ □ ◀

   A: He puts one on top of the other.

146   The meaning of the prefix {sub} in the sentence "He *supposed* that the statement was true, but could not prove it" is that the *supposition* underlay his conduct. So, {sub} = _____

▶ □ ◀

   A: Under.

147 What is the allomorph of {**sub**} used in *suppose*? {_____}

▶ □□□ ◀

    A: {sup}

148 What is the technical name for the change of {**sub**} to the allomorph {**sup**} before the base {**pose**}? _____

▶ □□□ ◀

    A: Assimilation.

149 A synonym of the Latin derivative *supposition* is the Greek derivative *hypothesis*. You have seen the Greek prefix and suffix before. What does Greek {**hypo**} mean? _____

▶ □□□ ◀

    A: Under.

150 What class of word does the suffix {**sis**} indicate? _____

▶ □□□ ◀

    A: Noun.

151 Since *supposition* and *hypothesis* are synonyms, you can probably guess the meaning of the Greek base {**the**}. What is it? _____

▶ □□□ ◀

    A: Put (or place).

152 Greek {**hypo**} = Latin {_____}.

▶ □□□ ◀

    A: {sub}

153 Greek {**sis**} = Latin {_____}.

▶ □□□ ◀

    A: {ion}

154 There is a slight difference in meaning between *supposition* and *hypothesis*. What is it? (In your own words) _____

▶ □□□ ◀

    A: Hypothesis is a more learned word, used in science.

155 When one *reposes* in a chair, in what direction is one leaning, forward or back?

_____

▶ ◻◻ ◀

A: Back.

156 What class of word are the words *compose, expose, interpose, suppose,* and *repose?*

_____

▶ ◻◻ ◀

A: Verbs. (*Repose* can also be a noun, as in "My repose was broken by a loud shout.")

157 What class of word is *supposition,* as in "My *supposition* proved false"? _____

▶ ◻◻ ◀

A: Noun.

158 What class of word is *position* in the sentence "He *positioned* his men carefully"?

_____

▶ ◻◻ ◀

A: Verb.

159 Is it common or uncommon to have a word in English serve as both noun and verb?

_____

▶ ◻◻ ◀

A: Common.

160 {**post**} = behind. Where is something placed that is in *postposition* to something else?

_____

▶ ◻◻ ◀

A: It is behind it.

161 When does a *post-game* show start? _____

▶ ◻◻ ◀

A: After the game.

162 Where is something that has been placed in *anteposition* to something else? _____

▶ ◻◻ ◀

A: It is ahead of that something else.

163 When one is in *opposition* to some people or some ideas, he puts himself _____ them.

▶ □ ◀

    A: Against.

164 What is the allomorph of the prefix {ob} which was used in the last frame? _____

▶ □ ◀

    A: {op}

165 What is the change from {**ob**} to the allomorph {**op**} before {**posit**} called? _____

▶ □ ◀

    A: Assimilation.

166 Is assimilation of the prefix common or rare in Latin prefixes? _____

▶ □ ◀

    A: Common.

167 Is this kind of assimilation more common in Greek prefixes than in Latin prefixes, or less common? _____

▶ □ ◀

    A: Less common.

168 What does *contraposition* mean? (In your own words) _____
_____

▶ □ ◀

    A: A position opposite something.

169 What is an *opponent?* (In your own words) _____
_____

▶ □ ◀

    A: Someone who has been placed opposite you (and hinders you).

170 Do Latin prefixes have one meaning, several meanings, or many meanings? _____

▶ □ ◀

    A: "Several" and "many" are loose terms, but "several" is probably the best answer.

NICE-TO-KNOW ■ The reason for this, as we explained earlier, is that Greek words were normally borrowed into English directly, while the Latin words frequently were partly changed because they had been used in French, Italian, and a few other languages.

Four More Latin Prefixes
(Frames 171–186)

{**extra**} = without, outside   {**intro**} = into, inward
{**intra**} = within   {**retro**} = back

171   The basc {**mur**} = wall. In *intramural* sports, where do the opponents come from, inside or outside the walls of the institution? _____

▶ □□□ ◀

    A: Inside.

172   Where do *extramural* activities like a picnic take place? _____

▶ □□□ ◀

    A: Outside the usual place (outside the walls).

173–174   It is not common today to build a wall around an institution, but we still speak of <u>intra</u>_____ and <u>extra</u>_____ activities.

▶ □□□ ◀

    A: Intramural; extramural.

175   You have alrcady had the prefix {**inter**}. What are *intercollegiate* athletics?

_____

▶ □□□ ◀

    A: Those between different colleges.

176   An *extracurricular* activity is one that occurs _____ the regular curriculum.

▶ □□□ ◀

    A: Outside (in addition to).

177   Someone who is *introspective* is inclined to look _____ ___ his own feelings and motivation.

▶ □□□ ◀

    A: Into.

178   What does the prefix {**retro**} mean, as in "Your increase in salary, you will be glad to know, is *retroactive* to the first of the year"? _____

▶ □ ◀

    A: Back.

179–182   What do the four prefixes you have just studied, {**intra**}, {**extra**}, {**intro**}, and {**retro**} mean, respectively? _____, _____, _____, _____

▶ □ ◀

    A: Within; without, outside; into, inward; back.

183   In this sequence (frames 183–186), add one of the four new prefixes that the context requires to complete these words.

    A solution injected within the veins is called an _____venous solution.

▶ □ ◀

    A: Intravenous.

184   If a person tends to look back into the past, we say that he has a _____spective nature.

▶ □ ◀

    A: Retrospective.

185   Something which seems to us to be perceived outside our usual senses is said to be _____sensory.

▶ □ ◀

    A: Extrasensory.

186   A person whose thoughts, feelings, and interest are turned inward is said to be an _____vert.

▶ □ ◀

    A: Introvert.

Two Latin Prefixes Meaning "Not"
(Frames 187–204)

187   The next two Latin prefixes make words negative. How much alcohol does a drink that is *nonalcoholic* contain? _____

▶ □ ◀

    A: None.

188 The prefix {**non**} is a live morpheme and is found prefixed to many nouns, adjectives, and adverbs. Something which is *nonexistent* _____ (does / does not) exist.

▶ □□□ ◀

A: Does not.

189 Were someone to make up a new word with this {**non**} and say that your remarks were *nonfunny*, what would he mean? _____

▶ □□□ ◀

A: That he was not amused.

190 The second negating prefix is {**in**} with the allomorphs {**in / im / il / ir**}. The base {**litera**} = letter. What does someone know who is *literate*? _____

▶ □□□ ◀

A: Letters (i.e., he can read and write).

191 But what is someone who is *illiterate*? _____
_____

▶ □□□ ◀

A: He does not know his letters, that is, cannot read and write.

192 What characterizes something that is *irreplaceable*? _____
_____

▶ □□□ ◀

A: It cannot be replaced.

193 With some words, there is a difference in meaning between {**non**} and {**in**}. A *nonhuman* is something that is not human, as in "It was an environment where only certain *nonhumans* could live." What is a nonhuman? (There are several possible answers.)
_____

▶ □□□ ◀

A: Animal, creature, etc.

194   In your own words, what is someone who is *inhuman?* _____

_____

▶ □ ◀

A: A human who has none of the good qualities that we like to consider human.

195   What would the difference be between an act that was *nonlegal* and one that was *illegal?* _____

_____

▶ □ ◀

A: A nonlegal act is not within the realm of the law (that is, it is neither required by law nor forbidden by law), while an illegal one is against the law.

196   There is one big difficulty with this prefix {in}, meaning "not." There is another prefix {in}, spelled the same way and with the same allomorphs as the negative prefix {in}. This other {in} prefix you saw in *impose* and *infer.* The meaning of the {in} in *impose* is _____.

▶ □ ◀

A: In (or, on or into).

197   The base {lumin} = light. If we *illuminate* a room, we bring light _____ the room.

▶ □ ◀

A: Into.

198   In the word *illuminate* the prefix {il} = _____.

▶ □ ◀

A: Into.

199   The prefix {in} meaning "into" is found chiefly in words like *illuminate, induce* (as in "He *induced* his father to buy him another car"), and *imbibe* (as in "He had *imbibed* too many drinks to be able to converse intelligently"). What class of word are *illuminate, induce,* and *imbibe?* _____

▶ □ ◀

A: Verbs.

200   The negating prefix {in}, however, is attached chiefly to nouns, adjectives, and adverbs. *Gratitude* and *ingratitude* are _____ (synonyms / antonyms).

▶ □ ◀

A: Antonyms.

201   The verb *inflame* means "to cause to burst _____ flames."

▶ □□□ ◀

   A: Into.

202   There is an English adjective that means "easily bursting into flames." What is this word? _____

▶ □□□ ◀

   A: Inflammable.

203   But some people thought that the prefix {in} in *inflammable* was the negating prefix, and mistakenly interpreted the word to mean (in your own words) _____

   _____.

▶ □□□ ◀

   A: Something that will not burn (the exact opposite of its meaning).

204   In order to avoid confusion, the gasoline industry replaced the misleading word *inflammable* with the new word _____.

▶ □□□ ◀

   A: Flammable.

Four New Latin Prefixes
(Frames 205–219)

{**infra**} = below	{**preter**} = beyond, more than
{**per**} = through	{**ultra**} = beyond

205   The base {**ambula**} = walk. An *ambulatory* patient is one who can _____.

▶ □□□ ◀

   A: Walk.

206   The base {**ambula**} occurs in *perambulate*, as in "The official was appointed to *perambulate* the district and verify the boundaries." What was the official supposed to do?

   _____

▶ □□□ ◀

   A: Walk through the district (and check on the boundaries).

207–208   The base {col} = strain. When you *percolate* coffee, you _____ boiling water

_____ the coffee grounds.

▶ □ ◀

    A: Strain; through.

209   In certain parts of the country, it is essential for sanitary reasons to find out whether or

not waste water will _____ _____ the soil.

▶ □ ◀

    A: Percolate through.

210   A *preternatural* ability is one that is _____ what one would naturally expect.

▶ □ ◀

    A: Beyond.

211   What characterizes someone who is *preterhuman?* _____

_____

▶ □ ◀

    A: The person is superhuman, that is, extraordinary.

212   *Infrasonic* sounds are those sounds with frequencies that are _____
(above / below) those audible to the human ear.

▶ □ ◀

    A: Below.

213   What are *ultrasonic* sounds? _____

_____

▶ □ ◀

    A: Those beyond (above) the range audible to the human ear.

214   What is an *ultralightweight* tent? _____

_____

▶ □ ◀

    A: One whose lightness is beyond that of most other tents.

215 An ape is sometimes called an *infrahuman* because it is _____ humans on the evolutionary scale.

▶ □ ◀

   A: Below.

216 Add one of the four prefixes you just had to the word that the context requires in the next sequence of frames.

   The basic installations and services on which a community's existence depends arc called the _____ structure.

▶ □ ◀

   A: Infrastructure. (That is, the infrastructure is beneath everything else, in a figurative sense.)

217 The Duke's actions were so violent that he was thought to have _____ gressed all the laws of God and man.

▶ □ ◀

   A: Pretergressed.

218 The last innovation Uncle George approved of was the invention of money; he was an _____ conservative.

▶ □ ◀

   A: Ultraconservative.

219 The _____ foration had gone entircly through the material.

▶ □ ◀

   A: Perforation.

WORD LIST

Two concepts were presented in this unit:

assimilation 50   live morpheme 108

Here is a list of the words discussed in this unit. Use a dictionary if you need to.

abduct 14
aberrant 23
abstain 29
abstract 31
accede 49
adapt 48
adduce 23
adhere 15
adhesive 15
affluent 49
aggression 49
allocate 49
ambulatory 205
announce 49
antecedent 78
anteposition 162
appetite 49
assimilation 50
assume 49
attraction 49
cede 80
circumference 127
coauthor 86
collaborator 87
commensal 84
commotion 116
compose 141
concede 82
confer 139
conference 127
congress 65
contraposition 168
dedicate 92
deference 127
defrost 97
depose 90
differ 137
difference 127
digress 67
effusive 41
egress 69
eject 23
emit 45
empathy 28

eviscerate 44
exceed 79
ex-convict 115
exit 18
expel 38
expose 142
extracurricular 176
extramural 172
extrasensory 185
flammable 204
gratitude 200
hypothesis 149
illegal 195
illiterate 191
illuminate 197
imbibe 40
impel 37
impose 89
impulse 39
induce 199
induct 17
infer 127
inflame 201
inflammable 202
infrahuman 215
infrasonic 212
infrastructure 216
ingratitude 200
ingress 66
inhuman 194
inject 23
intercede 76
intercollegiate 175
interpose 143
interrupt 107
intramural 171
intravenous 183
introspective 177
introvert 186
irreplaceable 192
literate 190
nonalcoholic 187
nonexistent 188

nonfunny 189
nonhuman 193
nonlegal 195
offer 127
opponent 169
opposition 163
perambulate 206
percolate 208
perforation 219
position 158
post-game 161
postposition 160
precede 77
predetermine 112
pretergress 217
preterhuman 211
preternatural 210
proceed 71
procession 73
progress 64
propose 111
recede 70
redivide 106
refer 127
regress 62
relinquish 93
repose 155
repulsion 7
retroactive 178
retrospective 184
return 105
secede 74
secure 110
suffer 138
superimpose 145
suppose 146
supposition 146
transfer 127
transgress 68
transpose 144
ultraconservative 218
ultralightweight 214
ultrasonic 213

REVIEW EXERCISES

Purpose: To review some of the Latin prefixes

Directions:
With the aid of a dictionary find one word beginning with each of the following prefixes. Easily confused prefixes have been grouped. Choose a word that you wish to learn.
Write the word and at least one meaning.
Write the meaning that the prefix has in your word.
Use the word in a sentence.

1. {**ante**} _____

   _____

2. {**anti**} __(a Greek prefix)_____

   _____

3. {**extra**} _____

   _____

4. {**infra**} _____

   _____

5. {**inter**} _____

   _____

6. {**intra**} _____

   _____

7. {**intro**} _____

   _____

8. {**retro**} _____

   _____

9. {**de**} _____

   _____

10. {**re**} _____

    _____

11. {**se**} _____

    _____

12. {**ab**} _____

    _____

13. {**ad**} _____

    _____

14. {**per**} _____

_____

15. {**pre**} _____

_____

16. {**preter**} _____

_____

17. {**pro**} _____

_____

WORDS OF INTERESTING ORIGIN

Directions: Find in your dictionary the origins of the italicized words. Then write down (a) the language of origin, (b) the etymological meaning (= early meaning), and (c) the modern meaning.

1. "The prison system in this state," said the governor, "is not working as a deterrent to crime; the number of *recidivists* is alarmingly high."

   Language of origin: _____

   Etymological meaning: _____

   Modern meaning: _____

2. *Influenza* reached epidemic proportions last winter.

   Language of origin: _____

   Etymological meaning: _____

   Modern meaning: _____

3. "*Jingoism* and sword-rattling by our politicians," said the Secretary of State, "have become so common as to be a danger to this administration."

   Language of origin: _____

   Etymological meaning: _____

   Modern meaning: _____

4. In America almost every child or youth of school age has a *nickname* like "Chuck" in place of "Charles" or "Peg" in place of "Margaret."

   Language of origin: _____

   Etymological meaning: _____

   Modern meaning: _____

5. To her dismay June discovered that because she was separated from her husband and children she was *ostracized* by most of the community.

    Language of origin: _____

    Etymological meaning: _____

    Modern meaning: _____

EASILY CONFUSED WORDS

Use a dictionary as needed.

1. **Desert / dessert.**   The word *desert*, when pronounced *di zúrt*, is a verb and means *leave* or *abandon*, as in "He *deserted* his friends just when they needed him." When pronounced *déz ərt* it is a noun meaning an uncultivated place, with few or no inhabitants. The word *dessert* (with two *s*'s), pronounced *di zúrt*, is the course served at the end of a meal, often something sweet. Once again, the verb *desert* means abandon, the noun *desert* means a place without much plant or animal life, while *dessert* is a noun and is a course of a meal.

2. **Innocuous / inoculate.**   Although these words look somewhat alike and both come from Latin, they are quite different. *Innocuous* means "harmless," as in "We had been told that the drink was *innocuous*, and indeed it refreshed us all." *Innocuous* comes from Latin {in} = not, {nocu} = harmful, and the adjective suffix {ous}. *Inoculate*, on the other hand, means to create immunity by injecting a disease agent into an animal or plant, as in "Kurt had been *inoculated* against influenza, but he caught the disease just the same." The word breaks down into {in} = into, {ocul} = eye, bud of a plant, and {ate}, a verb suffix. The word *inoculate* earlier meant to graft a bud onto a tree; the word was then transferred to the similar action of introducing a foreign body like a disease agent. The noun is *inoculation*.

3. **Ingenious / ingenuous.**   Both words come from Latin. *Ingenious* means "gifted," as in "Eric was so *ingenious* about household equipment that we never had to have a repairman come in." The word *ingenuous* comes from a Latin word meaning "free born" or "of noble birth." The common meaning now is "frank, open, simple, or naive," as in "The child's questions were so *ingenuous* that we were ready to do anything she asked."

Use the six words in the sentences where each makes sense.

1. The coach's _____ plays delighted the opposition and confused our boys.

2. His simple remarks certainly seemed _____ to us, but the members of the crowd were nevertheless frightened by them.

3. In place of the devious official we expected to have to deal with, we were met by a simple, _____ girl.

4. The great _____ in Africa has always interested me.

5. A mother bear is not likely to _____ her cubs when they are this young.

6. Because of the resemblance to grafting a bud onto a tree, the common preventative of disease has been labeled _____ .

7. The ice cream had melted, so we had no _____ .

LATIN PHRASES

First try to get the meaning of the Latin phrase from the context of the sentences below, choosing a meaning from the list that follows. Write the number of the Latin phrase beside the definition that fits.

1. *Pro forma,* as in "This meeting and the vote are really just *pro forma;* the decision has already been made by the committee."

2. *De jure,* as in "Much as the minority party argued, they could not escape the fact that the president and his advisers were the *de jure* government."

3. *Ad hoc,* as in "The chairperson quickly appointed an *ad hoc* committee to handle this matter."

4. *Ante meridiem,* as in "We will meet at nine o'clock *ante meridiem.*"

5. *In absentia,* as in "The mayor insisted on casting his vote *in absentia,* although the charter specifically outlawed absentee ballots."

_____ illegal   _____ in the manner of an expert

_____ before noon   _____ (formed) for the purpose

_____ legal   _____ although not present

_____ for the sake of appearance   _____ without power to act

_____ not absent   _____ against the government

Use a dictionary to find the word-by-word translation and the modern meaning for each phrase.

	Word-by-Word Translation	Modern Meaning
pro forma	_____	_____
de jure	_____	_____
ad hoc	_____	_____
ante meridiem	_____	_____
in absentia	_____	_____

UNIT SEVEN

Useful Suffixes, Greek and Latin

This unit will treat some common suffixes borrowed from Greek and Latin. We will emphasize those English suffixes which are {full}, that is, give a lot of information.

CONTENTS

1–13	Review
14–31	The Greek Suffix {oid}
32–74	Greek Suffixes Common in Medicine
75–102	Review Frames for Greek Suffixes
103–135	Seven Noun Suffixes from Latin
136–153	Review of Material in Frames 103–135
154–180	Five Adjective Suffixes from Latin
181–197	Review Frames for the Last Sequence

Review
(Frames 1–13)

1 What do we call the three basic parts of a word such as *opposition*? _____,

_____, _____

▶ □ ◀

A: Prefix, base, and suffix.

2–4 Identify the prefix, the base, and the suffix of *opposition:* prefix = {_____}; base =
{_____}; suffix = {_____}.

▶ □ ◀

A: {ob} or allomorph {op}; {posit}; and {ion}.

5–6 Which two of the three elements have we emphasized the most so far in the program?
_____ and _____.

▶ □ ◀

A: Prefixes; bases.

7 We will now work on suffixes. The information carried by {**ion**} in *opposition* is mainly
that *opposition* is a/an _____ (noun / verb / adjective / adverb).

▶ □ ◀

A: Noun.

8 However, in the context of a sentence such as "The revolution brought both benefits and
troubles to the common people," we know that *revolution* is a noun not only from the
suffix {**ion**} but from the fact that the word *revolution* fills (in your own words) _____

_____

▶ □ ◀

A: A noun slot in the sentence (that is, it is preceded by *the*).

9 When an English word is in isolation (= stands alone) we often cannot tell what class of
word it is. Take the word *walks*. We do not know whether it is noun or verb, but when we
put *walks* into the slot in the sentence "He sweeps the walks," we know what class of
word it is. What is it? _____

▶ □ ◀

A: A noun.

10 What class of word is *walks* in the context "He *walks* to work every morning"? _____

▶ □□ □ □□□□ □ □□□ □□□ □□ □□□ □□□ □ □□□□ □□□ □□□□ □□□□ □ ◀

   A: A verb.

11 However, there are many English words where a suffix alone indicates the class of word. What part of speech is the word *nation?* _____

▶ □□ □ □□□□ □ □□□ □□□ □□ □□□ □□□ □ □□□□ □□□ □□□□ □□□□ □ ◀

   A: Noun.

12 What morpheme tells us that this word is a noun? _____

▶ □□ □ □□□□ □ □□□ □□□ □□ □□□ □□□ □ □□□□ □□□ □□□□ □□□□ □ ◀

   A: The suffix {ion}.

13 There are many English suffixes that carry much more meaning than just an indication of the class of word. There are, for example, a number of English morphemes taken from Greek and Latin which form nouns that contain such concepts as "quality" or "condition." One suffix showing quality or condition is Latin {itas}, as in Latin *puritas*, which in English becomes {y}, as in *purity*. You have seen this English morpheme {y} in such words as

   dignity, which is the _____ or _____ of being worthy of honor or esteem.

▶ □□ □ □□□□ □ □□□ □□□ □□ □□□ □□□ □ □□□□ □□□ □□□□ □□□□ □ ◀

   A: Condition or quality.

The Greek Suffix {oid}
(Frames 14–31)

14 Here is an example of a {full} suffix which appears in English adjectives. It is the Greek derivative {oid}, which means "similar to." A *human-oid* in a science fiction book would

   be a bug-eyed monster that nevertheless resembles a _____ in appearance.

▶ □□ □ □□□□ □ □□□ □□□ □□ □□□ □□□ □ □□□□ □□□ □□□□ □□□□ □ ◀

   A: Human being.

15 What would an animal described as *anthrop-oid* resemble? _____

▶ □□ □ □□□□ □ □□□ □□□ □□ □□□ □□□ □ □□□□ □□□ □□□□ □□□□ □ ◀

   A: A human being.

16 Since *anthropoid* and *humanoid* have about the same meaning, what do we call them?

_____

▶ □ ◀

    A: Synonyms.

17 The base {**human**} is Latin; what language does the base {**anthrop**} come from? _____

▶ □ ◀

    A: Greek. (In case you forgot, you saw this in Unit 4.)

18 Is this suffix {**oid**} added to _____

(just Greek bases / just Latin bases / both Greek and Latin bases)?

▶ □ ◀

    A: Both Greek and Latin bases (but not common with Latin bases.)

19 What shape is a *spheroid*? _____

▶ □ ◀

    A: Similar to (or like) a sphere.

20 What is a *philanthropist*? _____

▶ □ ◀

    A: A person who gives money to worthy causes.

21 Some people who work in philanthropic institutions like the Ford Foundation or the Carnegie Corporation sometimes humorously refer to themselves as *philánthrop-oids*. This implies that they are not real philanthropists, because they are not wealthy. But who do

these executives resemble? _____

▶ □ ◀

    A: Philanthropists.

NICE-TO-KNOW ■ The meaning of the suffix {oid} is familiar enough that people can expect they will be understood if they make up a word like *philanthropoid*.

22 Latin base {**ov/ovi**} = egg. A bird is an *oviferous* animal. What does it do? _____

_____

▶ □ ◀

    A: It lays eggs.

23 What is an *ovoid* object shaped like? _____

▶ □ ◀

    A: An egg.

24 Greek base {**aster**} = star. *Asteroid* is the name given to small celestial bodies. From the meanings of the base and suffix, what does *asteroid* mean? _____

▶ □ ◀

    A: An object like a star.

25 But since we know that stars are large and burning, while asteroids are small and cold, a better name than asteroid might be *plánetoid*. What does *planetoid* mean? _____
_____

▶ □ ◀

    A: An object like a planet.

26 What shape is a *discoid* body? _____

▶ □ ◀

    A: Like a disc, that is, round and flat.

27 What is the shape of something described as *petaloid?* _____

▶ □ ◀

    A: Like a petal.

28 The name of the Greek letter for the sound /s/ is *sigma*. What, therefore, is the shape of the *sigmoid flexure*, the lower part of the colon? _____

▶ □ ◀

    A: It is shaped like the letter *s*.

29 The name of the Greek letter for the sound /d/ is *delta*. This Greek letter *delta* is a triangle standing on its base, like this: Δ. When a muddy river runs into the sea, it deposits its sediment like this:

What do we call this fan of sediment? _____

▶ □ ◀

    A: Delta.

30 The large muscle of the shoulder, whose function is to raise the arm, is called the *déltoid*. What is its shape? _____

▶ □ ◀

   A: Like the Greek letter *delta*.

31 An object which is described as *cylíndroid* is not a cylinder but _____

▶ □ ◀

   A: Shaped something like a cylinder.

Greek Suffixes Common in Medicine
(Frames 32–74)

32 Greek {**gastr / gastro**} = stomach. If you have *gastr-ítis*, what part of your body is inflamed? _____

▶ □ ◀

   A: The stomach.

33 Greek {**larynx / laryng / laryngo**} = larynx (upper part of the windpipe). A person who is hoarse may be suffering from *laryng-ítis*. Define *laryngitis:* _____
_____

▶ □ ◀

   A: An inflammation of the larynx.

34 Therefore, what does the suffix {**itis**} mean? _____

▶ □ ◀

   A: Inflammation.

35 Since almost any part of the body can become inflamed, it is obvious that there are _____ (few / many) derivatives with the {**itis**} suffix.

▶ □ ◀

   A: Many.

36 What is *tonsill-ítis?* _____

▶ □ ◀

   A: Inflammation of the tonsils. (Note the single rather than double *l*.)

37 If the tonsillitis becomes serious, a *tonsill-éc-tom-y* may be necessary. Greek {ek}, which becomes English {ec}, means "out." The base {tom} means "cut" and the suffix {y} means "act of." Therefore, what is a *tonsillectomy?* _____

_____

▶ □ ◀

A: The act of cutting out the tonsils.

38 Another suffix derived from Greek is much used in medicine and carries a great deal of meaning. This is {sis}, meaning either "condition" or "abnormal condition." Let us take examples of the "abnormal" meaning.

Latin {halito} = breath. *Halitó-sis* is the condition of having a / an _____ (pleasant / unpleasant) breath.

▶ □ ◀

A: Unpleasant.

39 Greek {hypno} = sleep. What kind of sleep is *hypnó-sis*, natural or unnatural? _____

▶ □ ◀

A: Unnatural.

40 Greek {neuro} = nerve. Define *neuró-sis* (in your own words): _____

_____.

▶ □ ◀

A: Abnormal condition of the nerves; today restricted to a nervous disorder without demonstrable physical cause.

41 Greek {psycho} = mind. Define *psychó-sis* (in your own words): _____

_____.

▶ □ ◀

A: A major mental disorder.

42 Greek {sclero} = hard. Define *scleró-sis* (in your own words): _____

_____.

▶ □ ◀

A: Abnormal hardening (as of the arteries).

43 Greek {oma} = an abnormal swelling; tumor. Greek {carcin} = crab; cancer. Define *carcin-óma* (in your own words): _____.

▶ □□ □ □ □□ □ □□ □ □ □ □□ □□ □ □ □□ □ □ □□ □ □□ □ □ □ □□ □□ □ □□ □ □ □□ □ ◀

    A: A cancerous swelling; a malignant tumor.

44 Greek {oste} = bone. *Oste-óma* means a swelling of _____.

▶ □ □ □ □□ □ □ □□ □□ □ □ □□ □ □ □□ □ □ □□ □ □□ □ □ □□ □□ □ □ □ □□ □ □ □ □ ◀

    A: Bone (a benign type of tumor).

45 What does a physician cut when he performs an *osteó-tomy?* _____

▶ □ □ □ □□ □ □ □ □□ □ □ □ □□ □ □ □□ □ □ □□ □ □□ □ □ □ □□ □ □ □□ □ □ □ □□ □ ◀

    A: Bone.

46 Greek {my} = mouse, muscle. Define *my-óma* (in your own words): _____
_____.

▶ □ □ □ □ □□ □ □ □□ □ □ □□ □ □ □ □□ □ □ □□ □ □□ □ □ □□ □ □ □□ □ □ □ □□ □ □ ◀

    A: A tumor found on muscular tissue.

47 Latin {lymph} = spring water. *Lymph* is a liquid in the body. Would you assume from its derivation that this liquid is clear or opaque? _____

▶ □ □ □ □□ □ □ □ □□ □ □ □□ □ □ □ □□ □ □ □□ □ □ □□ □ □ □□ □ □ □□ □ □ □ □□ □ ◀

    A: Clear.

48 Define *lymph-óma* (in your own words): _____

▶ □ □ □ □□ □ □ □□ □ □ □□ □ □ □□ □ □ □□ □ □ □□ □ □ □ □□ □ □ □□ □ □ □□ □ □ □ ◀

    A: Abnormal growth in the lymph system.

49 Greek {card / cardio} = heart. What is *card-ítis?* _____

▶ □ □ □ □ □□ □ □ □□ □ □ □ □□ □ □ □□ □ □ □□ □ □ □□ □ □ □□ □ □ □□ □ □ □ □□ □ ◀

    A: Inflammation of the heart.

50 Greek {graph / gram} = write. What does a *cárdio-gram* record? _____
_____

▶ □ □ □ □□ □ □ □ □□ □ □ □□ □ □ □□ □ □ □□ □ □ □ □□ □ □ □□ □ □ □□ □ □ □ □□ □ ◀

    A: (The beating of) the heart.

51 What can a physician do with a *larýngo-scope?* _____

□ □

   A: Look at the larynx.

52 A physician using this instrument can perform a *laryngó-scop-y.* (Remember, {**y**} = act of.) Define *laryngoscopy* (in your own words): _____

_____.

□ □

   A: The act of visually examining the larnyx.

53 If a serious abnormality is found it may be necessary to perform a *laryng-éc-tom-y.* Define this operation (in your own words): _____

_____.

□ □

   A: The removal of part or all of the larynx.

54 Greek {**cyst/cysto**} = urinary bladder. A person who experiences a burning sensation while urinating may have *cyst-ítis.* Define this (in your own words): _____

_____

□ □

   A: Inflammation of the urinary bladder.

55 To examine this condition a physician may perform a *cystó-scop-y.* What does he do?

_____

□ □

   A: Visually examines the bladder.

56 This viewing is done by means of a special optical instrument. Can you form the word for this instrument? _____

□ □

   A: Cystoscope.

57 Greek {**metro / meter**} = measure. It may also be necessary to test the pressure in the bladder by performing a *cysto-métro-gram.* This is a procedure that makes a _____ record of the _____ of the pressure in the bladder.

□ □

   A: Written; measurement.

58 In extreme cases it may be necessary to perform a *cyst-éc-tom-y*. What is this operation?

_____

▶ □ ◀

  A: (Surgical) removal of the urinary bladder.

| **NICE-TO-KNOW** ■ The combining form that means "act of cutting out" is sometimes {**tomy**} and sometimes {**ectomy**}.

59 Greek {**ot / oto**} = ear; Latin {**media**} = middle. What is *ot-ítis média?* _____

_____

▶ □ ◀

  A: Inflammation of the middle ear.

60 Greek {**rhin / rhino**} = nose. What is *rhin-ítis?* _____

▶ □ ◀

  A: Inflammation of (the membranes of) the nose.

61 Greek {**ceros**} = horn. What gives a *rhinó-ceros* its name?

_____

▶ □ ◀

  A: It has a horn (or horns) on its nose.

62 What diseases does an *oto-rhino-laryngó-log-ist* specialize in? _____

_____

▶ □ ◀

  A: Diseases of the ear, nose, and throat.

63 Greek {**rrhea**} = flowing, discharge. Define *oto-rrhéa:* _____

_____

▶ □ ◀

  A: Discharge from the ear.

64 Greek {**logo**} = talk, words. What would you think a person does who is said to be suffering from *logo-rrhéa?* _____

▶ □ ◀

  A: He talks too much.

65 Define *rhino-rrhéa:* _____ .

▶ □□□ ◀

    A: Discharge from the nose.

66 Greek {**gastr** / **gastro**} = stomach. What kind of operation is a *gastr-éc-tom-y?* _____
_____

▶ □□□ ◀

    A: (Surgical) removal of the stomach.

67 Greek {**enter** / **entero**} = intestine. Define *gastro-enter-ítis:* _____
_____

▶ □□□ ◀

    A: Inflammation of the stomach and intestinal system.

68 What is an *enteró-tom-y?* _____

▶ □□□ ◀

    A: Removal of part or all of an intestine.

69 What does a *gastro-enteró-logist* specialize in? _____
_____

▶ □□□ ◀

    A: Diseases of the stomach and intestines (that is, of the digestive system).

70 What is the suffix that means a person who is skilled in a field? {_____}

▶ □□□ ◀

    A: {ist} or {logist}

71 One of the most common Greek suffixes in English is {**ize**}, which makes a verb out of nouns and adjectives. For example, "He *sterilized* the bottle carefully" means that he caused the bottle to become _____ .

▶ □□□ ◀

    A: Sterile.

72 To *theorize* about the origins of life is to make up _____ on the subject.

▶ □□□ ◀

    A: Theories.

73 Several {ize} words are avoided by some speakers of English. An example of one of these inferior words, as they appear to some, is the word used to mean "go to *social* events," as in "During their first year in Washington they _____ a great deal."

▶ □□ ◀

A: Socialized.

74 Another {ize} word looked down upon by some people is a word that means "bring to completion," as in "In order to present a complete report this morning, they worked all night to _____ it."

▶ □□ ◀

A: Finalize.

Review Frames for Greek Suffixes
(Frames 75–102)

■ We will now ask you to do a more difficult task, namely, to produce some of the words you have just used in frames 32–74. Here is a menu of these words; you may have to refer to it often.

carcinoma	*cystoscope*	*gastroenterologist*
cardiogram	*cystoscopy*	*halitosis*
carditis	*enterotomy*	*hypnosis*
cystectomy	*finalize*	*laryngectomy*
cystitis	*gastrectomy*	*laryngitis*
cystometrogram	*gastritis*	*laryngoscope*

75 What is the medical term for "bad breath"? _____

▶ □□ ◀

A: Halitosis.

76 What is the medical term for "cancer"? _____

▶ □□ ◀

A: Carcinoma.

77 What word is used for an operation where the larynx is removed? _____

▶ □□ ◀

A: Laryngectomy.

78 What is the name of the instrument by which visual examination of the bladder is possible? _____

▶ □□ ◀

   A: Cystoscope.

79 What is the name of the act of using such an instrument? _____

▶ □□ ◀

   A: Cystoscopy.

80 Inflammation of the larynx = _____.

▶ □□ ◀

   A: Laryngitis.

81 An instrument for visual examination of the larynx = _____.

▶ □□ ◀

   A: Laryngoscope.

82 A doctor who specializes in the disorders of the digestive system = _____.

▶ □□ ◀

   A: Gastroenterologist.

83 A tracing of the action of the heart = _____.

▶ □□ ◀

   A: Cardiogram.

84 Sleep which is psychically induced = _____.

▶ □□ ◀

   A: Hypnosis.

85 Inflammation of the bladder = _____.

▶ □□ ◀

   A: Cystitis.

■ Repeat this task using the following menu of words, still from frames 32–74. Use the menu as much as you like; after all, "otorhinolaryngologist" is quite a mouthful.

laryngoscopy	*otitis media*	*rhinorrhea*
logorrhea	*otorhinolaryngologist*	*sclerosis*
lymphoma	*otorrhea*	*socialize*
myoma	*psychosis*	*sterilize*
neurosis	*rhinitis*	*tonsillectomy*
osteoma	*rhinoceros*	*tonsillitis*
osteotomy		

86   What word is used for a major mental disorder? _____

▶ □ ◀

   A: Psychosis.

87   What word describes a mental disorder less severe than psychosis? _____

▶ □ ◀

   A: Neurosis.

88   What word means surgical removal of the tonsils? _____

▶ □ ◀

   A: Tonsillectomy (spelled with two *l*'s).

89   What is the name for an inflammation of the tonsils? _____

▶ □ ◀

   A: Tonsillitis.

90   What is the suffix meaning "inflammation"? {_____}

▶ □ ◀

   A: {itis}

91   Inflammation of the middle ear = _____ _____

▶ □ ◀

   A: Otitis media.

92   A tumor found on muscular tissue = _____.

▶ □ ◀

   A: Myoma.

93   Abnormal swelling in the lymphatic system = _____.

▶ □ ◀

    A: Lymphoma.

94   Excessive use of words = _____.

▶ □ ◀

    A: Logorrhea.

95   Make something free from germs = _____.

▶ □ ◀

    A: Sterilize.

96   Inflammation of the nose = _____.

▶ □ ◀

    A: Rhinitis.

97   Animal with one or two horns on the nose = _____.

▶ □ ◀

    A: Rhinoceros.

98   Discharge from the ear = _____.

▶ □ ◀

    A: Otorrhea (spelled with two *r*'s).

99   Hardening of part of the body, such as the arteries = _____.

▶ □ ◀

    A: Sclerosis.

100   Go out frequently to social gatherings = _____.

▶ □ ◀

    A: Socialize.

101   A doctor who specializes in the ear, nose, and throat = _____.

▶ □ ◀

    A: Otorhinolaryngologist.

102 Benign bone tumor = _____.

▶ □ ◀

A: Osteoma.

Seven Noun Suffixes from Latin
(Frames 103–135)

103 Refer to this menu of morphemes (suffixes and bases) that will occur in the series of frames that follow. Look them over first, if you like, but don't try to memorize them now.

NOUN SUFFIXES:

{**ence**} = quality, state, condition, as in *competence*
{**ion**} = action, condition caused by an action, as in *correction*
{**ity**} = condition, state, as in *acidity*
{**or**} = agent, doer, as in *inventor*
{**or**} = condition, as in *pallor*
{**tude**} = condition, state, as in *magnitude*
{**ure**} = action or result of action, as in *aperture*

TWENTY-TWO LATIN BASES (note that in some cases the base is combined with a prefix):

{**acid**} = sharp	{**grati / grate**} = thanks
{**alti**} = high	{**humid**} = wet
{**apert**} = open	{**invent**} = come upon, find
{**arid**} = dry	{**invest**} = put (something) into
{**compet**} = strive in competition with someone, be qualified to strive	{**liberal**} = generous
	{**magni**} = large
{**confid**} = trust	{**object**} = throw against
{**conscript**} = enroll, enlist	{**pall**} = pale
{**correct**} = rule, guide	{**sculpt**} = carve
{**eras**} = rub out	{**sequ**} = follow
{**ferv**} = heat, glow	{**stup**} = be motionless
{**fus**} = melt, flow	

In frames 103–135 you will need to rely on both the context and the menu in order to obtain the answers.

{**ity**} = condition or state. This suffix is found in numerous words.

First example: "The lab tests showed that George's stomach trouble was due to excessive *acíd-ity*." Define *acidity*: _____

▶ □ ◀

A: Condition of having too much acid in the system, particularly in the stomach.

104 Second example: "The extreme *aríd-ity* of the region made enterprises like farming, which need water, virtually impossible." What does the suffix {**ity**} mean? _____

▶ □ ◀

A: Condition or state.

105 What does *arid* mean? _____

▶ □□ ◀

A: Dry.

106 Third example: "Jones' *liberal-ity* in gifts to his old college raised its standards so high that his son was refused admission because his grades were too low." What is a synonym of *liberality?* _____

▶ □□ ◀

A: Generosity.

107 What is the condition of being wet or humid called? _____

▶ □□ ◀

A: Humidity.

108 We just had an antonym of *humidity*. What was it? _____

▶ □□ ◀

A: Aridity.

109 What is the Anglo-Saxon synonym for *aridity?* _____

▶ □□ ◀

A: Dryness.

110 {or} = agent or doer.

First example: "Edison, because of his many scientific discoveries, is one of the world's best known *in-vent-or-s*." Which word, *invention* or *inventor*, describes the person who does something? _____

▶ □□ ◀

A: Inventor.

111 Second example: "Because John thought that all wars were wrong, he became a conscientious *ob-ject-or*." What morpheme in the word *objector* tells us that it refers to a person who objects, not the thing objected to? {_____}

▶ □□ ◀

A: {or}

112   Third example: "Through his lucky speculations in the stock market he acquired the reputation of being a shrewd *in-vést-or*." If you wanted advice on investing your money, would you consult an *investor* or an *investment?* _____

▶ □□□ ◀

   A: Investor.

113   What does the morpheme {or} in these three examples mean? (In your own words):

   _____

▶ □□□ ◀

   A: Actor or doer (that is, a person—or thing—which does something).

114   What do we call a person who collects things?   _____

▶ □□□ ◀

   A: Collector.

115   There is another Latin {or} suffix with an entirely different meaning; this {or} shows condition.

   First example: "Diane had been in bed so many weeks without ever seeing the sun that the *páll-or* of her skin was in contrast with that of her well-tanned friends." *Pallor* is the _____ of being a _____ color.

▶ □□□ ◀

   A: Condition; pale.

116   Second example: "Mary was so astounded that she stood there in a *stúp-or*." Define *stupor* (in your own words). Use the menu for the meaning of the base.   _____

   _____

▶ □□□ ◀

   A: Condition of being unable to move or talk.

117   Third example: "Ann brought such *férv-or* to the new problem that she spent all her time and energy in the laboratory." Which does *fervor* describe, the condition of being excited or the agent who excites others?   _____

▶ □□□ ◀

   A: The condition of being excited.

118 {**tude**} = condition, state.

First example: "The *mágni-tude* of the task before Dan quite discouraged him." *Magnitude* is the _____ of being _____.

▶ □□ ◀

A: Condition; large.

119 The Anglo-Saxon suffix {**ness**} means about the same as {**tude**} borrowed from Latin. There arc four Anglo-Saxon synonyms for *magnitude* that use this {**ness**} suffix. Give *one* of them. _____

▶ □□ ◀

A: Largeness (or greatness, or hugeness, or bigness).

120 Second example: "The plane was unable to gain sufficient *álti-tude* to clear the mountain pass." The condition that the plane failed to meet was being _____ enough.

▶ □□ ◀

A: High.

121 Third example: "Jane was full of *gráti-tude* for the assistance that had been given her." If we were to use a word with the {**grati / grate**} base but with the Anglo-Saxon {**ness**} suffix, we would say that the emotion Jane felt was _____.

▶ □□ ◀

A: Gratefulness.

122 {**ence**} = quality, state, condition.

First example: "Ron did not acquire necessary *cóm-pet-ence* in German to be appointed to the position in Berlin." *Competence* is the quality that a person shows who is _____ to do something.

▶ □□ ◀

A: Qualified.

123 How good was Ron's command of German in the sentence given as an example of the word *competence?* _____

▶ □□ ◀

A: Not good enough.

124 Second example: "Mary had great *cón-fid-ence* in her ability to pass the course." Mary felt that she _____ (had / did not have) the skills necessary to get a passing grade in the class.

▶ □ ◀

    A: Had.

125 Fill in the blank: "Because of her good grades, Mary was _____ that she could do well on the examination."

▶ □ ◀

    A: Confident.

126 What class of word is *confident?* _____

▶ □ ◀

    A: Adjective.

127 What class of word is *confidence?* _____

▶ □ ◀

    A: Noun.

128 Third example: "The Smiths' trip was a *séqu-ence* of minor disasters, all of them comical in retrospect." We describe things as occurring in a *sequence* when they _____ one another regularly.

▶ □ ◀

    A: Follow.

129 {**ion**} = action, or a condition caused by action.

First example: "Mr. Winters wrote on the blackboard a list of the students' errors with the *cor-réct-ion-s*." What did Mr. Winters do to the students' errors he wrote on the board? _____

▶ □ ◀

    A: Corrected them.

130 Second example: "The *con-script-ion* of poor farmers to fight an enemy overseas was not popular, and these soldiers who had been forced into service were hard to train." Define *conscription* (in your own words): _____

_____.

▶ □ ◀

A: Compulsory enrollment of people into the army or navy.

131 Third example: "The unprecedented *fús-ion* in America of so many races, creeds, and languages was accompanied by some difficulties." *Fusion* occurs when two metals are heated and _____ together.

▶ □□ ◀

A: Flow.

132 {**ure**} = action or result of action.

First example: "Because the light on the snow at this altitude was so bright, Alec knew he should reduce the *ápert-ure* of his camera one stop more than his light meter indicated." An *aperture* is an _____ in a camera that lets in light.

▶ □□ ◀

A: Opening, that is, it is the result of opening.

133 Second example: "The Chartres Cathedral is distinguished for three separate kinds of beauty: its architecture, its stained glass, and its *scúlpt-ure*." What is a person called who carves in stone? _____

▶ □□ ◀

A: Sculptor.

134 What do we call the result of his carving? _____

▶ □□ ◀

A: Sculpture.

135 Third example: "The responsibility for unfortunate (or fortunate) *de-lét-ions* of an important segment of the tape has never been satisfactorily assigned." What is a synonym for *deletion* that contains the base {**ras**}? _____

▶ □□ ◀

A: Erasure.

Review of Material in Frames 103–135
(Frames 136–153)

■ In this sequence you will produce some of the words you have just practiced in Frames 103–135. The menu of them is on the next page; refer to it as needed.

altitude	*erasure*	*magnitude*
aperture	*fervor*	*objector*
competence	*fusion*	*pallor*
confidence	*gratitude*	*sculpture*
conscription	*inventor*	*stupor*
correction	*investor*	

136 What do we call a person who discovers a new way of doing something?

_____

▶ □□ ◀

   A: Inventor.

137 What do we call someone who is opposed to something? _____

▶ □□ ◀

   A: Objector.

138 What is a person called who puts money into property? _____

▶ □□ ◀

   A: Investor.

139 What is the word that means "condition of being unable to move or speak"? _____

_____

▶ □□ ◀

   A: Stupor.

140 What word with the {or} suffix means "condition of being in an aroused state of excitement"? _____

▶ □□ ◀

   A: Fervor.

141 What does the suffix in the word *magnitude* mean? _____

▶ □□ ◀

   A: Condition of being.

142 What word is a synonym of "height"? _____

▶ □□ ◀

   A: Altitude.

143 What word means "condition of being thankful or of showing thanks"? _____

▶ □□ ◀

    A: Gratitude.

144 "Ron did not have the ability to learn a foreign language." What word with the suffix {**ence**} is a synonym of "ability"? _____

▶ □□ ◀

    A: Competence.

145 What quality does a person have who is "confident"? _____

▶ □□ ◀

    A: Confidence.

146–147 Give the meanings of the morphemes of the word *correction*: {**cor**} = an intensifying prefix; {**rect**} = _____; and {**ion**} = _____.

▶ □□ ◀

    A: Rule or guide; action or condition.

148 What word means "compulsory enrollment for military service"? _____

▶ □□ ◀

    A: Conscription.

149 What word means "act of flowing together"? _____

▶ □□ ◀

    A: Fusion.

150 What do we call the opening in a camera through which light passes into the camera? _____

▶ □□ ◀

    A: Aperture.

151 What does an artist create who carves statues? _____

▶ □□ ◀

    A: Sculpture.

152 What word means "result of removing something by rubbing out"? _____

▶ □ ◀

   A: Erasure.

153 What noun means "condition of being without color"? _____

▶ □ ◀

   A: Pallor.

Five Adjective Suffixes from Latin
(Frames 154–180)

154 Below are five adjective suffixes from Latin, combined with both old and new bases. Use this menu as you wish.

ADJECTIVE SUFFIXES:

{**ble**} = having capability or capacity, as in *audible*
{**id**} = in the condition of, as in *pallid*
{**ile**} = having capability or capacity, as in *fragile;*
    also similar to, as in *senile*
{**ine**} = having the nature of, as in *asinine*
{**ose / ous**} = full of, as in *glorious*

NINETEEN BASES:

{**asin**} = donkey	{**leon**} = lion
{**audi**} = hear	{**morb**} = sick
{**can**} = dog	{**naviga**} = sail a boat
{**flex**} = bend	{**pall**} = pale
{**frag**} = break	{**pecuni**} = money
{**gel**} = frost, ice	{**sen**} = old
{**glori**} = fame	{**stup**} = be motionless
{**infant**} = young child	{**ven**} = vein
{**juven**} = young	{**verb**} = word
	{**vir**} = man, male

{**id**} = in the condition of.

First example: "Diane had been so many weeks without even seeing the sun that her *pàll-id* skin was in contrast with that of her well-tanned friends." If this frame sounds familiar, don't be surprised. It was much like frame 115 of this unit, but instead of speaking of Diane's "pallid skin" we said earlier that it was the _____ of her skin that made Diane noticeable.

▶ □ ◀

   A: Pallor.

155 Second example: "Don dove into the lake, but a second's contact with the *gél-id* water sent him splashing and sputtering back to shore." What was the temperature of the water in this lake? _____

▶ □ ◀

A: Cold, freezing, icy.

156 Third example: "A *mórb-id* belief that he was responsible for his brother's low grades in school led to Harry's own scholastic failure." Does this mean that Harry's worry about his brother was normal or abnormal? _____

▶ □ ◀

A: Abnormal.

157–158 What class of word has {or}, as in *ríg-or?* _____ What class of word has {id}, as in *ríg-id?* _____

▶ □ U □ ◀

A: Noun. Adjective.

159 Many {or} nouns have adjectives with the suffix {id}, meaning "in the condition of." What adjective means "having pallor"? _____

▶ □ ◀

A: Pallid.

160 What is the adjective of *splendor* that has the suffix {id}? _____

▶ □ ◀

A: Splendid.

161 What adjective with the {id} suffix describes someone in a *stupor?* _____

▶ □ ◀

A: Stupid. (A more common sense of *stupid* is, of course, "lacking intelligence.")

162 {ile} = having capability or capacity, similar to.

First example: "Betty was particularly careful in wrapping the teacups she was sending Sue because they were so *frág-ile.*" These teacups had the capability of being _____ .

▶ □ ◀

A: Broken.

163 Second example: "It was pitiful to see a man so young now looking and acting *sén-ile*." This young person was acting like an _____ man.

▶ □ ◀

    A: Old.

164 Third example: "The critic was much embarrassed to discover that the author of the poem that he had described as *júven-ile* was actually a ten-year-old." Someone described as acting like a *juvenile* is exhibiting the worst features of people who are _____.

▶ □ ◀

    A: Young.

165 The adjective *senile* describes people who show the _____ aspects of old age.

▶ □ ◀

    A: Worst.

166 However, when we describe a man as *vír-ile*, we mean that he exhibits some of the best qualities of a mature _____.

▶ □ ◀

    A: Male, man.

167 How does a person act who is *ínfant-ile?* _____

▶ □ ◀

    A: Like a baby.

168 {**ble**} = having capability or capacity.

First example: "The class gave *aúdi-ble* approval of the teacher's announcements about postponing the test." The response of the students was one that could be _____.

▶ □ ◀

    A: Heard.

169 Second example: As the name suggests, the old *Fléxi-ble* Flyer sleds could _____ with the bumps in the snow.

▶ □ ◀

    A: Bend.

170 Third example: One of the great adventure stories of all time was the search for the Northwest Passage, a *náviga-ble* route from Europe to the fabled east by going to the north of the land mass of America. The explorers were looking for a route that could be

_____ by _____s.

▶ □ ◀

A: Traveled (navigated, sailed); ships.

171 {**ine**} = having the nature of. This suffix is unusual in that it is attached almost exclusively to bases that refer to people or animals, and particularly to animals. Use the menu in frame 154 where necessary for the following sequence of frames.

First example: "Personally I find Tom's sense of humor invariably *ásin-ine!*" In the speaker's opinion, what animal does Tom act like? _____

▶ □ ◀

A: A donkey.

172 Second example: "Major Rollins was not only one of the leading lion-hunters of his time but he was perfectly formed for the role: his *léon-ine* head would have graced the walls of any hunting lodge." What animal did the Major look like? _____

▶ □ ◀

A: A lion.

173 Third example: "The Count's evil smile (if one can call it a smile) revealed *cán-ine* teeth that were much longer and sharper than usual or necessary." The *canine* teeth in a human are the four teeth on either side of the upper and lower jaws, between the incisors and the bicuspids. Why have they received this name? _____

_____

▶ □ ◀

A: They look like the teeth of a dog.

NICE-TO-KNOW ■ One of the words which has this {ine} suffix meaning "having the nature of " but which does not refer to people or animals is *marine,* meaning "belonging to the ocean."

174 {**ose / ous**} = full of. Use the menu in frame 154 for the meanings of the bases if you wish.

First example: "The team's victory was so *glóri-ous* that everyone could share in the rewards." *Glorious* means _____ of _____.

▶ □ ◀

A: Full; glory.

175   Second example: "At that time Rick was so *im-pecúni-ous* that he ate at the Elite Cafe." Considering Rick's finances, how did the prices at the Elite Cafe probably compare with those of other restaurants in town? _____ (higher / lower / about the same)

▶ □ ◀

   A: Lower.

176   The prefix {**in**} in *impecunious* means _____.

▶ □ ◀

   A: Not.

177   {**pecuni**} = _____ and {**ous**} = _____ _____.

▶ □ ◀

   A: Money; full of.

178   *Pecunious* is not a common word but it means _____.

▶ □ ◀

   A: Having money.

179   Third example: "The speaker was so long-winded and *verb-óse* that most of the audience went to sleep." What was the speaker full of? _____

▶ □ ◀

   A: Words.

180   Certain insects have *vén-ous* wings. Describe the wings of these insects: _____
_____.

▶ □ ◀

   A: They have prominent veins.

Review Frames for the Last Sequence
(Frames 181–197)

   ■ In this drill you will produce the following words. Study this menu first, if you like, and refer to it as necessary.

asinine	*glorious*	*navigable*
audible	*impecunious*	*pallid*
canine	*infantile*	*senile*
flexible	*juvenile*	*venous*
fragile	*leonine*	*verbose*
gelid	*morbid*	*virile*

Choose a synonym from this menu to replace the words in parentheses.

181 "As he heard the list of accusations his face became (white) and glistened with perspiration." Synonym: _____.

▶ □ ◀

    A: Pallid.

182 "To our surprise, our host showed none of the symptoms of (old age) deterioration we had been led to expect from our inquiries." Synonym: _____.

▶ □ ◀

    A: Senile.

183 "With a (lion-like) roar Mr. Dawson leaped to his feet; I could almost see his tail lashing." Synonym: _____.

▶ □ ◀

    A: Leonine.

184 "Such a talent for using unnecessary words can hardly be described as just being (talkative)." Synonym: _____.

▶ □ ◀

    A: Verbose.

185 "Sue was much impressed by the (manly) appearance of the guide." Synonym: _____.

▶ □ ◀

    A: Virile.

186 "At Priscilla's words I thought mournfully that truly my only real friends were (dogs)." Synonym: _____.

▶ □ ◀

    A: Canines. (In frame 173 *canine* was an adjective; here it is a noun.)

187   "The first year we were so (poor) that we lived in a cold water apartment with our books displayed in orange crates." Synonym: _____.

▶ □ ◀

   A: Impecunious.

188   "Tim's interest in accidents seemed (sick) to the rest of us." Synonym: _____.

▶ □ ◀

   A: Morbid.

189   "There was praise for all in the (magnificent) victory." Synonym: _____.

▶ □ ◀

   A: Glorious.

190   "The environment of much of the Arctic is particularly (subject to damage)." Synonym: _____.

▶ □ ◀

   A: Fragile.

191   "Blood that is (carried by the veins) is darker in color than arterial blood because it has released its oxygen and taken up carbon dioxide." Synonym: _____.

▶ □ ◀

   A: Venous.

192   "Phil's (donkey-like) remarks had ceased to be a joke at this point." Synonym: _____.

▶ □ ◀

   A: Asinine.

193   "'Our rules here are (not rigid),' said Mr. Peterson." Synonym: _____.

▶ □ ◀

   A: Flexible.

194 "Art should have realized that the water in the shower in the hut, coming directly from the glacier, was (cold)." Synonym: _____.

▶ □□□ ◀

   A: Gelid.

195 "Frank seemed doomed to play the part of a (young man) in all his plays." Synonym: _____.

▶ □□□ ◀

   A: Juvenile.

| **NICE-TO-KNOW** ■ While *fragile, senile,* and *infantile* are used only as adjectives, *juvenile* can be both an adjective, as in "juvenile delinquent," and a noun, as in "He played the part of a juvenile."

196 "'Are you sure that this bay is (fit for sailing) for our boat when the tide is out?' asked the captain." Synonym: _____.

▶ □□□ ◀

   A: Navigable.

197 "Jim's injuries were so serious that his directions to us were hardly (able to be heard)." Synonym: _____.

▶ □□□ ◀

   A: Audible.

WORD LIST

Here is a list of the words discussed in this unit. Refer to a dictionary if you need to.

acidity 103	fusion 131	pallid 154
altitude 120	gastritis 32	pallor 115
anthropoid 15	gelid 155	pecunious 178
aperture 132	glorious 174	petaloid 27
arid 105	gratefulness 121	philanthropist 20
aridity 104	gratitude 121	planetoid 25
asinine 171	halitosis 38	psychosis 41
asteroid 24	humanoid 14	purity 13
audible 168	humidity 107	rhinoceros 61
canine 173	hypnosis 39	sclerosis 42
carcinoma 43	impecunious 175	sculptor 133
cardiogram 50	infantile 167	sculpture 133
collector 114	inventor 110	senile 163
competence 122	investor 112	sequence 128
confidence 124	juvenile 164	sigmoid 28
confident 125	largeness 119	spheroid 19
conscription 130	laryngitis 33	splendid 160
correction 129	leonine 172	socialize 73
cylindroid 31	liberality 106	sterilize 71
cystitis 54	logorrhea 64	stupid 161
delta 29	lymph 47	stupor 116
deltoid 30	magnitude 118	theorize 72
dignity 13	morbid 156	tonsillectomy 37
erasure 135	navigable 170	tonsillitis 36
fervor 117	neurosis 40	venous 180
finalize 74	objector 111	verbose 179
flexible 169	oviferous 22	virile 166
fragile 162	ovoid 23	

OPTIONAL WORDS (MEDICAL TERMS)

carditis 49	gastroenteritis 67	osteoma 44
cystectomy 58	gastroenterologist 69	osteotomy 45
cystometrogram 57	laryngectomy 53	otorhinolaryngologist 62
cystoscope 56	laryngoscope 51	otorrhea 63
cystoscopy 55	laryngoscopy 52	otitis media 59
discoid 26	lymphoma 48	rhinitis 60
enterotomy 68	myoma 46	rhinorrhea 65
gastrectomy 66		

REVIEW EXERCISES

Directions: Match the definitions in the right-hand column with the morphemes in the left-hand column by writing the correct letters in the spaces provided.

SUFFIXES

I. _____ 1. {or}
   _____ 2. {oid}
   _____ 3. {ile}
   _____ 4. {ence}
   _____ 5. {oma}

a. having the capability or capacity
b. quality, state
c. abnormal swelling
d. agent, doer
e. similar to

II. _____ 1. {ine}
    _____ 2. {ose, ous}
    _____ 3. {ble}
    _____ 4. {itis}
    _____ 5. {tude}

a. full of
b. condition
c. having the nature of
d. having the capability
e. inflammation

BASES

III. _____ 1. {gastr / gastro}
     _____ 2. {fus}
     _____ 3. {graph}
     _____ 4. {ferv}
     _____ 5. {scope}
     _____ 6. {tom}

a. bent
b. cut
c. see
d. flow
e. young
f. stomach
g. heat
h. write

IV. _____ 1. {frag}
    _____ 2. {enter}
    _____ 3. {pecuni}
    _____ 4. {oto}
    _____ 5. {metro}
    _____ 6. {sequ}

a. sick
b. measure
c. follow
d. break
e. intestine
f. money
g. be motionless
h. ear

Directions: Match the definitions in the right-hand column with the words in the left-hand column.

V. _____ 1. carcinoma
   _____ 2. aperture
   _____ 3. oviferous
   _____ 4. sclerosis
   _____ 5. pallor
   _____ 6. gastritis

a. inflammation of the stomach
b. condition of being pale
c. opening
d. egg-laying
e. a cancerous swelling
f. removal of an intestine
g. abnormal hardening
h. swelling of nerves

VI. _____ 1. deltoid
   _____ 2. audible
   _____ 3. asteroid
   _____ 4. erasure
   _____ 5. otorrhea
   _____ 6. sigmoid

a. deletion
b. like the letter *s*
c. planetoid
d. discharge from the ear
e. triangular shaped muscle of the shoulder
f. can be heard

VII. _____ 1. fusion
   _____ 2. asinine
   _____ 3. enterotomy
   _____ 4. conscription
   _____ 5. impecunious
   _____ 6. verbose

a. draft
b. like a donkey
c. without money
d. joining
e. talkative
f. surgical removal of an intestine

WORDS OF INTERESTING ORIGIN

Here are biographical notes for ten more eponymous persons.

Louis *Braille* (1809–1852), a blind teacher in France, invented a system of printing for the blind consisting of a pattern of raised dots.

Anders *Celsius* (1701–1744) invented a temperature scale in which 0° is the freezing point and 100° the boiling point of water.

Nicolas *Chauvin* was a general notorious for his unreasoning support of the lost cause of Napoleon.

Gabriel *Fahrenheit* (1686–1736) invented a scale for measuring heat in which 0° was the freezing point of snow and salt equally mixed by weight and 100° was the (approximate) normal temperature of the human body. The freezing point of water on this scale is 32°, the boiling point 212°.

Frankenstein was a medical student in a novel by Mary Wollstonecraft Shelley, wife of the poet. The student created a monster who eventually killed him.

F. A. *Mesmer* (1734–1815) was a German physician who experimented with hypnotism.

Madam *Pompadour* (1721–1764) was the glamorous mistress of the French king Louis XV, known for her elaborate hair styles.

The 4th *Earl of Sandwich* (1718–1792) was said to have been so keen a gambler that he would not leave the gambling table to eat but had a special fast food item brought to him.

William A. *Spooner* (1844–1930) was an English clergyman known for his unintentional transposing of sounds, like "our queer old Dean" in place of "our dear old Queen."

Around 1850 in San Francisco, *Levi* Strauss produced pants of heavy denim, reinforced with copper rivets.

Use these eponymous words to answer the questions.

Braille	*Fahrenheit*	*mesmerized*	*sandwich*
Celsius	*Frankenstein*	*pompadour*	*spoonerism*
chauvinistic	*Levis*		

1. On what scale does water freeze at 32° and boil at 212°? _____

2. What do we call the substitution of "A well-boiled icicle" for "a well-oiled bicycle"? _____

3. What do we call pants made of heavy denim, often blue? _____

4. What do we call a common light meal consisting of a slice of cheese, ham, and so forth between two slices of bread? _____

5. On what scale does water freeze at 0° and boil at 100°? _____

6. What is the name of the system of printing for the blind? _____

7. How would you describe a person who seemed hypnotically fascinated with something? _____

8. What do we call a hairdo in which the hair is brushed up high from the forehead? _____

9. What was the name of the scientist who created a monster? _____

10. What kind of a pig is a man who refuses women their proper rights? _____

EASILY CONFUSED WORDS

Use a dictionary as needed.

1. **Adapt / adopt.**   Both words are of Latin origin. *Adapt* (Latin {**ad**} + {**apt**} = fit) means "to change to meet a new situation," as in "The dinosaurs may have been unable to *adapt* themselves to climatic change." *Adopt* is from Latin {**ad**} + {**opt**} = choose. When we *adopt* something we choose it for ourselves. *Adopt* commonly has the meaning of bringing a child into a family and raising it as one's own child. "When we bear children, God gives them to us, but when we *adopt* a child we choose it for ourselves." If we were to *adopt* the customs of another culture we would act like a native, but if we *adapt* them we change them.

2. **Pore / pour.**   The verb *pore* is from Middle English of uncertain origin and means "read" and "study intensely," as in "Erick was a tireless scholar; he would *pore* over his books without a break until everyone else in the dormitory had gone to sleep." It is usually used with the word *over*. *Pour* is another Middle English word whose origin we are not certain of. It is a verb, both transitive and intransitive. An example of the transitive is, "He *poured* himself another glass of milk," while the intransitive is used in "It never rains but it *pours*."

3. **Accept / except.**   Both words are Latin in origin, and both have the base {**cept**} = take. When you *accept* something, you take it to yourself; when you *except* something, you take it out of the rest. Examples: "I gladly *accept* what you say" and "I *except* from my criticism the great state of New Hampshire."

Use the six words in the sentences where each makes sense.

1. John did his best to act the scholar; but whenever he got his book opened and his pipe lit he

   fell asleep before he had spent even half an hour _____ over his work.

2. You can't go out now; it's _____ cats and dogs.

3. You are the best American we have met; you have made a real attempt to _____ to our customs.

4. Fred _____ the criticism gracefully.

5. They all respected Melvin because of the effort he had made to _____ the customs of the islanders.

6. I wish you would _____ employees over 60 from your annual picnic.

LATIN PHRASES

First try to get the meaning of the Latin phrases from the context of the sentences below, choosing a meaning from the list that follows. Write the number of the Latin phrase beside the definition that fits.

1. *Ipse dixit*, as in "In reply to your criticism of Mr. Jones' decision, all I can say is that you must obey his *ipse dixit* or resign."

2. *Ipso facto*, as in "Professor Kitto has already announced to his classes that he will not meet with them again; and our opinion is that he has *ipso facto* resigned."

3. *Bona fide*, as in "Of course if this sum of money represents a *bona fide* offer and not just a fishing expedition, we will reconsider our position."

4. *Ad hominem*, as in "This entire matter has been argued *ad hominem* and we have not discussed the issue at all."

5. *Ad rem*, as in "I am glad that the opposition have now decided to stop talking *ad hominem* and are now addressing themselves *ad rem*."

_____ questionable evidence   _____ tactful suggestion

_____ toward the man   _____ by that very action

_____ arbitrary statement by a person in power   _____ trial

_____ in good faith   _____ for humane purpose

_____ away from the man   _____ to the point at issue

Use a dictionary to find the word-by-word translation and the modern meaning for each phrase.

	Word-by-Word Translation	Modern Meaning
ipse dixit	_____	_____
ipso facto	_____	_____
bona fide	_____	_____
ad hominem	_____	_____
ad rem	_____	_____

UNIT EIGHT

More Compound Words

So far we have spoken about words as being made up of morphemes; in this unit we will speak of certain words as being built of "combining forms." Some of these combining forms actually consist of several morphemes. Many of the words in this unit are not common words, and many will be new to you. They were carefully chosen to illustrate how English words are built.

You will also see that many words can have both "literal" and "figurative" meanings, depending on the context in which they occur.

CONTENTS

1–4	Review
5–22	Ten Greek Combining Forms
23–32	Review of {logy} and {logist} Words
33–66	More Combining Forms
67–95	Review of Preceding Frames
96–131	Combining Forms, Both Old and New, Derived from Latin
132–143	Six Latin Bases
144–161	Six More Latin Bases
162–178	Literal and Figurative Meanings

Review
(Frames 1–4)

1   What is a minimal unit of meaning called? _____

▶ □ ◀

A: Morpheme.

2   The word *morpheme* is a compound word made up of a Greek base {**morph / morpho**} = form, shape, and a French suffix {**eme**} = irreducible unit. In your own words, define *morphology*. _____

_____

▶ □ ◀

A: It is the study of the smallest pieces of words that convey meaning.

│ **NICE-TO-KNOW** ■ The study of morphology is not simple. In fact, a course in morphology constitutes a whole se-
│ mester of study at upper-class college or graduate level.

3   Take for example the word *morphology* itself. What does {**log**} mean? _____

▶ □ ◀

A: Study of.

4   The {**y**} is essentially an {**empty**}, serving mainly to show what class of word *morphology* is. What class of word is it? _____

▶ □ ◀

A: Noun.

Ten Greek Combining Forms
(Frames 5–22)

■ In this sequence we will deal with types of words that we say are made up of two **combining forms,** although each combining form may sometimes be composed of two or more morphemes, like {**logy**}.

5–6   For example, we can divide the word *tonsillectomy* into two parts, which we call combining forms, namely {_____} and {_____}.

▶ □ ◀

A: {tonsill} and {ectomy}.

7 How many morphemes are in fact present in the combining form {**ectomy**}? _____

▶ ◻◻◻ ◀

A: Three.

8–10 The three morphemes in the combining form {**ectomy**} are {_____}, {_____}, and {_____}.

▶ ◻◻◻ ◀

A: {ec}, {tom}, and {y}.

11 We will also use braces, which strictly indicate *morphemes* (elements that cannot be further divided), for *combining forms* consisting of two or more _____.

▶ ◻◻◻ ◀

A: Morphemes.

12 Here are ten combining forms from Greek that are found with {**logy**}, meaning "study of," and {**logist**}, meaning "person who studies." Familiarize yourself with this menu and use it for reference in the series of frames that follows. You have already encountered some of these morphemes.

{**anthropo**} = man	{**geo**} = land, earth
{**bio**} = life	{**horo**} = hour, time
{**entomo**} = notched animal, insect	{**neuro**} = nerve
{**ethno**} = a race or nation of people	{**patho**} = suffering, disease, feeling
{**etymo**} = basic meaning of a word	{**psycho**} = soul, mind

Identify these fields of study, using the menu if you wish. Usually, you will not use exactly the same words as those given in the answer. If in doubt, go to your dictionary.

Biology is the study of all types of _____ things.

▶ ◻◻◻ ◀

A: Living (both plants and animals).

13 In your own words, define *geology*. _____

_____

▶ ◻◻◻ ◀

A: Study of the earth (its nature and its history, as well as the development of its crust).

14 What is *ethnology*? _____

▶ ◻◻◻ ◀

A: Study of different races of mankind.

15 What field is *ethnology* a branch o, anthropology or psychology? _____

▶ □□□ ◀

    A: Anthropology.

16 What does an *etymologist* study? _____

▶ □□□ ◀

    A: The history of words.

17 However, the word *entomology*, which looks so much like *etymology*, means the

_____ .

▶ □□□ ◀

    A: Study of insects.

18–19 *Horology* is both the science of measuring _____ and the art of manufacturing

_____s.

▶ □□□ ◀

    A: Time; clocks (watches).

20 *Pathology* is a term for a broad area of study. Define it. _____

_____

▶ □□□ ◀

    A: Study of disease (and the changes caused by disease).

21 What does a *neurologist* study? _____

_____

▶ □□□ ◀

    A: Structure and diseases of the nervous system.

22 What does a *psychologist* study? _____

▶ □□□ ◀

    A: The mind.

Review of {logy} and {logist} Words
(Frames 23–32)

23 We will now ask you to produce the {**logy**} and {**logist**} words you just practiced. Review the last sequence if you need to.

Here is the menu of the words from which you will be asked to choose in the next sequence. Refer to this menu as necessary.

anthropology *etymology* *neurologist*
biology *geology* *pathology*
entomology *horology* *psychologist*
ethnology

What is a doctor called who specializes in the nervous system? (Choose from the menu.)
_____

▶ □ ◀

   A: Neurologist.

24 What do we call a person who studies the mind? _____

▶ □ ◀

   A: Psychologist.

25 What is the name of the study of diseases in general? _____

▶ □ ◀

   A: Pathology.

26 What is the study of living things, both plants and animals? _____

▶ □ ◀

   A: Biology.

27 Study of the derivations of words = _____ .

▶ □ ◀

   A: Etymology.

28 Study of insects = _____ .

▶ □ ◀

   A: Entomology.

29 Study of the races of mankind = _____ .

▶ □ ◀

   A: Ethnology.

30   Of what larger field is *ethnology* a branch?   _____

▶ □ ◀

    A: Anthropology.

31   Study of the earth = _____.

▶ □ ◀

    A: Geology.

32   Study of the measurement of time = _____.

▶ □ ◀

    A: Horology.

More Combining Forms
(Frames 33–66)

33   You will now be asked to recognize some of the combining forms from frames 5–22, used with new combining forms taken from Greek. You will also encounter some words where all the combining forms will be new to you. Do this carefully; you will be asked to produce these words in the sequence after this.

A *hóro-scope*, which is based on the apparent position of the planets and stars at a

person's _____ of birth, looks into the person's future.

▶ □ ◀

    A: Hour (or time).

34   What does *geó-graphy* describe?   _____

▶ □ ◀

    A: The earth.

35   An *éthn-ic* festival is one that features the costumes, foods, music, and so forth of one or

more particular _____.

▶ □ ◀

    A: Races or nationalities.

36   What is a *bió-graphy?*   _____

▶ □ ◀

    A: The record of someone's life.

37 A person who is *sym-pathétic* shares in another person's _____.

▶ □ ◀

   A: Emotions, feelings.

38 What sort of ailment is *neur-ítis?* _____

▶ □ ◀

   A: Inflammation of a nerve.

39 What does a *psycho-ánalyst* analyze? _____

▶ □ ◀

   A: Someone's mind.

I **NICE-TO-KNOW** ■ The term *psychoanalysis* refers to the methods developed by Sigmund Freud and others.

40–41 A *psycho-path* is a person who _____s from a disorder of the _____.

▶ □ ◀

   A: Suffers; mind.

42 Greek {**phag**} = eating. What does an *entomó-phagous* animal eat? _____

▶ □ ⊓ ⊓ □ □ □ □ ◀

   A: Insects.

43 Greek {**ichthyo**} = fish. What does *ichthyó-phagous* mean? _____

▶ □ ◀

   A: Fish-eating.

44–45 *Ichthy-ósis* is an _____ condition of the skin in which the skin resembles that of a _____.

▶ □ ◀

   A: Abnormal; fish.

46 Greek {**sapro**} = rotten. What is the food of a *sapró-phagous* animal or plant?

_____

▶ □ ◀

   A: Decaying (rotten) matter.

47   What does someone suffering from *dys-phágia* have difficulty in doing? _____

▶ □□□ ◀

   A: Eating (or swallowing).

48   Greek {**rhizo / rhiz**} = root. What does a *rhizó-phagous* animal do? _____
_____

▶ □□□ ◀

   A: It eats roots.

49   Why are the filaments of certain mosses called *rhíz-oid?* _____
_____

▶ □□□ ◀

   A: Because they resemble roots.

50   What does the etymology of the word *geó-metry* show about the original use of this branch
of mathematics? What did it measure? _____

▶ □□□ ◀

   A: Land.

51   What is an *íchthy-oid* animal? _____

▶ □□□ ◀

   A: One that resembles a fish.

52   Greek {**iatr / iatro**} = doctor or treatment. What does a *psych-íatrist* try to treat?
_____

▶ □□□ ◀

   A: Disorders of the mind.

53   Greek {**hipp**} = horse. What is *hipp-íatry* the study of? _____

▶ □□□ ◀

   A: Diseases of horses.

54   Greek {**pus / pod**} = foot. What does a *pod-íatrist* specialize in? _____

▶ □□□ ◀

   A: Disorders of the feet.

55 How many feet does an *ócto-pus* have? _____

▶ □□□ ◀

    A: Eight.

56–57 From the morphemes you can see that a *gástro-pod* is a mollusk—a snail, for example—whose _____ seems to be located on its _____.

▶ □□□ ◀

    A: Foot; stomach.

58 Greek {**ornith / ornitho**} = bird. What does an *ornithó-logist* do? _____

▶ □□□ ◀

    A: Studies birds.

59 Define *órnith-oid*. _____

▶ □□□ ◀

    A: Like a bird.

60 Greek {**ger**} = old. What is the field of *ger-iátrics?* _____

_____

▶ □□□ ◀

    A: Study of the diseases or problems of old people.

61 Greek {**carcin / carcino**} = cancer. What does a *carcíno-gen* do? _____

_____

▶ □□□ ◀

    A: It causes cancer.

62 Greek {**partheno**} = virgin. The *Parthenon* in Athens received its name because it was sacred to Athena, who was a _____ goddess.

▶ □□□ ◀

    A: Virgin.

63 *Partheno-génesis* is reproduction of seed, ovum, or spore without fert _____ tion.

▶ □□□ ◀

    A: Fertilization.

64 What is a disease that is identified as *iatro-génic?* _____

_____

▶ □□□ ◀

    A: It is caused by medical treatment.

65 That is, the treatment by the doctor (a) cured it, (b) had no effect on it, (c) brought it on, or (d) removed the symptoms of it. _____

▶ □□□ ◀

    A: (c), brought it on. (Used especially of imaginary symptoms induced by a physician's words or actions.)

66 *Ichthyo-phóbia* is the _____ of _____ for religious reasons.

▶ □□□ ◀

    A: Avoidance, rather than fear, of fish. (There is no way you could know this; count "fear of fish" correct.)

Review of Preceding Frames
(Frames 67–95)

67 In this sequence you will choose a word from the following menu to fit the definitions presented in the frames.

biography	geography	iatrogenic
carcinogen	geometry	ichthyophagous
dysphagia	geriatrics	ichthyophobia
entomophagous	hippiatry	ichthyoid
ethnic	horoscope	ichthyosis
gastropod		

What is an adjective that means "designating races of man"? _____

▶ □□ ◀

    A: Ethnic.

68 Science of treating horses = _____.

▶ □□ ◀

    A: Hippiatry.

69 Caused by a physician = _____.

▶ □□ ◀

    A: Iatrogenic.

70   Something that causes cancer = _____.

▶ □□ ◀

    A: Carcinogen.

71   Astrological forecast = _____.

▶ □□ ◀

    A: Horoscope.

72   A snail with a stomach that is used as a means of locomotion = _____.

▶ □□ ◀

    A: Gastropod.

73   Account of someone's life = _____.

▶ □□ ◀

    A: Biography.

74   Fish-eating = _____.

▶ □□ ◀

    A: Ichthyophagous.

75   Fishlike = _____.

▶ □□ ◀

    A: Ichthyoid.

76   Insect-eating = _____.

▶ □□ ◀

    A: Entomophagous.

77   Difficulty in swallowing = _____.

▶ □□ ◀

    A: Dysphagia.

78   Branch of mathematics dealing with measurements of points, lines, surfaces, and solids = _____.

▶ □□ ◀

    A: Geometry.

79 What word means "measurement of the earth"? _____

▶ □□□ ◀

   A: Geometry.

80 Study of the problems of the elderly = _____.

▶ □□□ ◀

   A: Geriatrics.

81 Study of the surface of the earth, the climate, crops, and so on = _____.

▶ □□□ ◀

   A: Geography.

82 Disease that causes the skin to look like fish scales = _____.

▶ □□□ ◀

   A: Ichthyosis.

83 Avoidance of fish (for religious reasons) = _____.

▶ □□□ ◀

   A: Ichthyophobia.

84 Here are the rest of the words used in frames 33–66. Follow the same directions and use the following menu of words.

neuritis	*podiatrist*	*rhizoid*
octopus	*psychiatry*	*rhizophagous*
ornithoid	*psychoanalyst*	*saprophagous*
ornithologist	*psychopath*	*sympathetic*
parthenogenesis		

Inflammation of nerves = _____.

▶ □□□ ◀

   A: Neuritis.

85 A doctor who follows the teachings of Freud in treating disorders of the mind = _____.

▶ □□□ ◀

   A: Psychoanalyst.

86 Having the same feelings as someone else = _____.

▶ □□□ ◀

    A: Sympathetic.

87 Branch of medicine concerned with the study of disorders of the mind =

_____.

▶ □□□ ◀

    A: Psychiatry.

88 Rootlike = _____.

▶ □□□ ◀

    A: Rhizoid.

89 A marine animal with eight feet = _____.

▶ □□□ ◀

    A: Octopus.

90 A person suffering from mental disorders, especially when characterized by defective character or personality, = _____.

▶ □□□ ◀

    A: Psychopath.

91 A person specializing in disorders of the feet = _____.

▶ □□□ ◀

    A: Podiatrist.

92 A person studying birds = _____.

▶ □□□ ◀

    A: Ornithologist.

93 Production of young by a female without fertilization by a male =

_____.

▶ □□□ ◀

    A: Parthenogenesis.

94   Resembling a bird = _____.

▶ □□ ◀

     A: Ornithoid.

95   Eating rotting organic matter = _____.

▶ □□ ◀

     A: Saprophagous.

Combining Forms, Both Old and New, Derived from Latin
(Frames 96–131)

96   Use this menu as you feel the need. Also, use your dictionary when necessary for better understanding.

{**carni**} = meat or flesh	{**insecti**} = insect	{**pisci**} = fish
{**cide**} = kill	{**magni**} = big	{**rani**} = frog
{**febri**} = fever	{**omni**} = all	{**sui**} = self
{**frugi / fructi**} = fruit	{**pater / patri**} = father	{**vermi**} = worm
{**fuge**} = drive away, flee	{**pesti**} = troublesome animal,	{**vor / vore**} = eating
{**fy**} = make	plant, etc.	
{**herbi**} = grass		

What does an animal that is *omnivorous* eat? _____

▶ □□ ◀

     A: Everything.

97–98   *Omnivorous* can be divided into two combining forms, namely {_____} and {_____}.

▶ □□ ◀

     A: {omni} and {vorous}.

99–100   Into what two morphemes can the combining form {**vorous**} be divided? {_____} and {_____}.

▶ □□ ◀

     A: {vor} and {ous}.

101   What does an *omnivore* eat? _____

▶ □□ ◀

     A: Everything.

102 What class of word is *omnivore*? _____

▶ □□ ◀

A: Noun.

103 What does a *frugivorous* animal eat? _____

▶ □□ ◀

A: Fruit.

104 What is a *herbivore?* _____

▶ □□ ◀

A: An animal that eats grass.

105 Can you guess the adjective that means "grass-eating"? _____

▶ □□ ◀

A: Herbivorous.

106 What is a *carnivore?* _____

▶ □□ ◀

A: An animal that eats meat.

107 What kind of poison is a *herbicide?* _____

▶ □□ ◀

A: One that kills plants.

108 What is *patricide?* _____

▶ □□ ◀

A: The killing of one's father.

109 What has a person committed who has killed himself? _____

▶ □□ ◀

A: Suicide.

110 Why are some snakes called *ranivorous?* _____

▶ □□ ◀

A: They eat frogs.

111 What does a *pesticide* do? _____

▶ □□ ◀

   A: Kills pests (unwanted plants, animals, insects).

112 What kind of medicine is a *vermifuge*? _____
_____

▶ □□ ◀

   A: It drives worms out of the body.

113 Define an *insectivore*. _____

▶ □□ ◀

   A: An animal or plant that eats insects.

114 What kind of medicine is a *febrifuge?* _____

▶ □□ ◀

   A: One that drives away fever.

115 What do we do if we *magnify* something? _____

▶ □□ ◀

   A: Make it bigger.

116 A *vermicide* is a medicine. What does it do? _____

▶ □□ ◀

   A: Kills (intestinal) worms.

117 Some of you will have noticed an overlap in this unit and Unit Four. There are two words for "insect-eating," one Latin and one Greek. What is the Greek derivative you learned in Unit Four? _____

▶ □□ ◀

   A: Entomophagous.

118 What is the Latin derivative that means "insect-eating"? _____

▶ □□ ◀

   A: Insectivorous.

119 Latin {**pisci**} = fish. The Latin derivative *piscivorous* and the Greek derivative *ichthyophagous* are synonyms and mean _____.

▶ □ ◀

   A: Fish-eating.

■ Use these words, taken from the sequence of frames 96–119, to answer the questions below. The words all come from Latin.

carnivore	insectivore	pesticide
febrifuge	insectivorous	piscivorous
frugivorous	magnify	ranivorous
herbicide	omnivorous	suicide
herbivore	patricide	vermicide
herbivorous		

120 First we will take the words that mean "eating." What means "eating everything"?

_____

▶ □ ◀

   A: Omnivorous.

121 Certain animals live mostly on fruit. What adjective describes them? _____

▶ □ ◀

   A: Frugivorous.

122 What describes an animal, such as a seal, that eats fish? _____

▶ □ ∩ ∩ ∩ □ ◀

   A: Piscivorous.

123 What type of animal, classified by the food it eats, is a cow? It is a _____.

▶ □ ◀

   A: Herbivore.

124 An animal whose diet is like a lion's is called a _____.

▶ □ ◀

   A: Carnivore.

125 What is an animal that eats frogs called? _____

▶ □ ◀

   A: Ranivorous.

126 What kills undesirable weeds, bugs, and so on? _____

▶ □□□ ◀

    A: Pesticide.

127 What is the act of killing oneself called? _____

▶ □□□ ◀

    A: Suicide.

128 What does a person commit who kills his father? _____

▶ □□□ ◀

    A: Patricide.

129 What do we call a medicine that kills worms? _____

▶ □□□ ◀

    A: Vermicide.

130 What word is given to a medicine like aspirin that drives away fever? _____

▶ □□□ ◀

    A: Febrifuge.

131 What word means "make large"? _____

▶ □□□ ◀

    A: Magnify.

Six Latin Bases
(Frames 132–143)

132 In the next series of frames you are to choose a form of the word from the menu below, and to match it with the synonyms in parentheses in the sentences that follow.

{**ag** / **act**} = do, as in *agent* and *reaction*
{**frang** / **fract**} = break, as in *frangible* and *fracture*
{**grav**} = heavy, serious, pregnant, as in *gravity* and *gravid*
{**host**} = enemy, as in *hostile* and *hostility*
{**neglig** / **neglect**} = disregard, as in *negligence* and *neglect*
{**sap** / **sip**} = taste, as in *insipid* and *sapid*

"I see your female guppy is (pregnant); will you try to save me some of the babies?" What word in the menu is a synonym of "pregnant"? _____

▶ □□□ ◀

    A: Gravid.

133 "I never saw a yard looking so (uncared for)." Synonym from menu: _____.

▶ □□□ ◀

    A: Neglected.

134 "The new recipe for pudding turned out to be completely (tasteless)." Synonym: _____.

▶ □□□ ◀

    A: Insipid.

135 "As the crowd closed in, I could see that their feelings toward us were entirely (unfriendly)." Synonym: _____.

▶ □□□ ◀

    A: Hostile.

136 "Once we peeled off the unattractive skin we found the fruit to be cool, juicy, and remarkably (tasty)." Synonym: _____.

▶ □□□ ◀

    A: Sapid.

137 "As we realized the (seriousness) of the situation, our laughter died away." Synonym: _____.

▶ □□□ ◀

    A: Gravity.

138 "John's ski vacation was spoiled by a bad (break) in his leg—from falling off a stool in the bar." Synonym: _____.

▶ □□□ ◀

    A: Fracture.

139 When the senator finished his speech, the (response) from his colleagues was strongly positive. Synonym: _____.

▶ □□□□ □□□□ □□□□ □□□□ □□□□ □□□□ □□□□ □□□□ □□□□ □□□□ □□□□ ◀

    A: Reaction.

140 "All these matters were supposed to be taken care of by Seth, whom I had appointed as my (representative)." Synonym: _____.

▶ □□□□ □□□□ □□□□ □□□□ □□□□ □□□□ □□□□ □□□□ □□□□ □□□□ □□□□ ◀

    A: Agent.

141 "I never would have mailed the package if I had known how (breakable) the contents were." Synonym: _____.

▶ □□□□ □□□□ □□□□ □□□□ □□□□ □□□□ □□□□ □□□□ □□□□ □□□□ □□□□ ◀

    A: Frangible.

142 "I cannot understand this sudden (unfriendliness) that Ann now displays toward us both." Synonym: _____.

▶ □□□□ □□□□ □□□□ □□□□ □□□□ □□□□ □□□□ □□□□ □□□□ □□□□ □□□□ ◀

    A: Hostility.

143 "Through Wayne's (carelessness) I had lost almost all the money I had saved for a new suit." Synonym: _____.

▶ □□□□ □□□□ □□□□ □□□□ □□□□ □□□□ □□□□ □□□□ □□□□ □□□□ □□□□ ◀

    A: Negligence.

Six More Latin Bases
(Frames 144–161)

144 We will use a different technique with six more bases. Again, do not try to learn this menu now but refer to it as you do the series. Consult your dictionary where necessary.

        {**brevi**} = short, as in *brevity* and *abbreviation*
        {**joc**} = jest, fun, as in *jocose* and *jocularity*
        {**nebul**} = cloud, as in *nebula* and *nebulous*
        {**rect**} = right, as in *correct* and *rectitude*
        {**simil / simili**} = like, as in *similar* and *similitude*
        {**squal**} = rough, dirty, as in *squalor* and *squalid*

Using both the meanings of the bases and the context, give the meanings of the following series of words.

Brévi-ty, as in "Jill had not expected a long letter of explanation from her boss, but the *brevity* of his note shocked her." *Brevity* = _____.

▶ □□□ ◀

A: Shortness, briefness.

145 *Simíli-tude,* as in "The *similitude* between the two brothers who had been separated so long was remarkable." *Similitude* = _____.

▶ □□□□□□□□□□□ЦЦЦЦ□□□□□□□□□□□□□□□□□□□□□□□□□□□□□□□□□□□□□□□ ◀

A: Resemblance, likeness.

146 *Squál-or,* as in "Never had Rose believed that any human could live in such disgusting *squalor.*" *Squalor* = _____.

▶ □□□ ◀

A: Dirtiness, filth.

147 *Récti-tude,* as in "It was amusing to see the notorious Horace posing as a model of *recti-tude.*" *Rectitude* = _____.

▶ □□□□□□□□□□ПП□□□□□□□□□□□□□□□□□□□□□□□□□□□□□□□□□□ЦЦЦ□□□□ ◀

A: Uprightness, correctness.

148 *Joc-óse,* as in "Mr. Dibbs turned out to be a great deal of fun, and his *jocose* comments on the dinner had us in stitches." *Jocose* = _____.

▶ □□□ ◀

A: Jolly.

149 *Nébul-ous,* as in "The noted speaker's remarks were so *nebulous* and obscure that only Professor Sims understood the point of the talk." *Nebulous* = _____.

▶ □□□ ◀

A: Cloudy, unclear.

150 We will now ask you to produce these same six words without any clues. Give each word as a synonym for the word or words in parentheses.

"The (filth) in which these people live is unbelievable." Synonym: _____.

▶ □□□ ◀

A: Squalor.

151 "His talk, although (humorous) in manner, had an important message." Synonym:

_____.

A: Jocose.

152 "It has been well said that (shortness) is the soul of wit." Synonym: _____.

A: Brevity.

153 "I see no (resemblance) between the two cases." Synonym: _____.

A: Similitude.

154 "'It was a pleasure,' John said sweetly, 'to have as a speaker someone as (vague) as you.'"
Synonym: _____

A: Nebulous.

155 "The mayor was the picture of civic (correctness) as he rose to speak." Synonym:

_____.

A: Rectitude.

156 You will now use six words with these same bases. Replace the word in parentheses with
a synonym from the menu in frame 144.

"The house and furnishings are (filthy) beyond belief." Synonym: _____.

A: Squalid.

157 "I do not understand the (shortened forms) you used in your paper." Synonym:

_____.

A: Abbreviations.

158 "The two men are really quite (alike) in their views." Synonym: _____.

▶ □□□ ◀

    A: Similar.

159 "In the constellation of Orion there is a great (mass of interstellar dust)." Synonym:

_____.

▶ □□□ ◀

    A: Nebula.

160 "His letter was cold, formal, and quite (according to rules)." Synonym: _____.

▶ □□□ ◀

    A: Correct.

161 "Uncle Reuben's (joking manner) became tiresome after a while." Synonym:

_____.

▶ □□□ ◀

    A: Jocularity.

Literal and Figurative Meanings
(Frames 162–178)

162 Latin {**radic**} = root. When we *e-rádic-ate* a plant, we tear it out by its _____.

▶ □□□ ◀

    A: Roots.

163 If we *eradicate* a problem we (a) completely remove it, (b) make it worse, (c) improve it a little, (d) leave it unchanged. _____

▶ □□□ ◀

    A: (a), completely remove it.

164 We say that *root* in "root of a plant" is used in a **literal** sense because this is its etymological meaning so far as we can determine. In contrast, in "root of a problem" the meaning of *root* is **figurative**; it does not have its etymological meaning or sense.

In which sense is *eradicate* used in "The new mayor *eradicated* the traffic problem"?

_____ (literal / figurative)

▶ □□□ ◀

A: Figurative. (While the concepts of "literal" and "figurative" are useful, it is sometimes difficult to distinguish between them. Not all people agree that *literal* meaning is tied closely to etymological meaning. Subjective judgment often enters.)

165 In what sense is *root* used in "They hope to get at the *root* of the problem"?

_____ (literal / figurative)

▶ □□□ ◀

A: Figurative.

166 In what sense is *root* used in "It did not rain enough to soak down to the *roots* of the tree." _____ (literal / figurative)

▶ □□ ◀

A: Literal.

167 In the next sequence of twelve frames, identify the italicized words as either figurative or literal in meaning.

"Tom gathered *flexible* evergreen branches to make a bed for himself on the ground." Is *flexible* used in a figurative or literal sense? _____

▶ □□ ◀

A: Literal.

168 "When Jim heard these words, he *dissolved* into tears." Figurative or literal?

_____

▶ □□ ◀

A: Figurative. (Jim didn't melt away like ice.)

169 "Henry *navigated* his young friend through all the people at the party to the hostess." Figurative or literal? _____

▶ □□ ◀

A: Figurative. (*Navigate* in its literal sense applies to boats.)

170 "The peace agreement between the two countries was *fragile* indeed." Figurative or literal? _____

▶ □□ ◀

A: Figurative. (Peace does not break the way glass does.)

171 {**ferv**} = heat. "As Milton says, 'The mounted sun shot down direct his *fervid* rays.'" Figurative or literal? _____

▶ □ ◀

    A: Literal. (The sun can burn.)

172 "Marie was not an easy subject to *hypnotize*, and the doctor was unable to put her in a trance." Figurative or literal? _____

▶ □ ◀

    A: Literal.

173 "'Be careful of that box! The contents are *fragile*,' warned Sue." Figurative or literal? _____

▶ □ ◀

    A: Literal.

174 "Smith was a *fervid* supporter of the local football team." Figurative or literal? _____

▶ □ ◀

    A: Figurative.

175 "The admission requirements were more *flexible* than we had thought." Figurative or literal? _____

▶ □ ◀

    A: Figurative.

176 "The opposing team was *hypnotized* by Frank's handling of the ball." Figurative or literal? _____

▶ □ ◀

    A: Figurative.

177 "It took great skill to *navigate* the sailboat through the reef." Figurative or literal? _____

▶ □ ◀

    A: Literal.

178 "The liquid *dissolved* the unknown powder almost immediately." Figurative or literal?

_____

▶ □ ◀

A: Literal.

WORD LIST

The following concepts were presented in this unit:

combining form 5–6   figurative 164   literal 164

Here is a list of the words discussed in this unit. Refer to a dictionary if you need to.

abbreviation 157	geometry 50	octopus 55
agent 140	geriatrics 60	omnivore 101
anthropology 15	gravity 137	omnivorous 96
biography 36	herbicide 109	ornithologist 58
biology 12	herbivorous 105	Parthenon 62
brevity 144	horoscope 33	pathology 20
carcinogen 61	hostile 135	patricide 109
carnivore 106	hostility 142	pesticide 111
correct 160	hypnotize 172	piscivorous 119
dissolve 168	insectivore 113	podiatrist 54
entomology 17	insectivorous 118	psychiatrist 42
eradicate 164	insipid 134	psychoanalyst 39
ethnic 35	jocose 148	psychologist 22
ethnology 14	jocularity 161	psychopath 40
etymologist 16	magnify 115	reaction 139
febrifuge 114	morphology 2	rectitude 147
fervid 171	navigate 169	similar 158
flexible 167	nebula 159	similitude 145
fracture 138	nebulous 149	squalid 156
fragile 170	neglect 133	squalor 146
frangible 141	negligence 143	suicide 109
frugivorous 103	neuritis 38	sympathetic 37
geography 34	neurologist 21	vermifuge 112
geology 13		

OPTIONAL WORDS

dysphagia 47	ichthyosis 44
entomophagous 42	ornithoid 59
gastropod 56	parthenogenesis 63
gravid. 132	ranivorous 110
hippiatry 53	rhizoid 49
horology 18	rhizophagous 48
iatrogenic 64	sapid 136
ichthyoid 51	saprophagous 46
ichthyophagous 43	vermicide 116
ichthyophobia 66	

REVIEW EXERCISES

Each of the italicized words in the sentences below contains a base introduced in this unit. Using this information, try to determine the meaning of the word in context. Then look up the word in a dictionary to confirm your answer.

1. The movements of my grandmother were so *agile* that we all sat there spellbound.

   _____

2. Scientists do much research to identify the *carcinogenic* agents in our environment.

   _____

3. Janice was learning to use the new *centrifuge* in the laboratory.

   _____

4. This new process will require only a *fraction* of the time previously required.

   _____

5. All of the trees in this area of the garden are *fructiferous*.

   _____

6. Research by *geriatricians* has increased considerably in the last several decades.

   _____

7. Even in the face of her critics, Ms. Nelson retained her *magnanimity*.

   _____

8. The dictator considered himself to be *omnipotent*.

   _____

9. The *paternal* instincts of our teacher were apparent in many ways.

   _____

WORDS OF INTERESTING ORIGIN

Directions: Find in your dictionary the origins of the italicized words. Then write down (a) language of origin, (b) etymological meaning (= early meaning), and (c) modern meaning.

1. In a few hours the sails of our competitors had sunk below the *horizon*.

   Language of origin: _____

   Etymological meaning: _____

   Modern meaning: _____

2. The Russians are said to drink considerable amounts of *vodka*.

   Language of origin: _____

   Etymological meaning: _____

   Modern meaning: _____

3. A drink made from fermented mash of grain is called *whiskey* in the United States and Ireland, but *whisky* in Scotland.

    Language of origin: _____

    Etymological meaning: _____

    Modern meaning: _____

4. Keith had adopted a *sardonic* attitude which was most unattractive.

    Language of origin: _____

    Etymological meaning: _____

    Modern meaning: _____

5. Everything seems to be *OK* now.

    Language of origin: _____

    Etymological meaning: _____

    Modern meaning: _____

EASILY CONFUSED WORDS

Use a dictionary as needed.

1. ***Allusion / illusion.***   Both words have the Latin base {**lud / lus**} = mock, make a fool of. *Allusion* means reference to something or someone in an indirect or casual way, as in "Mr. Gooch's brief *allusions* to Larry's distinguished record were so slight as to be ridiculous." *Illusion* means a belief not in accord with the facts, as in "Jane, the very picture of innocence, had the *illusion* that she could portray an older and wicked woman in the new play."

2. ***Alteration / altercation.***   Both words have the Latin morpheme {**alter**} = other, another. *Alteration* means change from one thing to another, as in "After necessary *alterations* of the store we will be open again." *Altercation*, however, means a quarrel with another person, as in "After their brief *altercation* they shook hands, apologized, and had another drink."

3. ***Violation / volition.***   The base of *violation* is Latin {**violat**} = force or violence, but the meaning today is not usually as strong. The word often refers to the breaking of a law, not necessarily with violence, as in "He *violated* the ten-minute parking limit and got the maximum fine of three dollars." We also speak of *violating* someone's privacy. *Volition* has a base Latin {**vel / vol**} = wish, desire, as in "In spite of the rumors, Mary resigned from the team entirely of her own *volition*." In other words, Mary made a deliberate decision to resign.

Use the six words in the sentences where each makes sense.

1. To descend that awful cliff was contrary to Brad's _____.

2. You may pick up the suit as soon as we have made the necessary _____.

3. Erika didn't think Jack's _____ to the weight she had gained was a bit funny.

4. You stand in _____ of the law in three respects.

5. We are all optimistic that we can continue the debate without further _____.

6. When they entered the dimly lit hall, the _____ of being around a campfire in the mountains was perfect.

LATIN PHRASES

First try to get the meanings of the Latin phrases from the context of the sentences below, choosing a meaning from the list that follows. Write the number of the Latin phrase beside the definition that fits.

1. *Alter ego*, as in "Over the years Jud Hudson has become my *alter ego*, and more and more I turn important decisions over to him."

2. *Cum grano salis*, as in "We agree to take Mr. Howard's theories *cum grano salis*."

3. *In extremis*, as in "If we wish to get his signature on the page we must act with haste, for he is lying *in extremis* at his country home."

4. *Tempus fugit*, as in "Even as we speak, action is being taken elsewhere by those who wish us ill. As I said before, *tempus fugit* and the chance for victory will soon pass."

5. *Ex libris*, as in "The first Latin I ever recall seeing as a child was on some book plates my uncle sent, which said *ex libris* and then my name."

_____ with some reservation		_____ changed personality	
_____ former library copy		_____ wholeheartedly	
_____ a long distance away		_____ at the point of death	
_____ second self		_____ the temperature is changing	
_____ time flies		_____ from the library of (so-and-so)	

Use a dictionary to find the word-by-word translation and the modern meaning for each phrase.

	Word-by-Word Translation	Modern Meaning
alter ego	_____	_____
cum grano salis	_____	_____
in extremis	_____	_____
tempus fugit	_____	_____
ex libris	_____	_____

UNIT NINE
What Number, Please?

This unit is built around morphemes that relate to different types of numbers. You will also learn some irregular plural forms of English words, like "one neurosis" but "two neuroses."

CONTENTS

1–73 Latin Cardinal Numbers
74–106 Latin Ordinal Numbers
107–145 Greek Cardinal Numbers
146–150 Greek Ordinal Numbers
151–197 Other Words Showing Number
198–213 Irregular Plurals
214–231 Latin Words Like One *Alumnus* / Two *Alumni* and One *Alumna* / Two *Alumnae*
232–240 Latin Words like One *Stratum* and Two *Strata*
241–243 Greek Words like One *Analysis* / Two *Analyses*
244–256 Review of Greek and Latin Plurals

Latin Cardinal Numbers
(Frames 1–73)

1 First we should mention that Latin has two common sets of numbers. The most common kind in both Latin and English is the set called **cardinal numbers.** These are the ones that answer such questions as "How many fingers am I holding up?" In giving an answer like

six you are using a _____ number.

▶ □□□ ◀

  A: Cardinal.

2 On the other hand, the question "On which finger does a person wear a wedding ring?" gets the answer "On the fourth finger of the left hand." The word *fourth* is called an

ordinal number because the words *first, second, third, fourth* show the _____ in which objects are arranged.

▶ □□□ ◀

  A: Order.

| **NICE-TO-KNOW** ■ The word *cardinal* means "important," but it is hard to see the reasoning behind calling *one, two, three,* and so forth "cardinal numbers."

3 Which of these two is the ordinal number: *twelve* or *third?* _____

▶ □□□ ◀

  A: Third.

4 What kind of numerals do we call *seven* and *ten?* _____

▶ □□□ ◀

  A: Cardinal.

5 What kind of numerals do we call *first, second,* and *third?* _____

▶ □□□ ◀

  A: Ordinal.

6 Here is a menu of the combining forms of Latin cardinal numbers 1–10, as well as 100 and 1,000. Refer to this menu as necessary.

{uni} = 1	{quinqu / quinque} = 5	{nov / novem} = 9
{du}, {bi} = 2	{sex} = 6	{dec / deci / decem} = 10
{tri} = 3	{sept / septem} = 7	{cent / centi} = 100
{quadru / quadri / quadr} = 4	{octo / octi} = 8	{mill / milli} = 1,000

In the series that follows there will be some seldom-used words; in fact, some of them are not in desk dictionaries. They were chosen so that you would be able to practice analyzing words you had never seen before.

Greek {**pleg**} = paralysis. Define a *quadri-pleg-ic*. _____

_____

▶ □ ◀

   A: One who has lost the use of all four limbs.

7 Latin {**digit**} = finger. How many fingers on each hand does a *sex-digit-al* person have? _____

▶ □ ◀

   A: Six.

8 In early times, the calendar the Romans used began in March. Under that system, which number month was *Octo-ber* in the year? _____

▶ □ ◀

   A: Eighth.

9 In that early system, what number month was *Novem-ber?* _____

▶ □ ◀

   A: Nine.

10 What is the combining form that means *nine?* {_____}

▶ □ ◀

   A: {novem} or {nov}

11 What number month in this early calendar was *Decem-ber?* _____

▶ □ ◀

   A: Ten.

12 And what number month was *Septem-ber* in that calendar? _____

▶ □ ◀

   A: Seven.

❙ **NICE-TO-KNOW** ■ The origin of {ber} is not clear.

13 Latin {**foli**} = leaf. What makes a plant *quinque-fóli-ate?* _____

▶ □□□ ◀

   A: It has five leaves.

14 How many wheels does a *bí-cycle* have? _____

▶ □□□ ◀

   A: Two.

15 Greek {**cycle**} = English _____.

▶ □□□ ◀

   A: Wheel.

16 How many wheels are there on a *trí-cycle?* _____

▶ □□□ ◀

   A: Three.

17 How many wheels does a *úni-cycle* have? _____

▶ □□□ ◀

   A: One.

18 Latin {**anni / enni**} = year. How often is a *bi-énni-al* event held? _____

▶ □□□ ◀

   A: Every two years.

19 How often does a *quinqu-énni-al* event occur? _____

▶ □□□ ◀

   A: Every five years.

20 Latin {**pare / pari / para**} = produce children, as in *parent*. How many children does a woman have who is described as an *octí-para?* _____

▶ □□□ ◀

   A: Eight.

21 How many angles are in a *tri-angle?* _____

▶ □ ◀

   A: Three.

22 How many in a *quádr-angle?* _____

▶ □ ◀

   A: Four.

23 How many divisions would a *sex-párt-ite* arrangement have? _____

▶ □ ◀

   A: Six.

24 In ancient Rome there were committees called *septém-vir-ate-s.* How many men were on such a committee? _____

▶ □ ◀

   A: Seven.

25 {later} = side. In a *uni-láter-al* action, how many sides have participated? _____

▶ □ ◀

   A: One.

26 How many sides arc active in a *bi-láter-al* agreement? _____

▶ □ ◀

   A: Two.

27 How many days does one pray who offers a *nov-éna?* _____

▶ □ ◀

   A: Nine.

28 How many people sing in a *du-ét?* _____

▶ □ ◀

   A: Two.

29 A *décem-vir* in ancient Rome was a man who was a member of a board. How many men in all were on this board? _____

▶ □ ◀

A: Ten.

30 How many feet does a *cénti-pede* supposedly have? _____

▶ □ ◀

A: 100.

31 Latin {**pede** / **ped**} = English _____.

▶ □ ◀

A: Foot. (The Greek base is {pus / pod}.)

32 How long a period of time is a *mill-énni-um?* _____

▶ □ ◀

A: 1,000 years.

33 What part of a meter is a *mílli-meter?* _____

▶ □ ◀

A: One-thousandth.

34 A *cent-énni-al* is a celebration of something which happened _____ years ago.

▶ □ ◀

A: 100.

35 From the etymology, how many legs would you expect to find on a *mílli-pede?* _____

▶ □ ◀

A: 1,000. (There are actually far fewer than 1,000.)

36 Frames 36–73 review the Latin cardinal numerals that were presented in frames 1–35. We will now ask you to produce the words that were given as examples of Latin cardinal numbers combined with a base. Review frames 1–35 first if you like. Here is a menu of the words you will use.

bicycle	duet	October	septemvirate
biennial	millennium	quadrangle	sexdigital
bilateral	millimeter	quadriplegic	sexpartite
centennial	millipede	quinquefoliate	triangle
centipede	November	quinquennial	unicycle
December	novena	September	unilateral
decemvir	octipara		

What is the term for a woman who has borne eight children? _____

▶ □□□ ◀

   A: Octipara.

37   What was the name of a committee of seven men in Rome? _____

▶ □□□ ◀

   A: Septemvirate.

38   What is the animal whose name means "having 100 legs"? _____

▶ □□□ ◀

   A: Centipede.

39   And what do we call an animal with (apparently) ten times as many legs?

_____

▶ □□□ ◀

   A: Millipede.

40   What is a series of prayers for nine days? _____

▶ □□□ ◀

   A: Novena.

41   What was the eighth month of the early Roman calendar named? _____

▶ □□□ ◀

   A: October.

42   What was the name of the seventh Roman month? _____

▶ □□□ ◀

   A: September.

43 What was the ninth month in that calendar called? _____

▶ □ ◀

   A: November.

44 And the month that is now the twelfth month was then the tenth month; what was it called? _____

▶ □ ◀

   A: December.

45 What is the term for a person who is paralyzed in all four limbs? _____

▶ □ ◀

   A: Quadriplegic.

46 What kind of treaty is agreed to by two parties? _____

▶ □ ◀

   A: Bilateral.

47 What is the name of the most common two-wheeled vehicle? _____

▶ □ ◀

   A: Bicycle.

48 What is the one-wheeled device used for stunt riding? _____

▶ □ ◀

   A: Unicycle.

49 What word describes a celebration that occurs once every two years?

   _____

▶ □ ◀

   A: Biennial.

50 If an event is held every five years, what is it called? _____

▶ □ ◀

   A: Quinquennial.

51 What term means "having six fingers on one hand"? _____

▶ □ ◀

    A: Sexdigital.

52 What is the word that means "having five leaves"? _____

▶ □ ◀

    A: Quinquefoliate.

53 What is the name of the thousand-year period of peace predicted in Revelations in the New Testament? _____

▶ □ ◀

    A: The Millennium.

54 What is a two-dimensional figure with three sides and three angles called? _____

▶ □ ◀

    A: Triangle.

55 What is a flat figure with four sides and four angles called? _____

▶ □ ◀

    A: Quadrangle.

56 What adjective describes something divided into six parts? _____

▶ □ ◀

    A: Sexpartite.

57 What is the unit that is one-thousandth of a meter? _____

▶ □ ◀

    A: Millimeter.

58 What is a performance by two singers called? _____

▶ □ ◀

    A: Duet.

59 What is a one-hundredth anniversary called? _____

▶ □□□ ◀

   A: Centennial.

60 What was the title of a man on a ten-man board in Rome? _____

▶ □□□ ◀

   A: Decemvir.

61 If only one side has participated in making an agreement, what is the arrangement called? _____

▶ □□□ ◀

   A: Unilateral.

62–73 Give the meanings of the following combining forms showing number.

{quinqu / quinque} = _____   {uni} = _____

{mill / milli} = _____   {sept / septem} = _____

{dec / deci / decem} = _____   {du}, {bi} = _____

{sex} = _____   {tri} = _____

{nov / novem} = _____   {cent / centi} = _____

{quadru / quadri / quadr} = _____   {octo / octi} = _____

▶ □□□ ◀

   A: 5, 1,000, 10, 6, 9, 4, 1, 7, 2, 3, 100, 8.

Latin Ordinal Numbers
(Frames 74–106)

74 As before, refer to this menu of combining forms as necessary.

{primo} = 1st	{quint} = 5th	{non} = 9th
{second} = 2nd	{sext} = 6th	{decim / deci} = 10th
{terti} = 3rd	{sept} = 7th	{centi} = 100th
{quart} = 4th	{octav} = 8th	{milli} = 1,000th

When the custom of *primo-génit-ure* exists, which son gets the entire estate?

_____

▶ □□□ ◀

   A: The first one born.

75 If a woman gave birth to *quint-úplet-s*, how many children did she have at the same birth? _____

▶ □ ◀

A: Five.

76 Where does someone rank who is in the top *quárt-ile* of his class?

_____

▶ □ ◀

A: In the top fourth.

77 A *sécond-ary* road is one that is not a main road. What class of road is it? _____

▶ □ ◀

A: Second.

78 An *óctav-e* is the _____ full tone above a given tone.

▶ □ ◀

A: Eighth.

79 Our system of counting is based on the number 10 and multiples of 10. What name do we give to this system (the name has the morpheme {decim})? _____

▶ □ ◀

A: Decimal.

80 The morphemes {deci}, {centi}, and {milli} are found in many compounds where they mean "part of." For example, what part of a liter is a *deciliter*? _____

▶ □ ◀

A: One-tenth.

81 What part of a meter is a *centimeter*? _____

▶ □ ◀

A: One-hundredth.

82 The unit used to measure radioactivity is named a *curie* after Marie Curie. How large is a *millicurie?* _____

▶ □ ◀

A: One-thousandth of a curie.

83 A *non-ane* fever is one that recurs on the _____ day.

▶ □ ◀

    A: Ninth.

84 Something that is of primary importance is of first importance; what is something that is of *tertiary* importance? _____

▶ □ ◀

    A: Third in importance.

85 What part of a circle is a *sext-ant?* _____

▶ □ ◀

    A: One-sixth.

> **NICE-TO-KNOW** ■ An instrument used in navigation is called a *sextant* because it covers one-sixth of a circle, namely 60 degrees.

86 There are eight positions in fencing. Which of these positions is the one called the *sept-ime?* _____

▶ □ ◀

    A: The seventh.

87 Frames 87–106 are review frames. As in the last series, we will ask you to produce the words that you learned in frames 74–86. Review frames 74–86 if you need to; perhaps take notes. Here are the words you will use.

decimal	quartile	septime
nonane	quintuplets	sextant
octave	secondary	tertiary
primogeniture		

What is the name of a fever that has a nine-day cycle? _____

▶ □ ◀

    A: Nonane.

88 What is the seventh position in fencing called? _____

▶ □ ◀

    A: Septime.

89 What is the system that has the number 10 as its base? _____

▶ □ ◀

    A: Decimal.

90 Those who rank in the top quarter of their class are said to be in the top _____.

▶ □ ◀

    A: Quartile.

91 What is the name of the custom of leaving all the estate to the eldest son?

    _____

▶ □ ◀

    A: Primogeniture.

92 What do we call a set of five babies born at one time? _____

▶ □ ◀

    A: Quintuplets.

93 What is the eighth full tone above another musical note called? _____

▶ □ ◀

    A: Octave.

94 What is a road called that is not ranked as a main or primary road? _____

▶ □ ◀

    A: Secondary.

95 What is a sixth part of a circle called? _____

▶ □ ◀

    A: Sextant.

96 In linguistics, what does one call an accent that is weaker than a secondary accent?

    _____

▶ □ ◀

    A: Tertiary.

97–106   Give the meanings of the following prefixes, which show order.

{quart} = _____   {non} = _____

{primo} = _____   {sext} = _____

{octav} = _____   {quint} = _____

{sept} = _____   {decim / deci} = _____

{second} = _____   {terti} = _____

▶ □ ◀

   A: 4th, 1st, 8th, 7th, 2nd, 9th, 6th, 5th, 10th, 3rd.

Greek Cardinal Numbers
(Frames 107–145)

107   Refer to this menu of Greek morphemes as necessary in the next series.

{heno} = 1	{pent / penta} = 5	{ennea / ennead} = 9
{duo / dy} = 2	{hexa / hex} = 6	{deca} = 10
{tri} = 3	{hept / hepta} = 7	{hecto} = 100
{tetra / tetrad} = 4	{octo} = 8	{kilo} = 1,000

Some athletic coaches in ancient Greece used the *tetrad* system, in which workouts were repeated regularly on the basis of a certain cycle. How many days were in this cycle?

_____

▶ □ ◀

   A: Four.

108   Greek {agon} = angle. A *héx-agon* is a plane figure; how many angles does it have?

_____

▶ □ ◀

   A: Six.

109   A *pént-agon* was once a magical symbol—a type of star. How many points did the star have? _____

▶ □ ◀

   A: Five.

110   What do the believers in *heno-thé-ism* worship? _____

▶ □ ◀

   A: One god.

I **NICE-TO-KNOW** ▪ *Henotheism* is the belief in or worship of one god while not denying the existence of other gods.

111 How many meters are in a *kílo-meter* (also pronounced *kilo-méter)?* _____

▶ □ ◀

A: 1,000.

112 How many fingers on each hand does a person who is *hexa-dactýl-ic* have? _____

▶ □ ◀

A: Six.

113 There is a synonym for *hexadactylic* that is built on Latin morphemes; what is it?

_____

▶ □ ⊓ ⊓ □ □ □ □ □ □ □ □ □ ⊔ ⊔ ⊔ □ □ □ □ ◀

A: Sexdigital.

114 Greek {**cephal**} = head. How many heads does something that is *tri-cephál-ic* have?

_____

▶ □ ⊓ □ □ □ □ □ □ □ □ □ □ □ ⊔ ⊔ □ □ □ ◀

A: Three.

I **NICE-TO-KNOW** ▪ Cerberus, watchdog of the underworld in Greek mythology, was *tricephalic,* according to some ancient authorities.

115 A *hepta-hédron* is a solid figure. How many plane sides does it have? _____

▶ □ ◀

A: Seven.

116 How many legs does an *ócto-pus* have? _____

▶ □ ◀

A: Eight.

117 How many rulers are there in a *dý-arch-y?* _____

▶ □ ◀

A: Two.

118 How many liters are in a *hecto-liter?* _____

▶ □□□ ◀

A: 100.

119 The commandments given to Moses are sometimes called the *deca-log*. How many of these commandments are there? _____

▶ □□□ ◀

A: Ten.

120 The Muses (Greek goddesses like Clio and Calliope who presided over literature and the arts and sciences) are sometimes called the *ennead*. How many Muses were there? _____

▶ □□□ ◀

A: Nine.

121 Frames 121–145 review Greek cardinal numbers. We will now ask you to produce words, like *tetrad*, which you saw in frames 107–120. Review frames 107–120 if necessary. You will be asked to use the following words:

decalog	heptahedron	octopus
dyarchy	hexadactylic	pentagon
ennead	hexagon	tetrad
hectoliter	kilometer	tricephalic
henotheism		

Refer to this menu as needed in this next sequence.

What is another name for the Ten Commandments? _____

▶ □□□ ◀

A: Decalog.

122 What is rule by two people called? _____

▶ □□□ ◀

A: Dyarchy.

123 What do we call a set of nine, like the Greek Muses of music and literature? _____

▶ □□□ ◀

A: Ennead.

124 What was the name of the four-day cycle used by some Greek athletic trainers?

_____

▶ □□ ◀

    A: Tetrad.

125 A solid figure with seven sides = _____

▶ □□ ◀

    A: Heptahedron.

126 What kind of animal was the mythical Cerebrus, guardian of the gates of the underworld, if he was equipped with three heads? _____

▶ □□ ◀

    A: Tricephalic.

127 The word *sexdigital* is built on Latin morphemes. What is a synonym based on Greek morphemes? _____

▶ □□ ◀

    A: Hexadactylic.

128 How long is a thousand meters? _____

▶ □□ ◀

    A: One kilometer.

129 A plane figure composed of six sides = _____

▶ □□ ◀

    A: Hexagon.

130 What is the name of a mollusk with eight legs? _____

▶ □□ ◀

    A: Octopus.

131 What is the name of a five-pointed star, used in magic? _____

▶ □□ ◀

    A: Pentagon.

132 What measure is equal to one hundred liters? _____

▶ □ ◀

   A: Hectoliter.

133 What belief do people follow who worship only one god, even though they may concede that other gods exist? _____

▶ □ ◀

   A: Henotheism.

134–145 Give the meanings of the following Greek prefixes:

   {**duo / dy**} = _____   {**octo**} = _____   {**hecto**} = _____

   {**hept / hepta**} = _____   {**ennea / ennead**} = _____   {**tri**} = _____

   {**heno**} = _____   {**pent / penta**} = _____   {**tetra / tetrad**} = _____

   {**hexa / hex**} = _____   {**kilo**} = _____   {**deca**} = _____

▶ □ ◀

   A: 2, 7, 1, 6, 8, 9, 5, 1,000, 100, 3, 4, 10.

Greek Ordinal Numbers
(Frames 146–150)

■ There are only two Greek ordinals that occur with any frequency in English. They are {**prot / proto**} = first and {**deuter / deutero**} = second.

146 *Deuteró-gam-y* is a _____ marriage after death or divorce of the first spouse.

▶ □ ◀

   A: Second.

147 Greek {**gam**} = English _____.

▶ □ ◀

   A: Marry or marriage.

148 If we say that someone was the *proto-mártyr* in a cause, what does this mean? (In your own words) _____

▶ □ ◀

   A: This person was the first in the cause to be punished.

149 Greek {**nom**} = law. The name *Deutero-nom-y* is given to the fifth book of the Bible because in it the laws of Moses are described for the _____time.

▶ □ ◀

   A: Second.

150 Define *proto-type*, as in "Jim's Road Runner that we made so much fun of was a *prototype* of the successful electric automobile." (In your own words) _____
_____

▶ □ ◀

   A: The first of its kind; a model.

Other Words Showing Number
(Frames 151–197)

■ There are some productive combining forms from both Latin and Greek that indicate such concepts as "single," "many," and so on.

151 How many wings does a *mono-plane* have? _____

▶ □ ◀

   A: One, a single.

152 Single = Greek {_____}.

▶ □ ◀

   A: {mono}

153 A *poly-hedron* is a solid figure. How many sides does it have? _____

▶ □ ◀

   A: Many.

154 Many = Latin {**multi**}; many = Greek {_____}.

▶ □ ◀

   A: {poly}

155 What adjective describes a society in which people may have more than one spouse at a time? _____

▶ □ ◀

   A: Polygamous.

156 How many children has a woman borne who is *multi-para?* _____
(none / one / more than one)

▶ □ ◀

    A: More than one. (The meaning of the modern medical term is different from the etymological meaning, which is "many.")

157 Greek {olig / oligo} = few. Some caterpillars are described as *oligó-phagous.* How many kinds of food do such insects eat? _____

▶ □ ◀

    A: Few.

158 Define *ólig-archy.* _____

▶ □ ◀

    A: Rule by a few.

159 Greek {pan} = all; Greek {chromat} = color. How many colors is a *pan-chromát-ic* film sensitive to? _____

▶ □ ◀

    A: All of them.

160 *Pan-héllen-ism* was the belief held by some ancient Greeks that _____ Greeks should unite.

▶ □ ◀

    A: All.

161 Greek {orama} = sight. How much can one see in a *pan-oráma?* _____

▶ □ ◀

    A: Everything.

162 Greek {hemi} = half. How much of a sphere is a *hémi-sphere?* _____

▶ □ ◀

    A: Half a sphere.

163 In which hemisphere are the continents of North and South America located?

_____

▶ □ ◀

A: In the Western Hemisphere.

164 Where are Africa, Europe, and Asia located? _____

▶ □ ◀

A: In the Eastern Hemisphere.

165 As before, we will now ask you to use some words you just had. We have also mixed in some new words, as you can see by a glance at the menu.

biped	*monomania*	*panchromatic*
biplane	*monoplane*	*panorama*
deuteragonist	*monopoly*	*polygamy*
deuterogamy	*multipara*	*polyhedron*
hemisphere	*oligarchy*	*protagonist*
heptarchy	*oligophagous*	*tetrahedron*
monogamy	*oligopoly*	*triplane*

What do we call a plane that has only one wing? _____

▶ □ ◀

A: Monoplane.

166 What name is given to a plane with two sets of wings, one above the other?

_____

▶ □ ◀

A: Biplane.

167 How does a *bi-ped* walk? _____

▶ □ ◀

A: On two feet.

168 In the early days of aviation there were a few planes built with three sets of wings. What name would you guess was given to such contraptions? _____

▶ □ ◀

A: Triplane.

169 What kind of obsession is *mono-mánia?* _____

▶ □ ◀

A: An obsession with one subject.

170 *Polý-gamy* is the practice of having two or more husbands or wives at one time; what is *monó-gamy?* _____

▶ ◻◻◻ ◻◻◻ ◀

   A: Having only one husband or wife at a time.

171 What is the term for a second marriage after the death or divorce of the first spouse? _____

▶ ◻◻◻ ◻◻◻ ◀

   A: Deuterogamy.

172 Greek {**agon**} = contest, competition. In ancient Greek plays, the player of first importance was the _____.

▶ ◻◻◻◻ ◻◻ ◀

   A: Protagonist. (Today the word is used only in a figurative sense, meaning "most important person.")

173 Find in the menu the word you think was used for the player next in importance to the protagonist? _____

▶ ◻◻◻◻ ◻◻ ◀

   A: Deuteragonist.

174 The use of {**agon**} shows that the Greek plays were put on in a _____ for prizes.

▶ ◻◻◻◻ ◻◻◻◻◻◻◻◻◻◻◻◻◻◻◻◻◻◻◻◻◻◻◻◻◻◻◻◻◻◻◻◻◻◻◻◻◻◻◻ ◀

   A: Competition.

175 What Latin derivative describes the old woman who lived in a shoe and had so many children that she didn't know what to do? _____

▶ ◻◻◻◻ ◻◻ ◀

   A: Multipara.

176 What descriptive adjective is applied to animals that eat only a limited variety of food? _____

▶ ◻◻◻◻ ◻◻ ◀

   A: Oligophagous.

177 What do we call a solid with many sides? _____

▶ □□□ ◀

    A: Polyhedron.

178 How many sides does the solid called a *tetra-hedron* have? _____

▶ □□□ ◀

    A: Four. (The sides themselves are triangular in shape.)

179 In a *hept-arch-y*, how many rulers are there? _____

▶ □□□ ◀

    A: Seven.

180 What is rule by a few called? _____

▶ □□□ ◀

    A: Oligarchy.

181 Greek {**pol**} = sell. When only one person (or one company) is permitted to sell an item, we say that he has a _____ on the market.

▶ □□□ ◀

    A: Monopoly.

182 How many people are permitted to sell goods in an *oligo-poly?* _____

▶ □□□ ◀

    A: Few.

183 What do we call camera film which is sensitive to all colors? _____

▶ □□□ ◀

    A: Panchromatic.

184 What is a wide view or picture where we feel we can see everything? _____

▶ □□□ ◀

    A: Panorama.

185   North America is located in the Western _____.

▶ □ ◀

    A: Hemisphere.

186–197   Give the meanings of these combining forms.

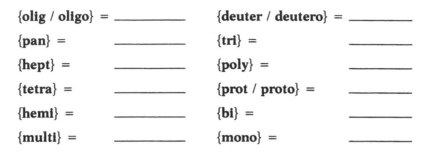

{olig / oligo} = _____	{deuter / deutero} = _____
{pan} = _____	{tri} = _____
{hept} = _____	{poly} = _____
{tetra} = _____	{prot / proto} = _____
{hemi} = _____	{bi} = _____
{multi} = _____	{mono} = _____

▶ □ ◀

    A: Few; all; seven; four; half; many; second; three; many; first; two; one.

Irregular Plurals
(Frames 198–213)

■ In English, the plural of a noun is usually formed by adding the plural morpheme {s}. In the great majority of nouns, this morpheme has one of three different sounds: / s /, / z /, or / ɨz /.

198   In the word *dogs*, which sound does the morpheme {s} have, / s /, / z /, or / ɨz /?   / ____ /.

▶ □ ◀

    A: / z /

199   In *cats* which sound does {s} have?   / ____ /.

▶ □ ◀

    A: / s /

200   And in *horses* which sound do you think {s} has?   / ____ /.

▶ □ ◀

    A: / ɨz /

I   NICE-TO-KNOW ■ The slashes mean that we are talking about *sounds*—that is, phonemes—rather than letters.

201 We will run through these common allomorphs of English {**s**} for nouns again. In *trees* the {**s**} form is / _____ /.

▶ □□ ◀

    A: / z /

202 In *docks* the allomorph of {**s**} is the sound / _____ /.

▶ □□ ◀

    A: / ˋs /

203 And in *hedges*, the allomorph is the sound / _____ /.

▶ □□ ◀

    A: / ɨz /

204 In all these examples, the *written* form of the plural morpheme is the letter _____.

▶ □□ ◀

    A: s

205 A small minority of English nouns have irregular forms for the plural. We say "one man" but "two _____."

▶ □□ ◀

    A: Men.

206 We have "one child" but "two _____."

▶ □□ ◀

    A: Children.

207 We say "one box" but "two _____."

▶ □□ ◀

    A: Boxes.

208 We speak of "one ox" but "two _____."

▶ □□ ◀

    A: Oxen.

209   If a man is a polygamist he has not one _____ but several _____ .

▶ □□ ◀

   A: Wife; wives.

210   We say not "many *mouses*" but "many _____ ."

▶ □□ ◀

   A: Mice.

211   When you add one *goose* to another, you have two what?   _____

▶ □□ ◀

   A: Geese.

212   What is the plural of *louse*?   _____

▶ □□ ◀

   A: Lice.

213   A child may be laughed at for saying "My foots hurt me." What should he have said hurt him?   _____

▶ □□ ◀

   A: His feet.

> **NICE-TO-KNOW** ■ What this use of *foots* shows is that the child understands the system of English (one *suit*, two *suits*; one *horse*, two *horses*) but has not learned the exceptions like *foot, feet*.
> A very small percentage of English words have an {s} which is borrowed from languages other than Latin or Greek. The word borrowed from Arabic for a kind of supernatural being is *jinni* for one and *jinn* for two or more.

Latin Words like One *Alumnus* / Two *Alumni* and One *Alumna* / Two *Alumnae*
(Frames 214–231)

214   English has a number of Latin and Greek borrowings that keep the plural form of the Greek or Latin originals. A common example is the word *alumnus*, which in Latin means a "foster son" (= a boy who is part of a family although a son neither by birth nor by adoption) and also a "pupil." In America today an *alumnus* of a school or college is one who has (in your own words) _____ .

▶ □□ ◀

   A: Attended that institution.

215   What is an association of former students of an institution often called? The _____
Association.

▶ □□ ◀

   A: Alumni.

| **NICE-TO-KNOW** ■ Note that the *i* in *alumni* is pronounced in English like "eye." This may cause trouble to those who have studied Latin, since in Latin the word *alumni* is pronounced differently: the *i* is pronounced to rhyme with "bee."

216   One male graduate is called an *alumnus;* what do we call two or more? _____

▶ □□ ◀

   A: Alumni.

217   The Latin word *alumna* means in Latin "a foster daughter or girl pupil." What do we call
a woman who has attended a school or college? She is an _____ of that institution.

▶ □□ ◀

   A: Alumna.

218   Which graduates are members of an *Alumnae Association,* men or women or both?
_____

▶ □□ ◀

   A: Women.

| **NICE-TO-KNOW** ■ In Latin *ae* rhymes with "eye." The *ae* of the plural form *alumnae* is in English pronounced to rhyme with "bee."

219   So we say "one alumna" but "two _____."

▶ □□ ◀

   A: Alumnae.

220   The former dominance of men in education is shown by the fact that when an association
includes both male and female graduates it is called an "_____ (Alumnae/
Alumni) Association."

▶ □□ ◀

   A: Alumni.

289

221 The singular/plural contrast shown by *alumna/alumnae* is not common in English, but the *-us/-i* contrast, as in *alumnus/alumni*, occurs with some frequency. We speak of "one *nucleus*" but of "two _____."

▶ □□□ ◀

A: Nuclei.

222 You all know about the *radius* of a circle, such as the spoke of a wheel. The plural form of *radius* follows the same pattern as *alumnus*, namely "one *radius*" but "two _____."

▶ □□□ ◀

A: Radii.

223 Like *radius* and *nucleus*, the noun *focus*, used in optics to describe the point at which light rays meet when they pass through a lens, also has the plural form _____.

▶ □□□ ◀

A: Foci.

> **NICE-TO-KNOW** ■ The Latin word *focus* means "fireplace." The connection between that and English *focus* is that if you focus the sun's rays with a lens, where the rays meet is where the paper, shavings, or other material will start to burn.

224 A statue much larger than life size is a *colossus*. The plural is _____.

▶ □□□ ◀

A: Colossi.

225 We could expand this list of words like *focus* and *nucleus* that keep the Latin signal ____ for a plural.

▶ □□□ ◀

A: i

226 But many of them have a second plural: there is *radius/radii* and *radius/radiuses*. In the same way, along with *nuclei* there is the variant _____.

▶ □□□ ◀

A: Nucleuses.

227 A *persona* is a character in a play. The plural of *persona* is like that of *alumna*, namely "one *persona*," "two _____."

▶ □□□ ◀

A: Personae.

228 Let us see if you know the meanings of the words whose plurals you have just examined. The Latin word for "staff, rod, or spoke of a wheel" is _____.

▶ □□ ◀

    A: Radius.

229 We say "one *radius*" and "two _____."

▶ □□□ ◀

    A: Radii (or radiuses).

230 Actors in Greek drama wore masks. The Latin word for both a mask and for a character in a play is _____.

▶ □□□ ◀

    A: Persona.

231 The plural form of *persona* is like the plural of *alumna*. What is it? _____

▶ □□□ ◀

    A: Personae.

Latin Words like One *Stratum* and Two *Strata*
(Frames 232–240)

232 In geology a *stratum* is a horizontal layer of sedimentary rock. We say "There are four visible _____ in this rock."

▶ □□□ ◀

    A: Strata.

233 The facts that we know about some subject are called the *data*. What is a single isolated fact called? _____

▶ □□□ ◀

    A: Datum.

234 Do we say "The data makes it clear" or "The data make it clear"? _____
_____

▶ □□□ ◀

    A: "The data make it clear." (You will also hear "The data makes it clear.")

235 The word *agenda*, as in "We will put it on the *agenda* and see that it is taken care of promptly," means in Latin "things (plural) which must be done." What is a single item on an *agenda*? _____

▶ □ ◀

A: An agendum. (But *agendum* is not common.)

236 However, the English word *agenda*, in spite of its original meaning as plural, is now treated as a singular noun. To say "The agenda for today are lengthy" is an awkward expression; virtually everyone would say, "The agenda for today _____ lengthy."

▶ □ ◀

A: Is.

237 And if there was one agenda brought in by one person and another by someone else, you would have two _____.

▶ □ ◀

A: Agendas.

238 Earlier in this unit you had the word *millennium*. The history of Europe covers 3,000 years, or three _____.

▶ □ ◀

A: Millennia.

NICE-TO-KNOW ▪ As with most of these words there are two acceptable plurals. We can say either "two *millennia*" or "two *millenniums*."

239 We say that radio is an important *medium* for informing the public. What is the plural form of *medium* that means "various means of giving information, including television and newspapers"? _____

▶ □ ◀

A: Media.

240 Do we say " 'The media is' or 'The media are' not honest in reporting the news"?

_____

▶ □ ◀

A: Most people would say "The media are," although you do occasionally hear "The media is." There is also an "extra" plural for *media*, namely *medias*. But the form *media* is more widely used.

Words Like One *Analysis* / Two *Analyses*
(Frames 241–243)

241 "The first *analysis* was negative, but further tests showed that all the other *analyses* contradicted the first." Following the general pattern of "one analysis" and "two analyses," we speak of "two indices" but of "one _____."

▶ □□□ ◀

    A: Index. *Index* also has a plural *indexes*.

242 Doctors speak of "one *neurosis*" but "several _____."

▶ □□□ ◀

    A: Neuroses.

243 "One *psychosis*" but "several _____."

▶ □□□ ◀

    A: Psychoses.

Review of Greek and Latin Plurals
(Frames 244–256)

244 Frames 244–256 will test what you learned in frames 214–243. In the following sequence you will be asked to produce Greek or Latin plurals, using the following new words which are listed below in their singular forms:

> Like *stratum* / *strata: centennium, memorandum*
> Like *persona* / *personae: formula, lacuna, sequela, vertebra*
> Like *focus* / *foci: stimulus, gladiolus*
> Like *analysis* / *analyses: synopsis, synthesis.*

Write in the space provided the word that makes sense in the context.

The boss says that he is tired of people saying that they don't know what is going on, so from now on there will be at least two _____ every day to inform us.

▶ □□□ ◀

    A: Memoranda (= things that should be remembered).

245 Your one-sentence summaries of the plots are much shorter than the one-page _____ that I had assigned.

▶ □□□ ◀

    A: Synopses.

246 It is hard to believe that between the discovery of America in 1492 and the Declaration of Independence in 1776 almost three full _____ had passed.

▶ □ □ □ □ □ □.□ ◀

    A: Centennia.

247 *Stimulus* in Latin meant a "spur" or a "goad" that caused pain to an animal. This is a reminder that in order to get some human beings to react properly, a person must apply painful _____.

▶ □ ◀

    A: Stimuli (like threats of failing a course).

248 In order to increase the speed of his car a mere five miles per hour, Jack has experimented with twenty different _____ for fuel.

▶ □ ◀

    A: Formulae. (An alternate plural is *formulas.*)

249 Latin {**seque**} = follow. You are familiar with the English word *sequel,* which means something which _____ something else.

▶ □ ◀

    A: Follows.

250 Doctors frequently use a word that resembles *sequel* in appearance and origin to describe a diseased condition that was caused by some injury or disease. For example, if after one has a tooth extracted pieces of tooth which still remain become infected, those inflammations are called the _____ of the extraction.

▶ □ ◀

    A: Sequelae.

251 Latin {**lac**} = lake, hole, or void. A *lacuna* is a space where something has been omitted. We use the word today in two senses. First, when a scholar edits a manuscript he may indicate places where there are gaps; these are called _____.

▶ □ ◀

    A: Lacunae.

252 This word *lacuna* is also used in anatomy and biology, where small cavities in bone that are filled with bone cells are called _____.

▶ □ ◀

    A: Lacunae.

253 While *analysis* is the act of pulling things apart, *synthesis* is its opposite. What does *synthesis* mean? _____

▶ □ ◀

    A: The act of putting things together.

254 The formation of water by combining oxygen and hydrogen is an example of the many _____ that chemists perform.

▶ □ ◀

    A: Syntheses.

255 "Well," said the doctor, "I have always prided myself on being one of God's *vertebrate* creatures. But after that fall," he continued, rubbing his lower back, "I am not sure that I have enough _____ left to qualify."

▶ □ ◀

    A: Vertebrae.

256 A Roman *gladiator* was so named because he used a sword, *gladius* in Latin. Latin *gladiolus* meant "small sword." Today, the shape of the leaves gives a name to the showy flowers we call _____.

▶ □ ◀

    A: Gladioli.

WORD LIST

The concepts presented in this unit were:

cardinal numbers 1   ordinal numbers 3

Here is a list of the words discussed in this unit. Refer to a dictionary if you need to.

agenda 235	kilometer 111	protagonist 172
alumna 216	medium 239	prototype 150
alumnus 215	memorandum 244	psychosis 243
bicycle 14	millennium 32	quadrangle 22
biennial 18	millimeter 33	quadriplegic 6
bilateral 26	millipede 35	quartile 76
biped 167	monogamy 170	quinquennial 19
biplane 166	monomania 169	quintuplets 75
centennial 34	monoplane 151	radius 222
centennium 246	monopoly 181	secondary 77
centimeter 81	neurosis 242	September 12
centipede 30	November 9	sextant 85
colossus 224	nucleus 221	stimulus 247
datum 233	octave 78	stratum 232
December 11	October 8	synopsis 245
decimal 79	octopus 116	synthesis 253
Deuteronomy 149	oligarchy 158	tertiary 84
duet 28	panchromatic 159	triangle 21
focus 223	panhellenism 160	tricycle 16
formula 248	panorama 161	triplane 168
gladiolus 256	pentagon 109	unicycle 17
hemisphere 162	polygamous 155	unilateral 25
hexagon 108	polygamy 170	vertebra 255
index 241	primogeniture 74	

OPTIONAL WORDS

decalog 119	hexadactylic 112	protomartyr 148
decemvir 29	lacuna 252	quinquefoliate 13
deciliter 80	millicurie 82	septemvirate 24
deuteragonist 173	multipara 156	septime 86
deuterogamy 146	nonane 83	sequela 250
dyarchy 117	novena 27	sexdigital 7
ennead 120	octipara 20	sexpartite 23
hectoliter 118	oligophagous 157	tetrad 107
henotheism 110	oligopoly 182	tetrahedron 178
heptahedron 115	persona 227	tricephalic 114
heptarchy 179	polyhedron 153	

REVIEW EXERCISES

Purpose: To learn more words which have "number" morphemes in them.

Directions: Consulting a dictionary where necessary, write a word using a combining form which shows number; then define the word. Do not use words which occurred in this unit. Use allomorphs when necessary. We have indicated with an asterisk forms that are rare. Some of these forms you will be able to find only in a large dictionary.

Latin Cardinal Numbers

uni _____: _____

du _____ or bi _____: _____

tri _____: _____

quadri _____: _____

quinque _____: _____

sex _____: _____

*septem _____: _____

octo _____: _____

nov _____: _____

dec _____: _____

cent _____: _____

milli _____: _____

Latin Ordinal Numbers

primo _____: _____

second _____: _____

terti _____: _____

quart _____: _____

quint _____: _____

sext _____: _____

*sept _____: _____

octav _____: _____

*non _____: _____

decim _____: _____

Greek Cardinal Numbers

hen _____: _____

duo _____: _____

tri _____: _____

tetra _____: _____

pent _____: _____

hexa _____: _____

*hept _____: _____

octo _____: _____

*ennea _____: _____

deca _____: _____

hecto _____: _____

kilo _____: _____

Greek Ordinal Numerals

proto _____: _____

deutero _____: _____

Use a dictionary that has the entry "plural."

a. Write five examples of irregular plurals. (Do not repeat words used in this unit.)

_____, _____, _____,

_____, _____

b. Write five words that are used only in the singular.

_____, _____, _____,

_____, _____

c. Write five words that occur only in the plural.

_____, _____, _____,

_____, _____

We say "one father-in-law"; in the plural we say "two fathers-in-law," not *"two father-in-laws." Find four more examples of the plural for similar phrases.

_____, _____,

_____, _____

WORDS OF INTERESTING ORIGIN

There are scores of words used to describe animals in groups. Fit these animal names into the appropriate slots.

ants	*cattle*	*fish*	*locusts*	*sheep*
bees	*chickens*	*lions*	*puppies*	*whales*

1. In the clear water we saw a *school* of _____.

2. In the fog and over the now invisible surface of the water came the grunting and whistling of a *pod* of _____.

3. There in a cardboard box on the back porch was Polly, licking the members of her *litter* of _____.

4. Anyone who has ever tried it agrees that there is nothing more exasperating than trying to drive a *flock* of _____, even with the help of a well-trained dog.

5. As we waited at the water hole there was suddenly a roar that shook the earth, and there, not a hundred feet away, was the leader of a *pride* of _____.

6. Louder and louder grew the humming of a *swarm* of _____.

7. We spent the morning driving the *herd* of _____through the narrow pass.

8. Considering how hard they work, it is reasonable that we speak of a *colony* of _____.

9. In the barnyard was a *brood* of clucking _____.

10. The Cub Scouts descended on the table of goodies like a *plague* of _____.

EASILY CONFUSED WORDS

Use a dictionary as needed.

1. ***Climactic / climatic.*** In spite of their similar appearance, these two words have quite different meanings. *Climactic* contains the Greek base {**climac / climax**} = ladder, climbing, climax. Today *climax* is the highest point of something. The word *climactic* is the adjective of *climax*, as in "The game came to a *climactic* finish with the first half and then lost all suspense," or "In Michigan the *climactic* stage in a forest's development is reached when it is dominated by oak and beech." *Climatic* is the adjective of *climate*; these words contain the Greek root {**clima**} = region, zone. The modern meaning of *climate* is the average of the weather conditions in a given zone, as in "The *climatic* conditions here are even and predictable—always lousy."

2. **Extant / extinct.** These two words are almost antonyms of each other. *Extant* is made up of Latin {ex} + {stant} = stand; the modern meaning is "still standing up" or "still existing," as in "Mountain lions are still *extant* in those uninhabited valleys." *Extinct* has the Latin base {stingu / stinct} = to put out (a fire), to destroy. The modern meaning is "no longer existing," as in "The mountain lions are all *extinct* in the mountains; not one has been seen for fifty years."

3. **Official / officious.** Both words come from Latin *officium*, meaning "duty or office." The word *official* can be either an adjective or a noun. As a noun, it means a person put in some position of authority, as in "The *officials* in charge of the game did a lousy job." *Officious* originally meant "ready to be of service," but today it refers to someone who offers unnecessary and unwanted services. For example: "Tim was so officious in his new job that he was insufferable. It was, 'Can I get you a more comfortable seat, Mrs. Evans?' and 'Let me freshen your drink, Mr. White,' until we were ready to throw him out."

Use the six words in the sentences where each makes sense.

1. There is serious concern that many species of whales will soon become _____.

2. Some people maintain that various pollution agents in the atmosphere will soon effect

   _____ changes that should concern us all.

3. Ten dollars was the _____ price printed on the ticket.

4. Tim, whose help had been so welcome a few minutes before, now became _____ and disagreeable.

5. The _____ end of our game did not escape the notice of the national press.

6. These are the only _____ manuscripts of this particular author.

LATIN PHRASES

First try to get the meaning of the Latin phrases from the context of the sentences below, choosing a meaning from the list that follows. Write the number of the Latin phrase beside the definition that fits.

1. *Mirabile dictu*, as in "As we rushed around the corner, there, *mirabile dictu*, was our train with the conductor waving us on."

2. *Inter nos* as in "I wouldn't want this to get out" said Jasper in a conspiratorial tone, "but just *inter nos* I think Perkins is about through here."

3. *Corpus delicti*, as in "Surely you must know," said the Inspector, "that we need proof of death. There is at present no *corpus delicti*."

4. *Habeas corpus*, as in "Don't worry, Jack," said Matt, "we will get a writ of *habeas corpus* so that you can be out of here for two weeks."

5. *Nota bene*, as in "And finally," said Foster, "you must go to the office and, *nota bene*, without anyone's seeing you, make off with that memo you spoke of."

_____ internally

_____ make careful note

_____ between us

_____ body of the victim

_____ wonderful to say

_____ splendid speaker

_____ pleasures of the body

_____ permission for an accused to be free before his examination

_____ favorable letter

_____ information about the corpse

Use a dictionary to find the word-by-word translation and the modern meaning for each phrase.

	Word-by-Word Translation	Modern Meaning
mirabile dictu	_____	_____
inter nos	_____	_____
corpus delicti	_____	_____
habeas corpus	_____	_____
nota bene	_____	_____

UNIT TEN
Cognates and Borrowings

So far we have concentrated on words derived from Greek or Latin, since these two languages have contributed so many words to our language. In this unit, you will learn how English is related to such languages as German, Russian, and Finnish. You will also see how we have borrowed words from other modern languages, like French *amateur,* Italian *soprano,* and Spanish *mosquito.*

All English words have one of these four origins:

1. They have been in the English language as far back as we can trace them, that is, back to Old English. Examples are *with, high,* and *tool,* as you saw in Unit One.
2. They have been invented in comparatively recent times, like the word *escalator* (originally coined as a trademark in 1895), *laser* (standing for *l*ight *a*mplification by *s*timulated *e*mission of *r*adiation), and the element *e*insteinium (discovered in the debris of atom bombs, and named after Albert Einstein).
3. They have been borrowed in historical times from some other language, frequently Latin or Greek. Examples are words you have been learning such as *secondary* and *patriarchy.*
4. They have been borrowed in modern times from many languages. An example is *encore,* from French.

CONTENTS

   1–10   Introduction
   11–72   The Indo-European Language System
   73–83   Review of Cognates and Borrowings
   84–97   Norman French Words in English
   98–173 Modern French Words in English
174–203   Italian Words in English
204–223   Spanish Words in English
224–252   Words from Other Languages

Introduction
(Frames 1–10)

1 In the first unit you learned that it is from Old English that Modern English inherited its two main structural signals. The first of these structural signals is seen in the contrast between "The dog sees the cat" and "The cat sees the dog." What do we call this signal?

_____

▶ □□ ◀

  A: Word order.

2 The second type of structural signal is seen in such words as *the*, *of*, and *with*. What do we call such words? _____

▶ □□ ◀

  A: Function words.

3 From what language do most of these function words come? _____

▶ □□ ◀

  A: Old English (also called Anglo-Saxon).

4 From what two languages do the majority of *content* words in Modern English come? _____ and _____

▶ □□ ◀

  A: Latin and Greek.

5 Look again at the first sentence in the Sample Text that you examined in Unit One:

> With all the recent emphasis on high interest rates for investment certificates, you may be overlooking a very important family financial tool.

What kind of words are *on*, *for*, *may*, and *very*? _____

▶ □□ ◀

  A: Function words.

6 *Very* comes from Latin through Old French. From what language do you guess the other three function words—*on*, *for*, and *may*—come? _____

▶ □□ ◀

  A: Old English.

7 From what language (or languages) do the content words *recent, emphasis,* and *interest* come? _____

A: Latin and Greek. (But we are going to modify that statement a bit in this unit.)

8 The content words *high, overlooking,* and *tool* in this Sample Text are Old English in origin. Would you say that these are common words? _____

A: Yes, extremely common.

9 The chances are that words which are both short and common are usually (but not always) from the language or languages we call _____.

A: Old English.

10 From what language or languages do English words which are both long and unusual often come? _____

A: Latin and Greek.

■ We are now going to present you with evidence that will show why these statements, while useful when you first learned about borrowings, must be modified.

The Indo-European Language System
(Frames 11–72)

■ The languages we have discussed in this program (English, Latin, and Greek) are all members of a language system that is called **Indo-European.** It has been well said that the history of the Indo-European language families is "complicated but systematic." We will simplify this history as much as we can. Unfortunately, simplification means a certain amount of distortion, and we hope that you will bear this in mind.

The ancestry of the English language can be traced back about 5,000 years, although we have written records for Old English only from A.D. 600 on. Written records of other languages in the Indo-European system go back to approximately 1500 B.C. But scholars have been able to reconstruct earlier forms of these languages by comparing different members of this family. It has been discovered that most (but not all) of the languages spoken in Europe today and some of those spoken in India are related: the resemblance between these languages is too great to be a matter of chance.

11 About how old are the earliest written records of Old English? _____
_____

▶ □ ◀

A: About 1,400 years. (Remember, this number is just an estimate.)

12 How old are the earliest written records of any Indo-European language? _____
_____

▶ □ ◀

A: About 3,500 years. (This number too is an estimate.)

13 Here are some examples of the similarities we mentioned. Consider the German cardinal numerals from 1 to 5, which somewhat resemble their English equivalents, in numerical order: *ein, zwei, drei, vier, fuenf.* Which one of these words most resembles the English word *one?* _____

▶ □ ◀

A: *Ein.* (Note: You do not need to memorize these German words.)

14–17 When we compare two languages, we sometimes find that there are numerous words in these languages that resemble each other, like English *one* and German *ein.* Such words have a common ancestor; we call such words **cognates.** Here are the other four German numerals (not in numerical order). After each number write the English cognate: *fuenf* = _____; *drei* = _____; *zwei* = _____; *vier* = _____.

▶ □ ◀

A: *fuenf* = five; *drei* = three; *zwei* = two; *vier* = four.

18 What relation do the words *drei* and *three* have to each other? _____
_____

▶ □ ◀

A: They are cognates (or, they have a common ancestor).

19–23 Here, in random order, are the German cardinal numbers from 6 through 10: *sieben, neun, zehn, sechs, acht.* Write the German numeral after the English cognate. Rely on word resemblances, slight as they may seem. For example, *sieben* is a two-syllable word beginning with *s.* What English word for a numeral between 6 and 10 is a two-syllable word beginning with *s?*

ENGLISH = GERMAN

six = _____

seven = _____

eight = _____

nine = _____

ten = _____

▶ □ □ □ ■ □ □ □ □ ■ □ □ □ □ □ ■ □ □ □ □ □ □ □ □ ■ □ □ □ □ □ □ □ ■ □ □ □ □ □ memorize □ □ □ □ ■ □ □ □ □ □ ◀

A: *Sechs, sieben, acht, neun, zehn.*

24 How much do the English numbers from 1 to 10 resemble the German cognate numbers?

_____ (not at all / somewhat / very much)

▶ □ □ □ ■ □ □ □ □ ■ □ □ □ □ □ ■ □ □ □ □ □ □ □ □ ■ □ □ □ ▢ □ □ □ ▢ □ □ □ □ □ □ □ □ □ □ □ □ □ □ □ ◡ □ □ □ □ ■ □ □ □ □ □ ◀

A: This is a value judgment; some might say "somewhat" and some might say "very much." But surely there is more than a chance resemblance.

25 What name is given to words in two languages which are so similar that we assume they

come from a common ancestor? _____

▶ □ □ □ ■ □ □ □ □ ■ □ □ □ □ □ ■ □ □ □ □ □ ▢ □ ◠ ◠ ◠ □ □ □ □ □ □ ■ □ □ □ □ □ ◡ ◡ □ □ □ □ □ □ □ □ □ □ □ □ ■ □ □ □ □ □ ◀

A: Cognates.

26 Here are the words for the numbers 1 through 10 from four different languages. Examine them and then proceed.

ENGLISH	LATIN	GERMAN	JAPANESE
one	unus	ein	ichi
two	duo	zwei	ni
three	tres	drei	san
four	quattuor	vier	shi
five	quinque	fuenf	go
six	sex	sechs	roku
seven	septem	sieben	shichi
eight	octo	acht	hachi
nine	novem	neun	ku
ten	decem	zehn	juu

The German and Japanese words are for illustration only; do not memorize them.

Which is the one language of the four whose numbers are obviously *not* part of the

Indo-European language family? _____

▶ □ □ □ ■ □ □ □ □ ■ □ □ □ □ □ ■ □ □ □ □ □ □ □ □ ■ □ □ □ □ □ □ □ ■ □ □ □ □ □ □ □ □ □ □ □ □ □ ■ □ □ □ □ □ ◀

A: Japanese.

307

> **NICE-TO-KNOW** ■ We have already said that the relationship between members of the Indo-European family is "complicated but systematic." Words that look as different as English *four* and Latin *quattuor* can be shown to be cognates. However, to describe this relationship in detail is beyond the scope of this program.

27 Is Latin *novem* (9) a cognate of Japanese *ku?* _____

▶ □ ◀

  A: No.

28–33 We will now move to a study of cognates in which we use six kinship terms (*father, mother*, etc.). Here are six such terms in German, in scrambled order: *Bruder, Tochter, Vater, Mutter, Schwester, Sohn*. (German nouns are always capitalized.) Relying on resemblances (that is, what English words the German words look like), write down in the spaces provided what you think the German term is for each English kinship term.

  brother = _____   daughter = _____

  sister = _____   father = _____

  son = _____   mother = _____

▶ □ ◀

  A: *Bruder; Schwester; Sohn; Tochter; Vater; Mutter.*

34 Here are the words for these same kinship terms in Japanese, which is not an Indo-European language: *shimai, chichi, musoko, haha, musume*, and *kyoodai*. Can you identify which word means "father" in this list? _____

▶ □ ◀

  A: No (unless you already know Japanese).

> **NICE-TO-KNOW** ■ Here are the meanings of the Japanese terms, in case you were wondering: *shimai* = sister; *chichi* = father; *musoko* = son; *haha* = mother; *musume* = daughter; and *kyoodai* = brother.

35–40 Here are the same six kinship terms in Latin, in scrambled order. All of them have common English derivatives, so you can guess the meaning. Give the English meaning of each Latin word.

  mater, as in *maternal* = _____   *pater*, as in *paternal* = _____

  frater, as in *fraternity* = _____   *soror*, as in *sorority* = _____

  filia, as in *filial* = _____   *filius*, as in *filial* = _____

▶ □ ◀

  A: Mother; brother; daughter; father; sister; son.

41 Why did it seem easy to guess the meanings of the Latin words? (In your own words)

_____

▶ □ ◀

A: Because you already knew items borrowed from Latin: maternal, fraternity, filial, paternal, and sorority.

42–47 Here, in random order, are the same six kinship words from Sanskrit, an ancient literary and religious language of India. It is a member of the Indo-European language system, as you can see from the kinship terms listed below. Give the English meaning of each Sanskrit cognate:

matar = _____   _duhitr_ = _____

bhratar = _____   _svasr_ = _____

sunu = _____   _pitar_ = _____

▶ □ ◀

A: Mother; brother; son; daughter; sister; father.

NICE-TO-KNOW ■ In order to avoid unusual symbols and letters we have simplified the spelling of many of the examples we have given you.

48–53 Considering all these resemblances (as well as the evidence from scores of other languages), scholars have reconstructed forms that can account for the resemblances and differences these cognates have. Here are six Indo-European kinship terms. Write what you believe is the English meaning of each Indo-European word.

*peter_ = _____   *matar_ = _____

*bhrater_ = _____   *dhughter_ = _____

*sunu_ = _____   *swesor_ = _____

▶ □ ◀

A: Father; brother; son; mother; daughter; sister.

54 What does the asterisk (*) in front of these words mean? _____

_____

_____

▶ □ ◀

A: That this form has never been discovered but is a guess (an intelligent guess, to be sure) as to the possible form of the common ancestor of the cognates in different languages.

55 What do we call this language which is the common ancestor? _____

▶ □ ◀

A: Indo-European.

56 Scholars believe that speakers of Indo-European, the source of most of the languages of Europe, lived somewhere in southern Russia many millennia ago. For reasons not quite clear to us (possibly overpopulation, a shortage of fertile land, pressure from hostile neighbors, or a change of climate), many of them felt compelled to find new homes, and the tribe that spoke this Indo-European language split up in about 3000 B.C. Some went east to Persia and India. Where did those go who went west? _____

▶ □ ◀

A: To Europe.

I NICE-TO-KNOW ■ A recent alternate theory is that they lived around the Baltic Sea.

57 And some stayed where they were; they were the ancestors of the people who speak Russian and related languages. As these three great groups became separated from each other, and split into numerous smaller groups, what happened to the language they spoke? _____

▶ □ ◀

A: It changed.

58–61 Look at this diagram, which may help you understand the relationship of languages in the Indo-European system.

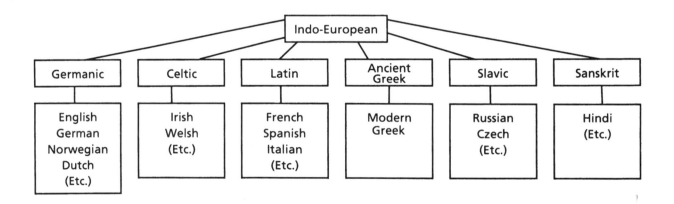

Note that this diagram is intended to help you see the relationship between some of the most well-known languages of the world. It omits dozens of other important languages and makes the whole system seem more regular than it is.

What are the four main branches of the Indo-European language family whose speakers moved *west*? _____, _____, _____, _____

▶ □ ◀

A: Germanic, Celtic, Latin, and Ancient Greek.

62 To which of these four branches does English belong? _____

▶ □ ◀

A: Germanic.

63–64 From what two languages has the English language borrowed extensively for content words? _____ and _____

▶ □ ◀

A: Latin and Greek.

65 What relationship do English *one*, Latin *unus*, and German *ein* have to one another? _____

▶ □ ◀

A: They are cognates of one another.

66 What relationship does the English morpheme {**uni**}, as in *unit, unity,* and *unify,* have to the Latin word *unus?* _____

▶ □ ◀

A: It is borrowed from Latin.

67 If all the speakers of Germanic had suddenly died in 1000 B.C., the English language:

    (a) would exist today in almost exactly its present form
    (b) would not exist today at all
    (c) would exist today but with substantial differences
    (d) would exist today in a form almost exactly like Germanic

(Choose one.) _____

▶ □ ◀

A: (b) would not exist today at all.

68 That is, in the chart is English descended *through* Germanic? _____ (yes / no)

▶ □ ◀

A: Yes.

69 If you were puzzled by the answers in the last two frames, consider this similar question about biological descent, stated in almost the same terms. If your great-great-ever-so-great grandfather had died in 1000 B.C. without producing any children,

(continued on next page)

(a) you would exist today in almost exactly your present form
(b) you would not exist today at all
(c) you would exist today but with substantial differences
(d) you would exist today and would look almost exactly like this childless ancestor

(Choose one.) _____

▶ □ ◀

A: (b) you would not exist today at all.

70 If the Italic tribes who spoke the language that later became Latin and who ruled the world had all been destroyed by a catastrophe in 1000 B.C., the English language

(a) would exist today in almost exactly its present form
(b) would not exist at all today
(c) would exist today but with substantial differences
(d) would exist today in a form almost exactly like Italic

(Choose one.) _____

▶ □ ◀

A: (c) would exist today but with substantial differences.

71 That is, in the chart is English descended *through* Latin? _____ (yes / no)

▶ □ ◀

A: No.

72 If Latin had never existed, which of these words would not exist in English, *brotherhood* or *fraternity?* _____

▶ □ ◀

A: Fraternity, because it comes from Latin.

Review of Cognates and Borrowings
(Frames 73–83)

73 A word which has some connection with a word in another language is either a **borrowing** or a **cognate.** In your own words define a borrowing: _____

_____

▶ □ ◀

A: A word that is borrowed directly from another language.

74 In the sentence "Joe and Bill may have been members of the same *fraternity*, but their feelings for each other were not brotherly," from what Latin word meaning "brother" is *fraternity* derived? (You can refer back to frame 35–40.) _____

▶ □ ◀

A: *Frater.*

75 Two words that are cognates of each other have some connection, like that of cousins in human kinship. Is English *father* a cognate of German *vater?* _____

▶ □ ◀

A: Yes.

76 What do German *Vater* and English *father* have in common in terms of etymology? (In your own words) _____

_____

▶ □ ◀

A: They are both descended at some point from a common ancestor *peter in the Indo-European language; that is, they are cognates of each other.

77 What is the nature of the relationship between English *mother* and Latin *mater?* (In your own words) _____

_____

▶ □ ◀

A: Same answer as that in frame 76: they are both descended at some point from a common ancestor *matar in the Indo-European language; they are therefore cognates of each other.

78 What is the nature of the relationship between English *maternal* and Latin *mater?*

_____

▶ □ ◀

A: *Maternal* is a borrowing from Latin *mater.*

79 Is the English word *sorority* a borrowing of Latin *soror* or a cognate? _____

▶ □ ◀

A: A borrowing.

80 Is English *sister* a borrowing or a cognate of Latin *soror?* _____

▶ □ ◀

A: A cognate.

81 Which are of more practical use in building a vocabulary, cognates or borrowings?

_____

▶ □ ◀

A: Borrowings, without question.

82 Finland has a common border with Russia on the north and east. Examine these examples of kinship terms.

ENGLISH	RUSSIAN	FINNISH
brother	*brat*	*veli*
sister	*sestra*	*sisar*
mother	*mat*	*aiti*
father	*atyets*	*isa*
daughter	*doch*	*tytar*
son	*sin*	*poika*

Which of these statements is true? (Choose one.) _____

(a) Russian and Finnish are both Indo-European languages.
(b) Neither Russian nor Finnish is an Indo-European language.
(c) Finnish is an Indo-European language but Russian is not.
(d) Russian is an Indo-European language but Finnish is not.

▶ □ ◀

A: (d) Russian is an Indo-European language but Finnish is not.

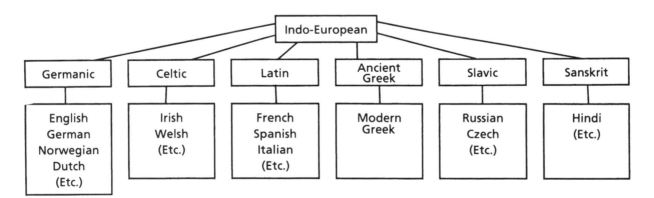

83 Look at this diagram of Indo-European languages. To which branch of the Indo-European languages does Russian belong? _____

▶ □ ◀

A: The Slavic.

Norman French Words in English
(Frames 84–97)

84 There have been *three* major invasions of England in historical times. First, the Romans occupied it in the first century A.D. and stayed for about 400 years. Although Latin was the official language for this long period, the natives, who spoke Celtic, adopted only a handful of Latin words, such as *wall* (<Latin *vallum*) and *wine* (<Latin *vinum*). The next invasion was actually a series of invasions over several centuries, when the Angles, the Saxons, and the Jutes crossed over from Europe and drove out the Romans. What is the name we give to the language spoken by these invaders? _____

▶ □ ◀

A: Old English (also called Anglo-Saxon).

85 Did this Old English language survive? (In your own words) _____
_____

▶ □ ◀

A: Yes; it exists to this day (much changed) in the form we call Modern English.

NICE-TO-KNOW ■ The language we call Old English was spoken from approximately A.D. 400 to A.D. 1100. It is so different that one cannot read it without studying it like a foreign language. Here are two lines from the poem *Beowulf,* written about A.D. 700:

> Stræt wæs stán-fáh, stig wisode
> Gumum ætgædere. gúþ-byrne scán.

This is translated:

> The street was stone-variegated, the path guided
> the men together. The war-mailcoat shone.

When we come to Middle English, spoken from approximately A.D. 1100 to A.D. 1500, we find something more familiar. Here is a quote from Chaucer, who died in A.D. 1400, taken from "The Knightes Tale" in *The Canterbury Tales:*

> Whylom, as olde stories tellen us,
> Ther was a duk that highte Theseus;
> Of Athenes he was lord and governour,
> And in his tyme swich a conquerour,
> That gretter was ther noon under the sonne.

Except for a few words, you hardly need a translation:

> Once upon a time, as old stories tell us,
> There was a duke that was called Theseus;
> Of Athens he was lord and governor,
> And in his time such a conqueror,
> That greater was there none under the sun.

---

86 The invaders drove the speakers of Celtic into out-of-the-way parts of Britain. What are two groups that still speak a form of Celtic? _____

▶ □ ◀

A: Irish, Welsh.

87 To what language group did Old English belong? _____
(Celtic / Germanic / Greek / Latin)

▶ □ ◀

A: Germanic.

88 To which of these language groups does Modern English belong? _____

▶ □ ◀

A: Germanic.

89 Is Modern English descended directly from Greek and Latin? _____ (yes / no)

▶ □ ◀

A: No.

90 What is the relationship of Latin and Greek to Modern English? _____
_____

▶ □ ◀

A: They have contributed much vocabulary.

91 The third (and last) military invasion of English occurred in A.D. 1066, when the Normans, under the leadership of William the Conqueror, occupied the island. The victors continued to use their own variety of French (called "Norman French"), and the English continued to use Old English. The two languages existed side by side, but the speakers of English gradually borrowed more and more forms from Norman French.

There is an interesting pattern of terms for animals in Norman French and Old English. When the animal we now call a pig was running around the farms of England after the Conquest, the farmers who spoke Old English called it a *swin*. What is the Modern English form of this word? _____

▶ □ ◀

A: Swine.

92 When the swine was butchered and cooked, the French owners of the farm who ate it called it *porc*. What is the Modern English form of this Norman French word? _____

▶ □ ◀

A: Pork.

93 From what language was *pork* borrowed? _____

▶ □ ◀

A: Norman French.

94 Four more terms for food borrowed from the Norman invaders are *beef, mutton, veal,* and *venison.* What was an English cow called when it was cooked and came to the Norman table? _____

▶ □□□ ◀

  A: Beef.

95 What word borrowed from Norman French is used to refer to the cooked meat of a sheep? _____

▶ □□□ ◀

  A: Mutton.

96 The Old English farmer called another animal a *calf;* what did the Norman owner call the meat when it was cooked? _____

▶ □□□ ◀

  A: Veal.

97 What is the word borrowed from the Norman French that means "flesh of deer"?

_____

▶ □□□ ◀

  A: Venison.

Modern French Words in English
(Frames 98–173)

■ "Modern French" is the term used for the language spoken in France from approximately A.D. 1600 to the present day. More words in English came from French than from any other language except Latin and Greek.

  In this sequence you will examine some of these words. We have indicated an approximate pronunciation of the words in English. Many people would pronounce them differently, however.

Now write in the correct answers to the following multiple choice questions.

98 *Savant* (pronounced *suh-vánt*), as in "Jill was surprised to see that the audience was not composed entirely of gray-bearded *savants,* but contained younger students as well."

  Savant = (a) young scholar, (b) older scholar, (c) illiterate person, or (d) children.

                                    Answer: _____.

▶ □□□ ◀

  A: (b) older scholar.

99   *Amateur* (pronounced *ám-uh-ter*), as in "The players in the tournament were half professional and half *amateur*."

Amateur = (a) one who plays for love of the activity, (b) an inferior competitor, (c) a young player, or (d) an official.

Answer: _____.

▶ □ ◀

A: (a) one who plays for love of the activity. (*Amateur* may also be pronounced in other ways. Many French words that were borrowed into English have acquired several different pronunciations.)

100   *Chef* (pronounced *shef*), as in "The entire elaborate meal was prepared by the *chef* in person."

Chef = (a) guest, (b) owner, (c) writer, or (d) head cook.

Answer: _____.

▶ □ ◀

A: (d) head cook.

101   *Protégé* (pronounced *pró-tuh-zhay*), as in "All those present knew that Brian was the senator's *protégé* and were therefore careful about what they said."

Protégé = (a) a young man who is assisted in his career by an influential person, (b) a person who protects those he respects, (c) one completely opposed, or (d) an assistant.

Answer: _____.

▶ □ ◀

A: (a) a young man who is assisted in his career by an influential person.

102   *Fiancée* (pronounced *fee-an-sáy*), as in "With great pride Bryan introduced his *fiancée* with the words, 'This is my future wife.' "

Fiancée = (a) a divorced woman, (b) an engaged man, (c) an engaged woman, or (d) a person who sells stocks and bonds.

Answer: _____.

▶ □ ◀

A: (c) an engaged woman.

103   *Raconteur* (pronounced *rah-kon-tér*), as in "Louis was such as skillful *raconteur* that he kept us spellbound with his stories until they turned out the lights."

Raconteur = (a) artist, (b) singer, (c) storyteller, or (d) listener.

Answer: _____.

▶ □ ◀

A: (c) storyteller.

---

104 *Protégée* (pronounced *pró-tuh-zhay*), as in "Everyone knew that Sharon was the governor's *protégée*, and that he supported her strongly."

Protégée = (a) a protector, (b) an opponent, (c) an assistant, or (d) a woman guided and helped by an older person.

Answer: _____.

▶ □ ◀

A: (d) a woman guided and helped by an older person.

---

105 *Fiancé* (pronounced *fee-an-sáy*), as in "As Ken danced with Lois, he forgot entirely that he was Margaret's *fiancé*."

Fiancé = (a) an engaged woman, (b) an engaged man, (c) an adviser on money matters, or (d) an ex-husband.

Answer: _____.

▶ □ ◀

A: (b) an engaged man.

---

106 *Emigré* (pronounced *ém-uh-gray*), as in "Because of her ancestors' loyalty to the king, they were forced to sell their extensive holdings in France and leave the country as *emigrés*."

Emigré = (a) criminal, (b) exile, (c) professional soldier, or (d) revolutionary.

Answer: _____.

▶ □ ◀

A: (b) exile.

---

107 *Divorcée* (pronounced *duh-vór-say*), as in "My family's welcome became as cold as ice when they discovered that Karen was a *divorcée*."

Divorcée = (a) a woman formerly married, (b) an engaged woman, (c) a girlfriend, or (d) a man formerly married.

Answer: _____.

▶ □ ◀

A: (a) a woman formerly married.

108–117 Match these words and phrases borrowed from Modern French with the correct definitions.

_____	*amateur*	a. older scholar
_____	*chef*	b. one who participates for pleasure
_____	*divorcée*	c. chief cook
_____	*emigré*	d. man assisted by an older person
_____	*fiancé*	e. engaged woman
_____	*fiancée*	f. teller of stories
_____	*protégé*	g. woman assisted by an older person
_____	*protégée*	h. engaged man
_____	*raconteur*	i. divorced woman
_____	*savant*	j. exile

▶ □ ◀

A: In order of occurrence: b, c, i, j, h, e, d, g, f, a.

118   In the following frames, write the French words that make the best sense in the sentences provided. Again, a menu of the French words:

amateur	divorcée	fiancé	protégé	raconteur
chef	emigré	fiancée	protégée	savant

"My family is very strict," said Jack, "and they will never consent to my marrying a woman who is twice a _____."

▶ □ ◀

A: Divorcée.

119   "Jeff's knees were knocking as he faced the eight serious and stately _____ who were to examine him."

▶ □ ◀

A: Savants.

120   "Herbert had always been interested in food, and it was no surprise to learn that he has become the _____ at the Plaza."

▶ □ ◀

A: Chef.

121   What is the antonym of *professional?*   _____

▶ □ ◀

A: Amateur.

122–123 What is the term used to describe an engaged man? _____ An engaged woman? _____

▶ □□□ ◀

A: Fiancé. Fiancée.

124–125 What French term means a woman assisted by a powerful person? _____ What is the corresponding term for a man so assisted? _____

▶ □□□ ◀

A: Protégée. Protégé.

126 "You will just love Harvey's stories," said Harriet. "He is the most amusing _____ I have ever met."

▶ □□□□□□□□□□□□□□□□□□□□□□□□□□□□□□□□□□□□□UU□□□□□□□ ◀

A: Raconteur.

127 "My ancestors were not common laborers like yours," said Diane. "They were not immigrants, they were aristocratic _____."

▶ □□□□□□□□□□□□□□□□□□□□□□□□□□□□□□□□□□□□□UU□□□□□□□ ◀

A: Emigrés.

■ Write the French words that are derived from the Latin words given below. The first five are comparatively simple.

128 Latin *amator* (= lover) > French _____.

▶ □□□ ◀

A: Amateur.

129–130 Latin *protego* (= protect) > French _____ and _____.

▶ □□□ ◀

A: Protégé (man) and protégée (woman).

131 Latin *divortium* (= divorce) > French _____.

▶ □□□ ◀

A: Divorcée.

132   Latin *emigrare* (= move away) > French _____.

□ □

A: Emigré.

■ The next five words are much changed. It is not one of the objectives of the course to try to explain such extensive changes. But you should be able to supply the right words after considering the meanings of the Latin words.

133   Latin *sapere* (= be wise) > French _____.

□ □

A: Savant. (The {ant} makes a noun or adjective out of a verb.)

134   Latin {**re**} (= again) plus Latin *computare* (= count, tell) > French _____.

□ □

A: Raconteur.

135–136   Latin *fidere* (= trust) > French *fiance* (= a promise) > French _____ and

_____.

□ □

A: Fiancé (man) and fiancée (woman).

137   Latin *caput* (= head) > French _____.

□ □

A: Chef.

NICE-TO-KNOW ■ The change from *caput* to *chef* is not as capricious as it looks. First, *caput* in Latin means not only "head" as part of the body but an important person. *Chef* in French means not only "head cook" but head of other jobs. Second, initial *c* in Latin often becomes *ch* in French, as French *chanter* (= sing) < Latin *cantare;* and, under certain conditions, Latin *p* becomes French *f.*

■ Following are ten more French words used in English. Remember that some people pronounce these words differently. Write the letter of the correct answer for each multiple-choice term.

138   *Encore* (pronounced *ón-kore*), as in "The tenor had to grant the audience's repeated requests for *encores."*

Encore = (a) bouquet, (b) repeat performance, (c) smile, or (d) welcome.

Answer: _____.

□ □

A: (b) repeat performance.

139 *Matinee* (pronounced *mat-tin-áy*), as in "Since Sue worked every evening until ten o'clock, she and Bill went mainly to *matinees*."

Matinee = (a) afternoon performance, (b) movie, (c) morning prayer, or (d) neighborhood bar.

Answer: _____.

A: (a) afternoon performance.

140 *Faux pas* (pronounced *fŏh-pah*), as in "How could I have been so stupid as to ask Mrs. Worthington about her husband? I have never made a *faux pas* like that in my life!"

Faux pas = (a) crime, (b) footprint, (c) social blunder, or (d) success.

Answer: _____.

A: (c) social blunder.

141 *Tour de force* (pronounced *ture-duh-fŏrce*), as in "Rolly's long and complicated answer to a question he didn't understand was a real *tour de force* and completely confused his questioner."

Tour de force = (a) journey by the police, (b) armed tower, (c) clever performance, (d) mistake.

Answer: _____.

A: (c) clever performance.

142 *Fait accompli* (pronounced *fet-tah-kom-plée*), as in " 'My friend,' said Martha's father, 'there is no point in your fussing about Martha's marriage. It is now a *fait accompli*.' "

Fait accompli = (a) difficult feat, (b) conspiracy, (c) accomplished fact, or (d) illegal marriage.

Answer: _____.

A: (c) accomplished fact.

143 *Ennui* (pronounced *ón-wee*), as in "Peter, we are so delighted to see you! We were all dying of *ennui*! Amuse us!"

Ennui = (a) boredom, (b) upset stomach, (c) dislike, or (d) too much exercise.

Answer: _____.

A: (a) boredom.

144 *Gauche* (pronounced *gohsh*), as in "When Ted combed his hair while my father was saying the prayer, I realized for the first time how *gauche* he could be."

Gauche = (a) lacking social grace, (b) amusing, (c) lovable, or (d) cruel.

Answer: _____.

▶ □□ ◀

A: (a) lacking social grace.

145 *Adroit* (pronounced *uh-dróyt*), as in "It was a pleasure to watch Jerry repair a typewriter. There was no wasted motion; his every move was *adroit*."

Adroit = (a) clumsy, (b) skillful, (c) startling, or (d) automatic.

Answer: _____.

▶ □□ ◀

A: (b) skillful.

146 *Menage* (pronounced *muh-náhzh*), as in "What a picture of confusion at the Wilson's! Children everywhere, pots boiling over on the stove, radio and TV competing at top volume! And yet I have never seen a happier *menage* than this group."

Menage = (a) zoo, (b) class, (c) children, or (d) household.

Answer: _____.

▶ □□ ◀

A: (d) household.

147 *Menagerie* (pronounced *muh-náh-zher-ree*), as in "The school also operates a small *menagerie*, a source of pleasure to the students and, we assume, to the occupants."

Menagerie = (a) nursing home, (b) collection of wild animals, (c) restaurant, or (d) reading service.

Answer: _____.

▶ □□ ◀

A: (b) collection of wild animals.

148–157 Match these French words and phrases with the correct equivalents.

_____ *adroit*	a. zoo
	b. household
_____ *encore*	c. skillful
	d. lacking social grace
_____ *ennui*	e. boredom
	f. accomplished fact
_____ *fait accompli*	g. clever performance
	h. social blunder
_____ *faux pas*	

(continued on next page)

_____ *gauche*

_____ *matinee*

_____ *menage*

_____ *menagerie*

_____ *tour de force*

i. afternoon performance
j. a repeat performance

A: In order of occurrence: c, j, e, f, h, d, i, b, a, g.

158 In the spaces provided below, write the French word or phrase from the last sequence that best fits the context.

"You're sitting on my hat!" cried Yvonne. "How can anyone be as _____ as you are!"

A: Gauche.

159 "The wound proved to be less serious than we had feared and was soon stitched up by the surgeon's _____ fingers."

A: Adroit.

160 "Surrounded by books, pictures, and recorded music, she still complained of _____."

A: Ennui.

161 "Sophie was gratified that her last set of songs had inspired the audience to ask for three _____."

A: Encores.

162 "Can you imagine trying to live in a _____ like the Dugans'?" cried Laura.

A: Menage.

163 "That settles it!" said Mr. Perkins. "Come with me. We're going to take you to the _____ to show you to the monkeys."

▶ □□□ ◀

    A: Menagerie.

164 "Let's see if we can get through lunch in time to catch the _____ at the Civic Center"

▶ □□□ ◀

    A: Matinee.

165 "What do you mean, you apologize for your 'little mistake'?" roared Mr. Gaspara. "Insulting my boss was more than just a little _____!"

▶ □□□ ◀

    A: Faux pas.

166 "In Ricardo's final game he played one inning at each position and got three hits. It was a real _____."

▶ □□□ ◀

    A: Tour de force.

167 "I would like to help you out," purred Mr. Jenkins, "but I am afraid that now that the judge has decided against you it is a real _____."

▶ □□□ ◀

    A: Fait accompli.

■ Using the words from the last sequence, give the French derivatives from Latin.

168 Latin *falsus* (= false) plus *passus* (= step) > French _____.

▶ □□□ ◀

    A: Faux pas.

169 Latin *matutinum* (= morning) > French _____.

▶ □□□ ◀

    A: Matinee.

170 In spite of the etymology, when are *matinees* performed? _____

▶ □□□ ◀

    A: In the afternoon.

171 Latin *ad* (= toward) plus Latin *dextra* (= right hand) > French _____.

▶ □□□ ◀

    A: Adroit.

172 For right-handed people, the right hand is the skilled one and *adroit* means "skillful." What French word do you think means "left-handed"? _____

▶ □□□ ◀

    A: Gauche.

173 Latin *factum* (= deed) plus Latin *ad* plus Latin *complere* (= fill up) > French _____
_____.

▶ □□□ ◀

    A: Fait accompli.

> **NICE-TO-KNOW** ■ Some of you have certainly been wondering exactly how we decide what words are "foreign words." The answer is that such a decision is highly subjective. If you were to compare dictionaries, you would see that they do not always agree on this matter. In general a word is "naturalized" (adopted into the language) if most people when using it are not aware of its origin. A word is regarded as a foreign word if people who use it are aware of its origin. In using such words people tend to give them their foreign pronunciation. Most people would consider *amateur* a completely naturalized word. *Fait accompli,* on the other hand, still seems foreign, and it is so marked in the dictionaries we have examined. In spite of these gray areas, the term "borrowing" is a useful one.

Italian Words in English
(Frames 174–203)

■ For centuries the land of Italy has been known for its accomplishments in the arts, particularly music. Consequently many musical terms have been borrowed from Italian. Choose a word from the menu below to answer the questions on musical terms.

allegro	*diminuendo*	*piano*
alto	*forte*	*pianoforte*
andante	*largo*	*soprano*
crescendo		

174 What Italian word comes from Latin *fortis* (= strong) and means "loud"? _____

▶ □□□ ◀

    A: Forte.

175 What Italian word comes from Latin *planus* (= smooth) and today means "soft"?
_____

▶ □ ◀

A: Piano.

176 What musical instrument has a name that describes the volume of sound it produces and means "soft and loud"? _____

▶ □ ◀

A: Pianoforte (usually shortened to piano).

NICE-TO-KNOW ■ With earlier keyboard instruments, like the harpsichord, one could not vary the volume by striking the keys harder or softer.

177 What Italian word comes from Latin *crescere* (= increase) and means "gradually increasing in sound"? _____

▶ □ ◀

A: Crescendo.

178 What Italian word comes from Latin *diminuere* (= decrease) and means "gradually decreasing in sound"? _____

▶ □ ◀

A: Diminuendo.

179 What Italian word comes from Latin *supra* (= above) and refers to the highest singing voice for women or boys? _____

▶ □ ◀

A: Soprano.

180 What Italian word comes from Latin *altus* (= high) and refers to the *lowest* singing voice for women or boys? _____

▶ □ ◀

A: Alto.

I **NICE-TO-KNOW** ■ Originally *alto* referred to the highest man's voice, now called a *countertenor.*

181 What Italian word comes from Latin *largus* (= large) and means the music should be played "in a stately manner"? _____

▶ □□□ ◀

   A: Largo.

182 What Italian word comes from Italian (not Latin) *andare* (= walk) and means "in moderate time"? _____

▶ □□□ ◀

   A: Andante.

183 What Italian word comes from Latin *alacer* (= quick) and means "in fast time"?
_____

▶ □□□ ◀

   A: Allegro.

184–193 Match the Italian musical term with the proper definition.

_____ *allegro*	a. musical instrument with keyboard
_____ *alto*	b. increasing in volume
_____ *andante*	c. highest singing voice for women or boys
_____ *crescendo*	d. in a stately manner
_____ *diminuendo*	e. loud
_____ *forte*	f. in fast tempo
_____ *largo*	g. decreasing in volume
_____ *piano*	h. soft
_____ *pianoforte*	i. lowest singing voice for women or boys
_____ *soprano*	j. in moderate tempo

▶ □□□ ◀

   A: In order of occurrence: f, i, j, b, g, e, d, h, a, c.

■ Using the same musical terms as in the last sequence, write in each space provided the word that fits the context.

194 "Easy, Jane; don't pound the keys. Don't you see the passage is marked _____?"

▶ □□□ ◀

   A: Piano.

329

195 "The scene opened with a magnificent procession of lords and ladies marching in dignified manner to the _____ movement of the music."

▶ □ ◀

A: Largo.

196 "We were enchanted by the high, true _____ voices of the women."

▶ □ ◀

A: Soprano.

197 "Not a rustle was heard in the concert hall as the music died away in a gradual _____."

▶ □ ◀

A: Diminuendo.

198 "Ann's rich, deep _____ voice filled the entire auditorium."

▶ □ ◀

A: Alto.

199 "The sudden transition between the passage marked piano and that marked _____ was startling."

▶ □ ◀

A: Forte.

200 "You are determined," said Mr. Fox, "to play either too fast or too slow. Obey the composer; he said play it _____."

▶ □ ◀

A: Andante.

201 "This is not a funeral march but a peasant dance the composer has put in. Play it in an _____ manner."

▶ □ ◀

A: Allegro.

202 "A player on the harpsichord cannot vary the volume as she can on a _____."

▶ □□□□□■□□□ ◀

    A: Pianoforte (or piano).

203 "What a thrill as the chorus crashed out the finale in a stirring _____."

▶ □□□ ◀

    A: Crescendo.

Spanish Words in English
(Frames 204–223)

■ Spanish words in English were mostly employed in the American Southwest. When Spanish words came into the language the pronunciation was much changed, as is true of French words that were borrowed. But the French loan words retained their spelling, while the Spanish words were often so changed that a speaker of modern Spanish would not recognize either the sound of the word or its appearance. How could a Spaniard guess that the word *hoosegow* means "jail" and is the American spelling of Spanish *juzgado*?

Here is a menu of words used in English that were originally Spanish. Write a word of Spanish origin in each space provided.

alligator	*loco*	*poncho*
bonanza	*mosquito*	*rodeo*
canyon	*mustang*	*savvy*
cigar		

204 "A crocodile much resembles an _____ in appearance."

▶ □□□ ◀

    A: Alligator.

205 "To give up a young lady like that," said Andy, "a man would have to be plumb _____."

▶ □□□ ◀

    A: Loco.

206 "Well, I'll be seeing you," said Judith, as she swung into the saddle of her _____."

▶ □□□ ◀

    A: Mustang.

207 "There was a big increase this summer in the number of competitors in calf roping at the annual _____ held in Three Forks."

▶ □□□ ◀

    A: Rodeo.

208   "It would sure be nice out here," said Slim, slapping his legs, "if it weren't for these pesky _____."

▶ □□ ◀

    A: Mosquitos.

209   "To get to the mine you must hike up this trail through the _____ until you reach its head."

▶ □□ ◀

    A: Canyon.

210   "I don't know when I have smoked a _____ as good as this."

▶ □□ ◀

    A: Cigar.

211   "Looks like rain, boys," sang out Luke. "Better get out your _____."

▶ □□ ◀

    A: Ponchos.

212   "This dude ranch we have developed has done well so far, but it promises next year to be a real _____, enough to make us all rich."

▶ □□ ◀

    A: Bonanza.

213   "I don't know about his table manners," said Mort, "but he sure has a lot of _____ about horses."

▶ □□ ◀

    A: Savvy.

■ Some of these words, like *mosquito*, are of Latin origin; other words, like *poncho*, were borrowed by the Spaniards from Indian languages. In this sequence, give the English word borrowed from Spanish.

214   Latin *mixtus* (= mixed, wild) > Spanish *mestengo* > English _____.

▶ □□ ◀

    A: Mustang.

215 Latin *ille* (= the) plus Latin *lacertus* (= lizard) > Spanish *el lagarto* > English

_____.

▶ □ ◀

A: Alligator.

216 Latin *musca* (= fly) > Spanish and English _____.

▶ □ ◀

A: Mosquito.

217 Latin *canna* (= tube) > Spanish *cañón* > English _____.

▶ □ ◀

A: Canyon.

218 Maya *sicar* (= to smoke tobacco) > Spanish *cigarro* > English _____.

▶ □ ◀

A: Cigar. (Maya is an Indian language spoken in Central America.)

219 Latin *ulucus* (= owl) > Spanish *loco* (= crazy) > English _____.

▶ □ ◀

A: Loco.

220 Vulgar Latin *bonacia* (= prosperity) > Spanish and English _____.

▶ □ ◀

A: Bonanza.

I   NICE-TO-KNOW ■ *Vulgar Latin* was the language spoken by the common people of Rome.

221 Latin *rotare* (= move in a circle) > Spanish *rodear* (= surround) > Spanish and English

_____.

▶ □ ◀

A: Rodeo.

222 Latin *sapere* (= be wise) > Spanish *sabe* (= do you know?) > English _____.

▶ □ ◀

A: Savvy.

223 Araucan *pontho* > Spanish and English _____.

▶ □□ ◀

    A: Poncho. (Araucan is an Indian language spoken in Chile.)

Words from Other Languages
(Frames 224–252)

■ For many reasons, speakers of English have come into contact with many different countries. When they met new objects or ideas for which there was no word in English, they often borrowed the term. Use the menu below to write in the words that fit the context.

blitzkrieg	*igloo*	*sauerkraut*
boomerang	*kangaroo*	*skunk*
canoe	*kayak*	*wigwam*
hurricane		

224 The Eskimos paddle a boat they call a _____.

▶ □□ ◀

    A: Kayak.

225 The name which the Abnaki Indians gave to a common black and white animal with a powerful defense weapon was _____.

▶ □□ ◀

    A: Skunk. (The Abnaki Indians lived in Maine.)

226 Some Eskimos build a winter shelter from snow called an _____.

▶ □□ ◀

    A: Igloo.

227 The Germans perfected a type of motorized attack in the Second World War that they called a _____.

▶ □□ ◀

    A: Blitzkrieg. (Although you were told earlier that German nouns are capitalized, *blitzkrieg* here is an English word borrowed from German.)

228 The Algonquin Indians in eastern and central North America lived in a domed shelter they called a _____.

▶ □□ ◀

    A: Wigwam.

229 The Australian aborigines use a throwing stick that they call a _____.

▶ □ ◀

    A: Boomerang.

230 Columbus in 1493 used a Carib Indian word to describe the small boats the natives used. What was the word? _____

▶ □ ◀

    A: Canoe.

231 A prominent animal in Australia is a marsupial (= bears young in pouch) called a _____.

▶ □ ◀

    A: Kangaroo.

232 In the West Indies the local name for a violent tropical cyclone is a _____.

▶ □ ◀

    A: Hurricane.

233 The Germans eat a dish of pickled chopped cabbage. What do they call it? _____

▶ □ ◀

    A: Sauerkraut.

234 Abnaki *segonku* > English _____.

▶ □ ◀

    A: Skunk.

235 Eskimo *igdlu* > English _____.

▶ □ ◀

    A: Igloo.

236 What is the native Australian term for a throwing stick? _____

▶ □ ◀

    A: Boomerang.

237 What German term means "lightning war"? _____

□□

A: Blitzkrieg.

238 What Eskimo term have we borrowed for a small double-ended boat? _____

□□

A: Kayak.

239 What animal with a strong odor is found only in North America? _____

□□

A: Skunk.

240 Ojibway *wigiwam* > English _____.

□□

A: Wigwam. (The Ojibway lived in the regions near the Great Lakes.)

241 Taino *huracan* > Spanish *huracán* > English _____.

□□

A: Hurricane. (The Taino were a tribe of the West Indies.)

242 Carib *canoa* > Spanish *canoa* > English _____.

□□

A: Canoe.

243–244 What two words in the sequence above come from Indians who lived in the Caribbean Sea, meaning "strong wind" and "little boat"? _____ and _____

□□

A: Hurricane and canoe.

245–246 What two words in the list came from German? _____ and _____

□□

A: Blitzkrieg and sauerkraut.

247–248   What two words were Eskimo? _____ and _____

▶ □ ◀

    A: Igloo and kayak.

249–250   What two words came from American Indian languages? _____ and _____

▶ □ ◀

    A: Wigwam and skunk.

251–252   What two English words came from languages spoken in Australia? _____
and _____

▶ □ ◀

    A: Kangaroo and boomerang.

WORD LIST

The following concepts were presented in this unit:

Indo-European languages   11   cognate   14

Here is a list of words discussed in this unit. Refer to a dictionary if you need to.

adroit 145	faux pas 140	piano 175
allegro 183	fiancé 105	pianoforte 176
alligator 204	fiancée 102	poncho 211
alto 180	filial 37	pork 92
amateur 99	forte 174	protégé 101
andante 182	fraternity 36	protégée 104
beef 94	gauche 144	raconteur 103
blitzkrieg 227	hurricane 232	rodeo 207
bonanza 212	igloo 226	sauerkraut 233
boomerang 229	kangaroo 231	savant 98
canoe 230	kayak 224	savvy 213
canyon 209	largo 181	skunk 225
chef 100	loco 205	soprano 179
cigar 210	maternal 35	sorority 39
crescendo 177	matinee 139	swine 91
diminuendo 178	menage 146	tour de force 141
divorcée 107	menagerie 147	veal 96
emigré 106	mosquito 208	venison 97
encore 138	mustang 206	wigwam 228
ennui 143	mutton 95	
fait accompli 142	paternal 38	

REVIEW EXERCISES

Purpose: To learn more about some words borrowed from different languages and cultures.

Directions: Look up these words in a dictionary to determine the language from which each has been borrowed. Do ten of your choice.

aloha	coyote	Sabbath	sofa
bronco	jubilee	sauerbraten	tamale
cherub	kibitz	schmaltz	tea
chipmunk	lasso	shampoo	tepee
chocolate	loot	sherbet	tulip
coolie	raccoon	snorkel	voodoo
cotton			

WORDS OF INTERESTING ORIGIN

Directions: Find in your dictionary the origins of the italicized words. Then write down (a) the language of origin, (b) the etymological meaning (= early meaning), and (c) the modern meaning.

1. *Hybrid*, as in "The *hybrid* corn was a brilliant invention and has increased our crop by 25 percent."

   Language of origin: _____

   Etymological meaning: _____

   Modern meaning: _____

2. *Discombobulated*, as in "Frank was completely *discombobulated* when we all jumped out of our hiding places and shouted 'Surprise!' and 'Happy Birthday!'"

   Language of origin: _____

   Etymological meaning: _____

   Modern meaning: _____

3. *Paradigm*, as in "From her very first day in school, Alice was a *paradigm* of industry and intelligence."

   Language of origin: _____

   Etymological meaning: _____

   Modern meaning: _____

4. *Scintilla*, as in "There is not a *scintilla* of evidence to support your preposterous story."

   Language of origin: _____

   Etymological meaning: _____

   Modern meaning: _____

5. *Lurid*, as in "As he slunk back home, Sam imagined that everyone was reading and commenting on the *lurid* headlines that described his shame."

   Language of origin: _____

   Etymological meaning: _____

   Modern meaning: _____

EASILY CONFUSED WORDS

Use a dictionary as needed.

1. ***Biweekly / semiweekly.*** These words contrast the Latin morphemes {**bi**} = twice, and {**semi**} = half. A *biweekly* magazine is one that is issued every two weeks, while a *semiweekly* comes out every half week, or we would probably say "twice a week." (Some people use *biweekly* to mean "twice a week.")

2. ***Unconscionable / unconscious.*** These both contain the base *conscious*, meaning "knowing" or "aware." *Unconscious* means "not being conscious, being deprived of one's own senses," as in "After that blow Rod lay *unconscious* for fifteen minutes, not moving a muscle." *Unconscionable* means not guided by one's conscience, as in "That *unconscionable* villain Dodge charged me at least twice what the room was worth."

3. ***Tortuous / tortured.*** Both are derived from Latin {**torqu /tort**} = twist. The word *tortuous* today means "twisted," full of curves either in a literal sense, as in "It was impossible to make time on this *tortuous* mountain road, with its narrow hairpin turns," or in a figurative sense, as in "His argument was so deceptive, so purposely vague, so *tortuous* that the jury was completely confused." The connection of *torture* with "twist" is that *torture* often consisted of various kinds of twisting. Today it broadly means any severe pain, as in "His body was so racked and *tortured* by his arthritis that we could only stay with him a short while." It also means "distorted" (much like *tortuous*), as in "His subject may have been interesting, but the *tortured* arguments that he dragged in as proof finally appeared just silly."

Use the six words in the sentences where each makes sense.

1. Clarence sat there eating his sandwich, totally _____ of the rattlesnake beside him.

2. Phil's paper came out twice a week, so it was truly a _____ publication.

3. The District Attorney gradually revealed the _____ connections between the accused and the mob.

4. The magazine appeared in 26 issues per year, that is, it was a _____ publication.

5. Alden had been _____ by pangs of remorse for his part in the joke that had proven so tragic.

6. A person would have had to be an _____ rascal not to have been touched by Gilda's story.

LATIN PHRASES

First try to get the meaning of the Latin phrases from the context of the sentences below, choosing a meaning from the list that follows. Write the number of the Latin phrase beside the definition that fits.

1st among equals

1. *Primus inter pares,* as in "It was a meeting of distinguished people, but they were all waiting for Mr. Knapp to take charge. It was a clear case of *primus inter pares.*"

fm eggs

2. *Ab ovo,* as in "Pardon me, Professor Rounds," said the Dean, "since we are not at all acquainted with the subject perhaps you should begin *ab ovo.*"

seize the day

3. *Carpe diem,* as in "My philosophy is simple," said Doug, "and borrowed from the Latin poet: *carpe diem.* Pour me another drink if you will."

4. *Caveat emptor,* as in "I agree," said the salesman, "that most people get a car that lasts longer than the one you bought from us. I am afraid that you are out of luck: *caveat emptor,* you know."

5. *Quid pro quo,* as in "In this business you do not get anything free. There is always a *quid pro quo* involved."

_____ an empty warning	_____ something (in return) for something
_____ from the very beginning	_____ enjoy (each) day
_____ first equals	_____ What helps who?
_____ (keeps) away from eggs	_____ increase daily
_____ let the buyer beware	_____ first among equals

Second, copy the word-by-word translation that you find for each phrase in your dictionary. Then check to see if the meaning you have selected seems to match the modern meaning.

	Word-by-Word Translation	Modern Meaning
primus inter pares	_____	_____
ab ovo	_____	_____
carpe diem	_____	_____
caveat emptor	_____	_____
quid pro quo	_____	_____

Supplementary Exercises

Unit 1

New Words with Familiar Morphemes

Each of the italicized words contains either a prefix or a base you have learned in this lesson. Use these words and sentences as directed by your instructor.

1. Our light permitted us to get a dim view of the statue in the *recess* in the wall.
2. The *retro* look in fashion is one of many fashion trends.
3. John explained to us the theory of rocket *propulsion*.
4. Although *expulsion* was listed in the catalog as one of the penalties, no one in the memory of the oldest student had ever been expelled.
5. The *dissolution* of the City Council threw the city into chaos.
6. All that time I felt the strongest *compulsion* to reveal the whole story to the police.
7. The next history unit will deal with the rise of the *confederacy*.
8. If you will submit a *requisition* in triplicate, we will see what we can do.
9. The villain was almost too *despicable* a character in that movie.
10. We are hoping that the teacher will *intervene* before it is too late.

More Easily Confused Words

Use as directed by your instructor.

advice/advise   evoke/invoke

eminent/imminent   expedite/extradite

Latin Phrases

Use a dictionary to find the word-by-word translation and the modern meaning for each phrase.

	Word-by-Word Translation	Modern Meaning
ex tempore	_____	_____
in camera	_____	_____
in loco parentis	_____	_____

Use the Latin phrases in the sentences where each makes sense.

Because of the sensational nature of the testimony, the judge admitted only qualified people to a session held _____ .

There is often a conflict between students who want fewer regulations and college officials who believe that the institution has _____ responsibilities.

No matter how well I know the subject matter, I never dare give a speech on that topic

_____ .

Topic: Education
Use as directed by your instructor.
    For many centuries Latin either was the language used in schools or was one of the subjects that was considered of prime importance. It is therefore not surprising that Latin (and Greek) terms were much used for academic events. Here is a letter that one student might have written to another.

Dear Michael,
    Tomorrow they are holding *commencement* at our school, and I really feel that the name of the *ceremony* is appropriate, for as far as I can see a whole new life will begin for me. After *graduation* I expect to attend our state *university*. I will take a program in *liberal arts* and expect to receive a *bachelor's degree,* along with a *diploma* to hang on the wall of my study. I hope to go on to get a *master's* and possibly a *Ph.D*. Did you know that my uncle is a *trustee* at State, which is much the same office as a *regent*. Naturally he is pleased that I want to go to school there.
    Our class has been very close ever since the ninth *grade*. Becky is *valedictorian,* and I am happy to be *salutatorian*. We are almost all going to different *colleges* and so will each acquire a new *alma mater*.

Cordially yours,
Joan

Unit 2

Exercise on Identifying Word Classes

Identify the class of each of the following italicized words, using both morphological and syntactical criteria.

1. The cat fell into the *well*.

2. That's all very *well* and good.

3. He writes quite *well* .

4. At these words, tears *welled* up in Jane's eyes.

5. I think you should drive more *slowly*.

6. *Slow* down; curve ahead.

7. That was a *slow* third lap.

8. The muddy third turn *slowed* the race considerably.

9. That cat is certainly *pretty*.

10. I am *pretty* certain about that.

More Easily Confused Words

Use as directed by your instructor.

ascribe/prescribe   entomology/etymology

emigrate/immigrate   exceed/excel

Latin Phrases

Use a dictionary to find the word-by-word translation and the modern meaning for each phrase.

	Word-by-Word Translation	Modern Meaning
mens sana in corpore sano	_____	_____
e pluribus unum	_____	_____
cum laude	_____	_____

(See also *magna cum laude, summa cum laude*)

Use the Latin phrases in the sentences where each makes sense.

Maria was proud to have on her graduate diploma a gold seal with the words

_____ .

The ideal student athlete could be characterized by the phrase _____ .

The legend on U.S. coinage that indicates that a single nation was formed from thirteen states is _____ .

Topic: Politics

Use as directed by your instructor.

The two *major political* parties in the United *States* are the *Democratic* and *Republican*. The national *legislature* is *bicameral*, having a *Senate* and a House of *Representatives*, which meet in the *nation's capitol*. The *administration* is headed by the *President* and *Vice President*. The task of interpreting the laws falls upon the *Supreme Court*. The chief *executive officer* in a state is the *governor*. Cities are usually run by a *mayor* and a *council*.

Where there is no system of government, a condition of *anarchy* exists. In this *situation* a *dictator* often emerges who rules with legal restrictions. This type of government in Italy was called *fascism,* from the Roman *symbol* of *authority,* the *axe*. A *prominent* form of government today is *communism,* a form of Marxism. Between communism and democracy we may place *socialism*.

Unit 3

New Words with Familiar Morphemes

Each of the italicized words contains either a prefix or a base you have learned in this lesson or a previous lesson. Use these words and sentences as directed by your instructor.

1. This *expository* material is clearly presented.
2. Although he learns quickly, his *retention* is poor.
3. Jack was forced to make *restitution* for what he took.
4. Uncle Bill became more and more *contentious* as we talked.
5. The *tension* of the wire was considerable.
6. The letters were *inscribed* very carefully into the marble.
7–8. Many people confuse the words *inductive* and *deductive*.
9. The police were able to *apprehend* the robber in a short time.
10. Most people considered the deed a *contravention* of the law.

More Easily Confused Words

Use as directed by your instructor.

iniquity/inequity   famous/infamous

implicit/explicit   elicit/illicit

Latin Phrases

Use a dictionary to find the word-by-word translation and the modern meaning for each phrase.

	Word-by-Word Translation	Modern Meaning
ante bellum	_____	_____
post bellum	_____	_____
curriculum vitae	_____	_____

Use the Latin phrases in the sentences where each makes sense.

Those of use who will be looking for teaching jobs after graduation will need to prepare a _____ .

Some people divide all of American history into two periods, the _____ and the _____ periods.

Topic: Photography

Use as directed by your instructor.

The art of *photography* is generally considered to have been invented in 1822 by Joseph Niepce. Most of the *technical* terms are derived from Latin and Greek. For example, the lightproof box in which the *film* is placed is called a *camera* from the Latin *camera obscura,* a popular feature at fairs.* Other than the box, the only thing needed for a simple camera is a *lens*. Although this lens may be just a pinhole, the lens is usually made of glass or plastic and receives its name from its resemblance to a beam. The light rays that are gathered by the lens meet at a point called the *focus*. The difference in meaning between English "focus" and Latin "focus" is an example of how the meaning of a word can change greatly.

The size of the *aperture* through which the light rays enter the camera is often controlled by a shutter called an *iris diaphragm*. The size of the opening determines the amount of *exposure* that the *film* receives. There are many kinds of film for different purposes. With most black-and-white pictures the film becomes a *negative* when it is exposed; it is then *reversed* again in a *positive* print.

The serious photographer will need more than one lens. A *telephoto* lens, for example, works like a *telescope*. For a large telephoto lens a *tripod* is necessary to prevent blurring through movement of the camera.

*A tent with a lens in one side that projects the outside scene upside down.

Unit 4

New Words with Familiar Morphemes

1. Charles now was entering his *manic* phase, and we did not know whether we could control him.

2. Whatever outsiders thought, the Fawcett family was a pure *matriarchy*.

3. Many physical handicaps are now recognized as *genetic* in origin.

4. The *hydraulic* pressure was not sufficient to bring water to the blaze.

5. Grandmother's last years were a retreat into a warm and gentle *theocentric* world.

6. Maria's *dyslexia* caused her teachers to underestimate her real intelligence.

7. Ever since his fall Mike has suffered *dysfunction* of his legs.

8 Muscular *dystrophy* is believed to be genetic in origin.

9. The reasons for *kleptomania* are neither obvious nor simple.

10. Pansies are one of the common *heliotropic* flowers.

More Easily Confused Words

diagnosis/prognosis   allude/elude

empathy/sympathy   contiguous/continuous

Latin Phrases

	Word-by-Word Translation	Modern Meaning
cogito ergo sum	_____	_____
mea culpa	_____	_____
stet	_____	_____

Use the Latin phrases in the sentences where each makes sense.

My confusion about what to leave in or take out of my research paper is indicated by the number of times the word _____ occurs in my rough draft.

After the way she mishandled the situation, we expected at least a _____ from her.

Taken from the world of philosophy, _____ is perhaps the best known Latin phrase.

Topic: The Theater

Drama was an invention of the Greeks, but its origins are shrouded in *mystery*. From its name, *tragedy* seems to have some *connection* with goats, but *classical scholars* do not agree on what this connection was. While a tragedy was a serous play with an unhappy ending, a *comedy* was a play with a happy ending. Ancient comedy did not have to be humorous, but some plays, particularly the Greek comedies of Aristophanes and the Latin ones by Plautus, are *hilarious*.

Dancing was important in ancient drama, and the place where this dancing took place was called the *orchestra,* a round area in front of the stage. From the Greek word for "stage" come the English words *scene* and *scenery*.

The *acoustics* in ancient theaters were excellent, and anyone in the last row of the *auditorium* could hear the slightest whisper from the stage. Greek *actors* (and perhaps Roman actors) wore masks, from which comes the English word *person*.

The number of actors was limited, and an actor played several parts. The principal actor was called the *protagonist*.

Unit 5

New Words with Familiar Morphemes

1. "Don't tell me," grunted Robert, "that a man like myself with a degree in *thermodynamics* can't get this fire going."
2. Among the less well known people on the movie set are the *cinematographers*.
3. One of childhood's greatest thrills is getting an *odometer* for your bicycle and watching the miles tick by.

4. Too much exposure to the sun may lead to a precancerous condition called "actinic *dermatitis.*"

5. Many colleges have changed the name of the Department of Physical Education to that of *Kinesiology.*

6. "There is no known *antidote* to the poison I have given you," snarled the mad scientist.

7. Danny's *antagonist* in the game was twenty pounds heavier than he was.

8. Sue has been subject to severe attacks of *hypochondria* that incapacitate her.

9. The *syncopation* in the accompaniment to this song is most effective.

10. NATO is the *acronym* for North Atlantic Treaty Organization.

More Easily Confused Words

inflict/afflict   analogous/anomalous

annual/perennial   affect/effect

Latin Phrases

	Word-by-Word Translation	Modern Meaning
a priori	_____	_____
Deo volente	_____	_____
nolo contendere	_____	_____

Use the Latin phrases in the sentences where each makes sense.

We decided to get together again next year at this time, _____ .

We often read in the newspaper that an accused person will change his plea from guilty to _____ .

It was clear that my instructor expected me to use _____ reasoning in dealing with this issue.

Topic: Communication

Communication can occur in many ways. When you go home at night, your dog may communicate his *delight* at seeing you. In a narrower *sense,* communication is by spoken *language* and by secondary systems of *transmitting* language.

We may define language as an *arbitrary* system of *verbal* symbols by means of which members of a community cooperate. The system may be *analyzed* on four *hierarchical* levels. First comes the *phonemic* level, that is, the meaningful contrast in the sounds of a language. Thus in English the word "pig" means one thing and "big" is something else. The next level is *morphemic,* the *minimum* units of meaning, like the division of "boys" into {boy} and {s}. There is the *syntax,* the meaningful arrangement of morphemes, like the contrast between "The boy sees the girl" and "The girl sees the boy." Finally there is the *lexicon,* the meaning of the morphemes. In this course we have dealt almost entirely with the lexicon, since as speakers of English you know the phonology, morphology, and syntax.

The most important secondary system is writing, by which something that someone said or might have said is conveyed onto paper by arbitrary *symbols,* twenty-six letters in English.

Both the spoken language and writing may be conveyed in various ways. We may transmit *oral-aural* messages by *telephone.* We receive *radio* and *television* messages in our homes. Written, personal messages are most commonly brought by the *postal* carrier, although messages are sent also by *telegraph* and through *computers.*

Unit 6

New Words with Familiar Morphemes

1. Prefixes and suffixes are types of *affixes.*

2. The mayor demanded—and got—a *retraction* of the article that had so offended him.

3. The rate of *recidivism* in young inmates is distressingly high.

4. We were required to wait a full hour in the *antechamber* before we could see the great man.

5. From the start we felt *circumscribed* by useless requirements.

6. The *aboriginal* inhabitants have developed some amazing skills.

7. The treatment you request is strongly *contraindicated* by your last examination.

8. An *ambulance* gets its name from the fact that it is a moving hospital.

9. The *translucent* panes of glass in the door gave a soft, diffused light to the room.

10. The attacks of fever were now only *intermittent.*

More Easily Confused Words

supplement/complement   deductive/inductive

abuse/misuse   antiseptic/aseptic

Latin Phrases

	Word-by-Word Translation	Modern Meaning
pro bono publico	_____	_____
de facto	_____	_____
requiescat in pace	_____	_____

Use the Latin phrases in the sentences where each makes sense.

Because there are so many powerful people on the advisory committee, they seem to have become a _____ executive committee.

My lawyer has volunteered his time to _____ cases involving the homeless.

One frequently sees inscribed on a tombstone the words _____ (abbreviated as _____ .)

Topic: Ancient Athletics

The origin of *athletics* is clouded in mystery. Who first thought of having a boxing match or a running race? Every four years, however, when we hold our *Olympic* Games we are reminded of our debt to Greece. In the Greek games there were several *equestrian* or *hippic* events, both bareback and chariot racing. The *prestige* for a *victorious* owner was *enormous*. The rest of the program consisted of eight events: four running events, a *pentathlon,* and three *combat sports*. There was a *stade* (about 200 meters), a double stade, a long-distance run (about three *miles*), and a hoplitodromos (a race in armor of about three miles*)*. The word *stadium* takes its name from the stade.

The pentathlon, as the etymology shows, consisted of five events. Two of these, a stade run and wrestling, were also competed for as separate events, but the other three, which were contested only in the framework of the pentathlon, were the long jump, the *discus,* and the *javelin.*

Unit 7

New Words with Familiar Morphemes

1. Scientists who study animal behavior are usually opposed to *anthropomorphic* explanations.
2. In linguistics, an *asterisk* before a word means that the word is not attested.
3. Dad has solved the problem of noise in our house. We have an *audiometer,* and when the noise reaches a certain level, the fuses blow out.
4. A symbol like $ or % is called a *logogram*.
5. *Impecunious* though I may be, I will not accept money from you.
6. A large percentage of diseases are at least partially *psychosomatic* in origin.
7. The causes of *arteriosclerosis* are not understood.
8. You will have to wait until next week for the *sequel* to this story.
9. The medical profession is asking whether all *hysterectomies* are really necessary.
10. Historically, a *metropolis* was a city that sent out colonies, as in ancient Greece. What is its modern meaning?

More Easily Confused Words

collect/collate	avocation/vocation
device/devise	amoral/immoral

Latin Phrases

	Word-by-Word Translation	Modern Meaning
ars gratia artis	_____	_____
artes, scientia, veritas	_____	_____
errare humanum est	_____	_____
post hoc, ergo propter hoc	_____	_____

Use the Latin phrases in the sentences where each makes sense.

Because Tim won the first race of the season wearing a bandage on his knee, he decided to wear it for the next race, too. Tim's reasoning can be explained by the Latin phrase
_____ .

My sculptor friend, who is a movie buff, has taken for his motto the MGM trademark
_____ .

Because of all the mistakes I seem to be making, I should take as my motto _____

A school with a broad liberal orientation would appropriately have as its motto
_____ .

Topic: Modern Athletics

In modern times we have borrowed some of the events in which the Greeks participated, like the discus and the javelin. At other times we have borrowed just the name. For example, the modern pentathlon does not have the same events as the ancient pentathlon. Our modern *decathlon* has a Greek name, but the event was not known in ancient times. The *marathon* takes its name from a battle near Athens in 490 B.C.; a later source says that a Greek warrior ran from the battle to Athens to *announce* the victory. When the Olympic Games were renewed in 1896, a distance run of about twenty-six miles was added to the program.

Perhaps the most popular sports today are those that use a *ball* of some sort. Although the Greeks and Romans had ball games, we cannot reconstruct from the *scanty evidence* how the games were played. Some of them seem to have been noncompetitive, like our own *frisbee* throwing, but others had some system of *scoring*. There is no direct link, however, between ancient and modern ball games.

Today there are games involving a large ball, like basketball; or a small hard one, like *golf;* or one *squashed* flat, like a *hockey puck*. The ball may be carried in games like football or *rugby,* kicked as in *soccer,* passed and bounced as in basketball, or hit with an *implement* as in baseball, *tennis,* or *lacrosse.*

Some sports involve ice and snow. *Prominent* is *skiing.* Thousands are *schussing* through *powder snow* or snaking between and over the *moguls* who have never entered a *slalom* or downhill run or *ascended* to the top of a jumping hill.

Unit 8

New Words with Familiar Morphemes

1. The whole approach in this book on Third World countries is *ethnocentric*.
2. One feature of the Civil War that everyone recognizes is its *fratricidal* nature.
3. Pete was recognized as a *psychopath* and is now receiving the care he needs.
4. The people of that region are progressing in *pisciculture* to improve their economic status.
5. Under abnormal stress the mast of the boat was showing signs of *flexure*.
6. The famous actor was in retirement, writing his *autobiography*.
7. The *carnage* in that battle was frightful.
8. The recognition that the *geocentric* theory of Ptolemy was false was a great shock to humankind.
9. The phylum of *arthropods,* which includes insects, is enormous.
10. "We must wait for the results of the *biopsy* before we can do anything else," said Dr. MacFarlane.

More Easily Confused Words

perpetuate/perpetrate   apposition/opposition

volition/violation   compose/compile

Latin Phrases

	Word-by-Word Translation	Modern Meaning
alma mater	_____	_____
ars longa, vita brevis	_____	_____
de novo	_____	_____
quod erat demonstrandum	_____	_____

Use the Latin phrases in the sentences where each makes sense.

The letters Q.E.D. at the end of a mathematical problem stand for _____ .

It was pleasant to return to my _____ for my 20th class reunion.

Because of all the problems we encountered on the project, we decided to cut our losses and begin _____ .

The newly created cultural arts center put on its stationery the Latin phrase _____.

Topic: The Earth

It was not until the sixteenth century that man realized that our *earth* was a *planet,* traveling in *orbit* around the sun like Mercury, Venus, and other bodies. As everyone now knows, the earth is a *globe* slightly flattened at the *poles.* On *maps* and globes, the earth's area is marked off into a *grid.* There are imaginary lines running from one pole to another called the *meridians* of *longitude;* the numbering *system* begins at Greenwich, England, which is therefore on *zero* longitude. The *equator* is an *imaginary* line *equidistant* from the two poles at all points. One of the countries through which the equator passes is called *Ecuador* for that reason. The equator divides the world into two *hemispheres,* north and south. Less exactly defined are the eastern and western hemispheres; *Europe, Asia,* and *Africa* are in the eastern hemisphere.

Much of the world is covered by water; the two largest *oceans* are the *Atlantic* and the *Pacific.* The *Antarctic* continent is almost entirely covered by enormous *glaciers,* while the Arctic is mostly sea, frozen over most of the year.

Climate is the average weather for a given place over a period of years. Roughly speaking there are five climate *zones:* antarctic, southern *temperate,* tropical, northern temperate, and arctic. The temperate zones are on the whole the *areas* most suited for man's survival, but they contain a wide diversity of climate.

Unit 9

New Words with Familiar Morphemes

1. The meteorological *phenomena* have been extraordinary this season. (What is the singular form of *phenomena?*)

2. There was only one *larva* in the box this morning. (What is the irregular plural of *larva?*)

3. The two plants were found to belong to the same *phylum.* (What is the irregular plural of *phylum?*)

4. He received an *honorarium* for his talk. (What is the irregular plural of *honorarium?*)

5. Our collection of *papyri* is the finest in the country. (What is the singular of *papyri?*)

6. The *amoeba* has started to separate. (What is the irregular plural of *amoeba?*)

7. Look at this unusual *fungus* I have just found. (What is the irregular plural of *fungus?*)

8. My favorite teacher at the university was given the title of Professor *Emerita* on her retirement. (What is the form of *emerita* if applied to a male?)

More Easily Confused Words

anonymous/autonomous   anacronism/anarchism

coherent/cohesive   misogamy/misogyny

Latin Phrases

	Word-by-Word Translation	Modern Meaning
errata	_____	_____
post partum	_____	_____
prima facie	_____	_____
sine qua non	_____	_____

Use the Latin phrases in the sentences where each makes sense.

Even after his hard work at proofreading, the revised edition of Tim's book still contains a surprisingly long list of _____ .

At this time of year, rain gear is a _____ when hiking in that region.

The documents found during the police search of the office were considered to be ample _____ evidence of illegal activity.

My cousin was warned that after the birth of her first child she might suffer _____ depression.

Topic: The Human Skeleton

There are five parts of the human *skeleton* that are more prominent than the others. First is the *skull,* which is on top of the *thorax.* Below the thorax is the *pelvis,* of which the hip bones or *ilia* [plural] are prominent. Set into ball and socket joints in the pelvis are the *femora* [singular: *femur*]. Below the knee are the *fibula*, in the front part of the lower leg, and the *tibia,* the bone behind the fibula.

The *clavicle* supports the arms, resembling the legs in having three prominent bones. Corresponding to the thigh bone (femur) is the *humerus* in the upper arm; in the lower part of the arm are the *ulna* and the smaller *radius*. The *spine,* comprised of thirty-three *vertebrae,* supports the *pelvic* girdle, the thorax, and the skull.

There are 206 bones in the skeleton, of which we will mention only a few. We are all conscious of our *patella,* or kneecap. The *scapula* is a large, broad bone know as the shoulder blade. The difficulty of remembering such *anatomical* terms is shown by the number of *mnemonic* devices used, such as the one for the twelve *cranial* nerves: "On Old Olympus' Towering Top A Finn And German Viewed A Hop."

Unit 10

More Easily Confused Words

biannual/biennial/semiannual   requisite/prerequisite/perquisite

infer/induce   interstate/intrastate

Latin Phrases

	Word-by-Word Translation	Modern Meaning
annuit coeptis	_____	_____
novus ordo seclorum *(saeclorum)*	_____	_____
viva voce	_____	_____
vox populi	_____	_____

Use the Latin phrases in the sentences where each makes sense.

Since there did not seem to be a need for a secret ballot, the vote was taken _____ .

A Latin phrase appearing on the American one dollar bill is _____ .

Politicians pay much attention to the results of polls which they look upon as the

_____ .

The Founding Fathers of the U.S. showed their belief in the help of God by placing on the obverse side of the dollar bill the words taken from Vergil, _____ .

Topic: The House of 1900

At the turn of the century a *domicile* in a small New England town generally consisted of two main floors, the first containing *kitchen, dining room,* living room, and *parlor.* The last was kept closed except when the *minister* or wealthy *relatives* came to call. There was an unfinished third floor, the *attic,* used for drying clothes and for *storage.* There was also a *cellar* used as a workshop and for storage of *bicycles,* lawn mowers, and so forth. Prominent was the *furnace,* which burned coal or wood. The second floor contained bedrooms and a *lavatory* generally called "the bathroom." Most houses were illuminated by *gas* or *electricity,* but the kitchen *stove* usually burned coal. *Telephones* in 1900 were used only by businesses and wealthy *citizens.* Many homes had *pianos,* but there were of course no *phonographs,* no *cassette recorders* or *radios,* and above all, no *televisions.* The *refrigerator* was cooled by ice.

At the front of the house was usually a *piazza,* also called a *veranda,* used in the evening when the weather was hot. Often out in the yard would be a grape or rose *arbor.*

List of Words Taught in This Course

■ The *page number* given for each word is the page on which the word first appears in the text.

A

abbreviation (p. 252)
abduct (p. 159)
aberrant (p. 161)
abstain (p. 162)
abstract (p. 162)
abuse (p. 75)
abusive (p. 75)
accede (p. 165)
access (p. 22)
account (p. 9)
accumulate (p. 21)
acidity (p. 210)
acquire (p. 77)
acrophobia (p. 110)
active (p. 77)
adapt (p. 164)
adduce (p. 161)
adhere (p. 160)
adhesive (p. 160)
administration (p. 70)
adroit (p. 324)
advent (p. 16)
aesthete (p. 135)
aesthetics (p. 135)
affluent (p. 165)
agenda (p. 292)
agent (p. 250)
aggression (p. 165)
agoraphobia (p. 106)
allegro (p. 327)
alligator (p. 331)

allocate (p. 165)
altitude (p. 213)
alto (p. 327)
alumna (p. 289)
alumnus (p. 289)
amateur (p. 318)
ambulatory (p. 187)
amphibious (p. 145)
amphitheater (p. 145)
anabatic (p. 128)
anabiosis (p. 139)
anabolism (p. 130)
anadromous (p. 128)
analysis (p. 137)
analyst (p. 148)
andante (p. 327)
anemia (p. 136)
anesthesia (p. 134)
anesthetist (p. 148)
Anglomania (p. 112)
Anglophobe (p. 105)
anhydrous (p. 133)
announce (p. 165)
annually (p. 8)
anonymous (p. 126)
antecedent (p. 169)
anteposition (p. 181)
anthropoid (p. 197)
anthropology (p. 106)
anthropophagy (p. 113)
antibiotic (p. 140)
antipathy (p. 127)

antonym (p. 126)
apanthropia (p. 145)
apathy (p. 127)
aperture (p. 215)
aphelion (p. 146)
apogee (p. 146)
apostate (p. 145)
appetite (p. 165)
arid (p. 211)
aridity (p. 210)
asinine (p. 221)
assent (p. 12)
assimilation (p. 165)
assume (p. 11)
asteroid (p. 199)
astrology (p. 107)
athletic (p. 148)
athletics (p. 148)
attract (p. 165)
audible (p. 220)

B

barbarian (p. 86)
beef (p. 317)
beneficial (p. 80)
bibliography (p. 105)
bibliomania (p. 112)
bibliophile (p. 106)
bibliophobe (p. 106)
bicycle (p. 266)
biennial (p. 266)

bilateral (p. 267)
biography (p. 238)
biology (p. 107)
biped (p. 283)
biplane (p. 283)
blitzkrieg (p. 334)
bonanza (p. 331)
boomerang (p. 334)
brevity (p. 352)

C

canine (p. 221)
canoe (p. 334)
canyon (p. 331)
carcinogen (p. 241)
carcinoma (p. 202)
cardiogram (p. 202)
carditis (p. 202)
carnivore (p. 247)
catabatic (p. 128)
catabolism (p. 130)
catadromous (p. 129)
cause (p. 10)
cede (p. 170)
cement (p. 76)
centennial (p. 268)
centennium (p. 293)
centimeter (p. 273)
centipede (p. 268)
century (p. 76)
certificate (p. 4)
chef (p. 318)
chronometer (p. 138)
cigar (p. 331)
cinema (p. 138)
circumference (p. 176)
civilize (p. 76)
coauthor (p. 171)
collaborator (p. 171)
collector (p. 212)
colossus (p. 290)
comic (p. 148)
commensal (p. 171)
commotion (p. 20)
compel (p. 19)
compete (p. 69)
competence (p. 213)
competition (p. 69)
compose (p. 179)
comprehend (p. 73)
comprehension (p. 73)
comprehensive (p. 73)
con (p. 24)

concede (p. 170)
concession (p. 80)
condition (p. 70)
conducive (p. 74)
conduct (p. 74)
conductor (p. 25)
confer (p. 178)
conference (p. 176)
confidence (p. 214)
confident (p. 214)
congress (p. 167)
conscription (p. 214)
conspicuous (p. 20)
constitution (p. 70)
consul (p. 77)
consume (p. 20)
contention (p. 21)
contradict (p. 24)
contraposition (p. 182)
convene (p. 17)
convention (p. 17)
correct (p. 252)
correction (p. 214)
council (p. 79)
counsel (p. 80)
course (p. 9)
creation (p. 25)
creator (p. 25)
crescendo (p. 327)
cumulate (p. 21)
cumulus (p. 21)
cylindroid (p. 200)
cystectomy (p. 204)
cystitis (p. 203)
cystometrogram (p. 203)
cystoscope (p. 203)
cystoscopy (p. 203)

D

datum (p. 291)
decalog (p. 278)
December (p. 265)
decemvir (p. 268)
deciliter (p. 273)
decimal (p. 273)
dedicate (p. 172)
deference (p. 176)
defrost (p. 173)
delta (p. 199)
deltoid (p. 200)
depose (p. 171)
dermatologist (p. 112)
dermatophagous (p. 110)

describe (p. 74)
description (p. 74)
descriptive (p. 75)
design (p. 79)
deuteragonist (p. 284)
deuterogamy (p. 280)
Deuteronomy (p. 281)
diachronic (p. 138)
diadromous (p. 131)
diameter (p. 129)
diathermy (p. 130)
differ (p. 178)
difference (p. 176)
dignity (p. 197)
digress (p. 168)
diminuendo (p. 327)
discoid (p. 199)
dismiss (p. 12)
dispel (p. 12)
dissolve (p. 11)
divorcée (p. 319)
dominion (p. 77)
duet (p. 267)
dyarchy (p. 277)
dysentery (p. 99)
dysgenics (p. 100)
dyslogistic (p. 101)
dyspepsia (p. 100)
dysphagia (p. 24)
dyspnea (p. 101)

E

earth (p. 68)
ectopic (p. 132)
effectually (p. 80)
effusive (p. 163)
egress (p. 168)
eject (p. 161)
emerge (p. 12)
emigré (p. 319)
emit (p. 164)
empathy (p. 162)
emperor (p. 77)
emphasis (p. 27)
emulation (p. 77)
encore (p. 322)
endermic (p. 136)
enhydrous (p. 132)
ennead (p. 278)
ennui (p. 323)
enterotomy (p. 205)
enthusiasm (p. 79)
entomologist (p. 111)

entomophagous (p. 114)
entopic (p. 132)
epidermis (p. 139)
epigene (p. 139)
epilogue (p. 140)
eponymous (p. 126)
eradicate (p. 255)
erasure (p. 215)
esthesia (p. 134)
ethnic (p. 238)
ethnology (p. 235)
etymology (p. 111)
eugenics (p. 99)
eulogy (p. 100)
eupepsia (p. 100)
euphemism (p. 101)
euphony (p. 101)
euthanasia (p. 101)
event (p. 10)
evict (p. 12)
eviscerate (p. 164)
exalt (p. 80)
exceed (p. 170)
ex-convict (p. 175)
execute (p. 73)
execution (p. 73)
executive (p. 73)
exit (p. 160)
exobiology (p. 145)
exodontist (p. 146)
exodus (p. 133)
exoskeleton (p. 145)
expel (p. 16)
expose (p. 81)
extend (p. 72)
extensive (p. 72)
extent (p. 72)
extracurricular (p. 183)
extramural (p. 183)
extrasensory (p. 184)

F

fairest (p. 68)
fait accompli (p. 323)
family (p. 4)
faux pas (p. 323)
febrifuge (p. 248)
federal (p. 27)
fervid (p. 257)
fervor (p. 212)
fiancé (p. 319)
fiancée (p. 318)
filial (p. 308)

finalize (p. 206)
financial (p. 7)
flammable (p. 187)
flexible (p. 220)
focus (p. 290)
formidable (p. 80)
formula (p. 293)
forte (p. 327)
fracture (p. 250)
fragile (p. 219)
frangible (p. 250)
fraternity (p. 308)
frontier (p. 76)
frugivorous (p. 247)
fusion (p. 215)

G

gastrectomy (p. 205)
gastritis (p. 200)
gastroenteritis (p. 205)
gastroenterologist (p. 205)
gastropod (p. 241)
gauche (p. 324)
gelid (p. 219)
geography (p. 238)
geology (p. 235)
geometry (p. 240)
geriatrics (p. 241)
gladiolus (p. 295)
glorious (p. 221)
government (p. 26)
gradually (p. 76)
gratefulness (p. 213)
gratitude (p. 186)
gravid (p. 250)
gravity (p. 250)

H

halitosis (p. 201)
hectoliter (p. 278)
heliophilia (p. 111)
hemisphere (p. 282)
henotheism (p. 276)
heptahedron (p. 277)
heptarchy (p. 285)
herbicide (p. 247)
herbivore (p. 247)
herbivorous (p. 247)
hexadactylic (p. 277)
hexagon (p. 276)
high (p. 3)
hippiatry (p. 240)

horology (p. 236)
horoscope (p. 238)
hostile (p. 250)
hostility (p. 250)
human (p. 10)
humanoid (p. 197)
humidity (p. 211)
hurricane (p. 334)
hydrodynamic (p. 109)
hydrophobia (p. 109)
hyperacidity (p. 131)
hyperesthesia (p. 134)
hyperkinesia (p. 138)
hyperthermia (p. 132)
hypnosis (p. 201)
hypnotize (p. 257)
hypoacidity (p. 132)
hypodermic (p. 136)
hypoesthesia (p. 134)
hypogene (p. 139)
hypokinesia (p. 139)
hypothermia (p. 132)
hypothesis (p. 180)

I

iatrogenic (p. 242)
ichthyoid (p. 240)
ichthyophagous (p. 239)
ichthyophobia (p. 242)
ichthyosis (p. 239)
igloo (p. 334)
illegal (p. 186)
illiterate (p. 185)
illuminate (p. 186)
imbibe (p. 163)
immigrate (p. 13)
impecunious (p. 222)
impel (p. 11)
important (p. 8)
impose (p. 171)
impulse (p. 14)
incline (p. 80)
index (p. 293)
induce (p. 186)
induct (p. 160)
infantile (p. 220)
infer (p. 176)
inflame (p. 187)
inflammable (p. 187)
influence (p. 76)
infrahuman (p. 189)
infrasonic (p. 188)
ingratitude (p. 186)

ingress (p. 167)
inhuman (p. 186)
inject (p. 13)
inquire (p. 14)
insectivore (p. 248)
insectivorous (p. 248)
insipid (p. 250)
inspect (p. 17)
intercede (p. 169)
intercollegiate (p. 183)
interest (p. 3)
interpose (p. 179)
interrupt (p. 174)
intramural (p. 183)
intravenous (p. 184)
introduce (p. 79)
introduction (p. 23)
introspective (p. 24)
introvert (p. 184)
invent (p. 14)
inventor (p. 25)
investment (p. 26)
investor (p. 212)
irreplaceable (p. 185)

J

jocose (p. 252)
jocularity (p. 252)
juvenile (p. 220)

K

kangaroo (p. 334)
kayak (p. 334)
kilometer (p. 277)
kinesics (p. 138)

L

lacuna (p. 293)
largeness (p. 213)
largo (p. 327)
laryngectomy (p. 203)
laryngitis (p. 200)
laryngoscope (p. 203)
laryngoscopy (p. 203)
Latinate (p. 68)
legacy (p. 88)
legion (p. 81)
leonine (p. 221)
liberality (p. 211)
literate (p. 185)
loco (p. 331)

logorrhea (p. 204)
lymph (p. 202)
lymphoma (p. 202)

M

magnify (p. 248)
magnitude (p. 213)
mankind (p. 68)
manners (p. 76)
martial (p. 77)
maternal (p. 308)
matinee (p. 323)
medical (p. 26)
medium (p. 292)
memorandum (p. 293)
menage (p. 324)
menagerie (p. 324)
metabolism (p. 130)
metachromatism (p. 140)
metamorphosis (p. 140)
metonymy (p. 143)
millennium (p. 268)
millicurie (p. 273)
millimeter (p. 268)
millipede (p. 268)
monarchy (p. 104)
monogamy (p. 284)
monomania (p. 283)
monoplane (p. 281)
monopoly (p. 285)
morbid (p. 219)
morphology (p. 234)
mosquito (p. 331)
motion (p. 20)
multipara (p. 282)
mustang (p. 331)
mutton (p. 317)
myoma (p. 202)

N

nation (p. 70)
nature (p. 10)
navigable (p. 221)
navigate (p. 256)
nebula (p. 252)
nebulous (p. 252)
neglect (p. 250)
negligence (p. 250)
neuritis (p. 239)
neurologist (p. 236)
neurosis (p. 201)
nonalcoholic (p. 184)

nonane (p. 274)
nonexistent (p. 185)
nonfunny (p. 185)
nonhuman (p. 185)
nonlegal (p. 186)
November (p. 265)
novena (p. 267)
nucleus (p. 290)

O

objector (p. 211)
obtain (p. 81)
ochlocracy (p. 112)
ochlophobia (p. 112)
octave (p. 273)
octipara (p. 266)
October (p. 265)
octopus (p. 241)
offer (p. 176)
oligarchy (p. 282)
oligophagous (p. 282)
oligopoly (p. 285)
omnivore (p. 246)
omnivorous (p. 246)
ophiologist (p. 113)
ophiophagous (p. 114)
ophiophobe (p. 111)
opinion (p. 10)
opponent (p. 182)
opposition (p. 182)
ornithoid (p. 241)
ornithologist (p. 114)
ornithophobia (p. 111)
osteoma (p. 202)
osteotomy (p. 202)
otitis media (p. 204)
otorhinolaryngologist (p. 204)
otorrhea (p. 204)
overlook (p. 4)
overturn (p. 22)
oviferous (p. 198)
ovoid (p. 199)

P

palindrome (p. 140)
palingenesis (p. 140)
palinode (p. 143)
pallid (p. 218)
pallor (p. 212)
panchromatic (p. 282)
panhellenism (p. 282)
panorama (p. 282)

parallel (p. 140)
paramedic (p. 142)
parapsychology (p. 140)
part (p. 77)
parthenogenesis (p. 241)
Parthenon (p. 241)
paternal (p. 308)
pathology (p. 236)
patriarchy (p. 104)
patricide (p. 247)
pecunious (p. 222)
pentagon (p. 276)
people (p. 10)
perambulate (p. 187)
per annum (p. 8)
percent (p. 8)
percolate (p. 188)
perforate (p. 189)
perigee (p. 146)
perihelion (p. 146)
perimeter (p. 129)
periodontist (p. 140)
periscope (p. 130)
person (p. 81)
persona (p. 290)
pesticide (p. 248)
petaloid (p. 199)
philanthropist (p. 106)
philharmonic (p. 106)
philhellene (p. 109)
philology (p. 106)
philosophy (p. 106)
phobia (p. 105)
piano (p. 327)
pianoforte (p. 327)
piscivorous (p. 249)
planetoid (p. 199)
podiatrist (p. 240)
policy (p. 78)
political (p. 10)
polygamous (p. 281)
polygamy (p. 284)
polyhedron (p. 281)
poncho (p. 331)
pork (p. 316)
portion (p. 70)
position (p. 181)
possess (p. 73)
possession (p. 74)
possessive (p. 73)
postgame (p. 181)
postposition (p. 181)
precarious (p. 80)
precede (p. 169)

predetermine (p. 175)
pregame (p. 23)
preserve (p. 79)
presuppose (p. 23)
pretergress (p. 189)
preterhuman (p. 188)
preternatural (p. 188)
prevent (p. 23)
primogeniture (p. 272)
principal (p. 77)
pro (p. 24)
proceed (p. 168)
procession (p. 169)
prognosis (p. 140)
progress (p. 167)
prologue (p. 140)
propel (p. 21)
prophylactic (p. 144)
propose (p. 175)
prorevolutionary (p. 24)
prosecution (p. 80)
protagonist (p. 284)
protégé (p. 318)
protégée (p. 319)
protomartyr (p. 280)
prototype (p. 281)
prudent (p. 80)
psychiatrist (p. 240)
psychoanalyst (p. 239)
psychologist (p. 236)
psychopath (p. 239)
psychosis (p. 201)
purity (p. 197)
pyrography (p. 113)
pyromaniac (p. 114)
pyrophile (p. 110)

Q

quadrangle (p. 267)
quadriplegic (p. 265)
quarter (p. 8)
quartile (p. 273)
quinquefoliate (p. 266)
quinquennial (p. 266)
quintuplets (p. 273)

R

raconteur (p. 318)
radius (p. 290)
ranivorous (p. 247)
rapid (p. 79)
rate (p. 3)

reaction (p. 250)
recede (p. 168)
recent (p. 3)
recreate (p. 25)
rectitude (p. 252)
redivide (p. 174)
reduce (p. 82)
reduction (p. 82)
refer (p. 176)
reflection (p. 80)
regress (p. 167)
reject (p. 13)
relinquish (p. 172)
remote (p. 80)
renown (p. 76)
repel (p. 16)
replacement (p. 25)
repose (p. 181)
republic (p. 77)
repulsion (p. 158)
require (p. 11)
requirement (p. 26)
reserve (p. 79)
respect (p. 9)
restitution (p. 81)
resume (p. 16)
retroactive (p. 23)
retrospect (p. 23)
retrospective (p. 184)
return (p. 13)
revolution (p. 70)
rhinitis (p. 204)
rhinoceros (p. 204)
rhinorrhea (p. 205)
rhizoid (p. 240)
rhizophagous (p. 240)
rodeo (p. 331)
Roman (p. 77)
Russophile (p. 105)
Russophobe (p. 105

S

salutary (p. 80)
sapid (p. 250)
saprophagous (p. 239)
satisfy (p. 79)
sauerkraut (p. 334)
savant (p. 317)
savvy (p. 331)
sclerosis (p. 201)
sculptor (p. 215)
sculpture (p. 215)
secede (p. 169)

secondary (p. 273)
secure (p. 80)
senate (p. 77)
senile (p. 220)
separation (p. 9)
September (p. 265)
septemvirate (p. 267)
septime (p. 274)
sequela (p. 293)
sequence (p. 214)
sexdigital (p. 265)
sexpartite (p. 267)
sextant (p. 274)
sigmoid (p. 199)
similar (p. 252)
similitude (p. 252)
situation (p. 80)
skunk (p. 334)
socialize (p. 206)
soprano (p. 327)
sorority (p. 308)
spheroid (p. 198)
splendid (p. 219)
splendor (p. 219)
squalid (p. 252)
squalor (p. 252)
station (p. 9)
sterilize (p. 205)
stimulus (p. 293)
stratum (p. 291)
stupid (p. 219)
stupor (p. 212)

subdue (p. 79)
succession (p. 79)
suffer (p. 178)
suicide (p. 247)
superimpose (p. 179)
suppose (p. 179)
supposition (p. 179)
swine (p. 316)
sympathetic (p. 239)
sympathy (p. 127)
synchronic (p. 138)
synchronize (p. 138)
synonym (p. 126)
synonymous (p. 126)
synopsis (p. 293)
synthesis (p. 137)

T

temper (p. 80)
tertiary (p. 274)
tetrad (p. 276)
tetrahedron (p. 285)
theocracy (p. 113)
theology (p. 107)
theophile (p. 113)
theophobe (p. 112)
theorize (p. 205)
tonsillectomy (p. 201)
tonsillitis (p. 200)
tour de force (p. 323)
transfer (p. 176)

transgress (p. 168)
transpose (p. 179)
triangle (p. 267)
tricephalic (p. 277)
tricycle (p. 266)
triplane (p. 283)
triumph (p. 79)
tropic (p. 85)

U

ultraconservative (p. 189)
ultralightweight (p. 188)
ultrasonic (p. 188)
unicycle (p. 266)
unilateral (p. 267)
union (p. 70)
upturn (p. 22)

V

veal (p. 317)
venison (p. 317)
venous (p. 222)
verbose (p. 222)
vermicide (p. 248)
vertebra (p. 293)
vicissitude (p. 88)
virile (p. 220)

W

wigwam (p. 334)

Glossary

■ This Glossary contains brief explanations of the technical terms that appear in the programmed material in the text. The Glossary is intended for the instructor and for interested students who seek a more complete (and in some cases more technical) definition of terms frequently used in the text. Such students should be aware, however, that some concepts are difficult to explain in precise terms.

active voice   (Not used in the programmed material in the book.) See **voice.**

adjective (p. 45)   A **word class.** In English it is marked morphologically by the ability to take the **suffixes** {er} and {est}, or the **function words** "more" and "most," to show comparison, as in "This book is *heavier* than that one."

adverb (p. 59)   A **word class.** In English some adverbs are formed from **adjectives** by adding the **suffix** {ly}, like "quickly," formed from the adjective "quick." Other adverbs that can fill the same syntactical **slot** as "quickly" are "well," "home," and "fast." In general, adverbs answer such questions as *How? Where? When? To what extent?* and the like.

allomorph (p. 14)   Variant form—that is, a different spelling—of a **morpheme.** For instance, the **prefix** {con} has the form {com} before the sound /p/ and the form {col} before the sound /l/, as in "compel" and "colloquial."

analyze (p. 10)   To break a word down into small parts. For example, we can analyze the word "commotion" as made up of a **prefix** {com}, a **base** {mot}, and a **suffix** {ion}.

Anglo-Saxon (p. 5)   The name of the English language in use between about A.D. 400 and A.D. 1100. Also called *Old English*. See also **Middle English.**

antonyms (p. 75)   Two words that have approximately opposite meanings. Thus "wet" and "dry" are antonyms. See also **synonyms.**

assimilation (p. 165)   The process by which two sounds next to each other take on the same or similar characteristics. For instance, the **prefix** {ad} plus the **base** {sume} yields not *"adsume" but "assume." (The change of {con} to the **allomorph** {com} in "combustion" is an example of *partial assimilation*.)

base (p. 11)   The part of a word to which **prefixes** and/or **suffixes** may be added. For instance, in the word "convention," the base is {vent}, meaning "come," the prefix is {con}, and the suffix is {ion}.

borrowing (p. 2)   A word known to have been brought into English from another language. For example, the English word "fraternity" is a borrowing from Latin "fraternitas." Also called *derivative*.

cardinal number (p. 264)   A number that indicates *quantity*—that is, tells *how many*, such as "one," "five," or "ten." Cardinal numbers can also indicate *order*, or *sequence*, when they follow the noun they modify, as in "Chapter One" or "Room 10." See also **ordinal number**.

cognate (p. 306)   Cognates are words in different languages that are related to one another because they are derived from a common ancestor. For example, German "Bruder," French "frère," and English "brother" are cognates of one another because they all can be shown to have come from the **Indo-European** form *"bhrater."

combining form (p. 234)   An inexact but useful term for a **morpheme** or combination of morphemes that joins with another morpheme or combination of morphemes without being further analyzed as **base, prefix,** or **suffix.** For instance, {ectomy} in "tonsillectomy" is a combining form meaning "cutting out"; it is made up of {ec}, {tom}, and {y}.

content word (p. 3)   A word that carries the major part of the meaning of a phrase or a sentence. Most content words are **nouns** (like "father"), verbs (like "seize"), **adjectives** (like "rapid"), or **adverbs** (like "quickly"). See also **function words.**

derivative (p. 2)   A word known to have been introduced into English from another language. Also called *borrowing*. The majority of English **content words** are derived from Latin and/or Greek.

etymology (p. 28)   The study of the history of words and their development from earlier times.

figurative meaning.   See **literal meaning.**

form class   (Not used in the programmed material in the text.) See **word class.**

function word (p. 3)   A word like "a," "with," and "but," which has semantic meaning and also indicates relationships between other words in a sentence or serves to link words in a sentence.

head (p. 50)   A word modified by another word. In the phrase "the big hill," "hill" is the head of the phrase and "big" is the **modifier.**

Indo-European (p. 305)   A family, or system, of languages that includes almost all the languages spoken today in Europe; in areas settled by Europeans, such as North America, South America, South Africa, Australia; and in Iran and India. Important European member languages are English, German, French, Italian, Spanish, the Scandinavian languages, and the Slavic languages (Russian, Polish, Czechoslovakian, and other languages of Eastern Europe). Important languages spoken in Europe that are *not* members of the Indo-European system are Finnish, Hungarian, Turkish, and Basque. In Iran, the Indo-European language is Persian (or Farsi); Hindi and Urdu are among the Indo-European languages spoken in India.

intransitive verb (p. 56)   A verb that does not have an object and cannot be transformed, or changed, from active **voice** to passive. Examples are "She *runs* every day" and "They *slept* in the living room." See also **transitive verb.**

language (Not defined in the programmed material in the text.) A system of spoken symbols—words and the means of combining them in sentences—used by members of a community or nation to communicate. Most languages now have a written as well as a spoken system.

literal meaning (p. 255) In general, the meaning of a word or phrase as determined by its **etymology,** or origin. For instance, the literal meaning of "The senator brought in *his big guns to demolish* members of the opposition" is that the senator used artillery to kill his opponents. Since this action is unlikely, we assume that a *figurative meaning* (p. 255) is intended; we might interpret the words to mean that the senator brought into his campaign prominent people to speak against his rivals.

live morpheme (p. 174) A **morpheme** that we may use to create new words, with some confidence that such words will be understood. An example is "pro-television," to refer to someone who is in favor of television.

Middle English (p. 5) The name of the English language in use between about A.D. 1100 and A.D. 1500. See also **Anglo-Saxon.**

modifier (p. 50) A word or group of words that modifies (limits or defines) the meaning of another word or group of words. In "The *brave* woman was rewarded," "brave" tells *which woman* was rewarded. Frequently used modifiers are **adjectives, adverbs,** and prepositional phrases. In the sentence *"The skillful* gardener *quickly* planted *the* flowers *in the garden,"* the adjective "skillful" modifies "gardener"; the adverb "quickly" modifies "planted"; and the prepositional phrase "in the garden" modifies "planted." The **function word** "the" modifies "gardener" and "garden."

morpheme (pp. 10, 18, 19, 174) A minimum unit of meaning. A *full morpheme* (p. 18) can be assigned a meaning; for instance, the {re} in "repel" means "back." An *empty morpheme* (p. 18) does not have a clear meaning; {re} in "revere" has no assignable meaning. An *intensifying morpheme* (p. 19) has no clear meaning but serves to make the word stronger, as {com} intensifies the meaning of "motion" to "commotion."

morphological criteria (p. 40) In English, these criteria, or rules, show, by morphology, such divisions as **word class.** For example, English nouns typically have a contrast between singular and plural. See also **syntactical criteria.**

noun (p. 40) A **word class.** In English, a noun is usually marked morphologically by a contrast between *one* and *more than one,* as in "one boy" but "two boys." In a few nouns this contrast is missing, as in "The *news* is good." An English noun is also marked syntactically by the ability to follow a **noun marker.** For example, in *"The news* is good," "the" is the noun marker and "news" is the noun.

noun marker (p. 42) A **function word** that precedes a **noun** in the same position, or **slot,** as "the" in *"The* cat caught the mice." Typical words of this class are "a" / "an," "even," "no," "my," "our," "each," "all," "both," "some," "many," "this," "these," "one," "two," and so forth. For some of the noun markers, the noun would take {s} to indicate *more than one:* "Both cats caught the mice."

noun modifier (p. 54) A **noun** that modifies (limits or defines) another noun, like "table" in "the *table* top."

object (p. 56) See **transitive verb.**

obsolete (p. 31) Describing a definition that is no longer used.

Old English.   See **Anglo-Saxon.**

ordinal number (p. 264)   A number that indicates *in what order*, like "first" or "tenth." See also **cardinal number.**

passive voice   (Not used in the programmed material in the text.) See **transitive verb** and **voice.**

past tense (p. 55)   A verb form showing action in past time, like "picked" in "Mary *picked* the flowers yesterday." This form contrasts with *present tense* (p. 55)—for example, "picks" in "John *picks* the flowers every morning." (The label *present tense* for "picks" in this sentence is conventional but sometimes misleading. In "John picks the flowers every morning," the tense is habitual action.)

phoneme (p. 286)   A minimum unit of distinctive sound. For example, the word "get" has the initial phoneme / g /, which distinguishes it from the word "pet," which has the initial phoneme / p /. An alphabet represents the phonemes in a language by means of letters.

phrase (p. 54)   An inexact but useful term for a group of words that are bound together in some way but do not form a sentence, like the two prepositional phrases "on top of the table."

prefix (p. 11)   A **morpheme** added to the beginning of a **base,** like {ad} in "advent."

present tense.   See **past tense.**

sentence   (Not defined in the programmed material in the text.) A group of words that is syntactically complete. In English, a sentence begins with a capital letter and ends with a period, question mark, or exclamation mark.

slot (p. 42)   A position in a sentence that can be filled by some **word classes** but not others. For instance, an adjective can fill the slot between **noun marker** and **noun,** as "big" does in the sentence "The *big* dog barks."

structure (p. 5)   The systematic organization of significant contrasts in a language.

subject   (Not used in the programmed materials in the text.) Label for a word that occupies the type of **slot** that "horse" fills in the sentence "That *horse* is a hard worker."

suffix (p. 25)   A **morpheme** added to the end of a **base,** like {ion} in the word "convention."

synonyms (p. 75)   Two words that have about the same meaning. For instance, "insect" and "bug" are considered synonyms, even though "bug" is less formal than "insect." Although inexact, the term *synonym* is useful in language study. See also **antonym.**

syntactical criteria (p. 40)   In English, these criteria, or rules, show, by syntax, such divisions as **word class.** This typically means, "What **slot** in a sentence can a word fill?" Thus, in the sentence "The dogs _____the cat," the word that could fill the slot is a **transitive verb.** See also **morphological criteria.**

syntax (Not used in the programmed material in the text.)   The meaningful distribution of morphemes. In English, this is achieved mostly by **word order** and **function words.**

tense (p. 53)   Morphological change in a verb to show when an action has occurred, is occurring, or will occur. There are only two tenses in English that are indicated by a change in the *form* of the verb itself: present tense, as in "He *runs* very fast," and **past tense,** as in "He *ran* very fast." Other tenses can be formed by using **function words** along with the verb: "He *will run* fast," "He's *going to run*," "He *used to run*," "He *should have run* faster," and so on.

transformation   (Not used in the programmed material in the text.) Changes in the **structure** of a language according to specific rules. For example, we can transform, or change, a statement ("Bears are scarce in some states") into a question ("Are bears scarce in some states?") by varying the **word order** according to established rules.

transitive verb (p. 56)   A verb that has an object, as in the sentence "The boy *sees* the *ball*," in which "sees" is the transitive verb and "ball" is the object. In addition, a transitive verb can be transformed, or changed, from the **active voice** to the passive voice: "The boy *sees* the ball," an active voice sentence, can be changed to "The ball *is seen* by the boy," a passive voice sentence. A verb that does not have an object is **intransitive,** like "fell" in "The boy *fell* down." Many verbs have both transitive and intransitive uses, like "reads" in "The girl *reads* the book" (transitive) and "The girl reads rapidly" (intransitive). See also **voice.**

voice   (Not used in the programmed material in the text.) There are two voices among English verbs, **active voice** and passive voice. An example of an active voice verb is "catches" in "The boy *catches* the dog." The verb "is caught" in the sentence "The dog *is caught* by the boy" is in the passive.

word   (Not defined in the programmed material in the text.) In a language, the smallest unit that can stand alone to communicate meaning. In English, words are usually written with space before and after them. (Note: Many **function words,** like "of," "the," and "but," cannot stand alone to convey meaning, but the definition given here is widely used nevertheless.)

word class (p. 40)   In English, there are four major word classes (sometimes called *form classes*): **noun,** verb, **adjective,** and **adverb.** They are marked by **morphological** and **syntactical criteria,** or standards for determining which class a word belongs in. The morphological criteria are distinctive **suffixes,** like {s} for nouns, {s} for verbs, {er / est} for adjectives, and {ly} for adverbs. The syntactical criterion is **word order.**

word order (p. 5)   The order in which words occur in a sentence. In English, word order determines the function of each element in an actor-action-goal sentence, as in "The *snake* saw the *boy*." In many cases, if the word order is changed, the sentence conveys an entirely different meaning: "The *boy* saw the *snake*." Word order also determines the direction of modification; for instance, it shows who is "smart" in "The *smart* girl helps the boy." Word order follows established rules; *"Saw the snake the boy" does not make sense in English.